Borderlines

Lewis Baston has written on British politics and the electoral landscape for more than thirty years, from polling analysis for the *Financial Times* to election results analysis for the *Guardian*. From 2003 to 2010 he was Research Director for the Electoral Reform Society, and from 2011 to 2015 he was Research Fellow at Democratic Audit. He has appeared on *BBC Breakfast*, *The One Show* and *Sunday Politics*, Radio 4's *PM* and *The World Tonight*, and as the border expert on Tim Marshall's series about borderlands for *The Compass*.

Borderlines

A History of Europe, Told From the Edges

LEWIS BASTON

hodder
press

First published in Great Britain in 2024 by Hodder Press
An imprint of Hodder & Stoughton Limited
An Hachette UK company

3

A CIP catalogue record for this title is available from the British Library

Hardback ISBN 9781399723763
Trade Paperback ISBN 9781399723770
ebook ISBN 9781399723800

Typeset in Bembo by Hewer Text UK Ltd, Edinburgh
Printed and bound in Great Britain by Clays Ltd, Elcograf S.p.A.

Hodder & Stoughton policy is to use papers that are natural, renewable
and recyclable products and made from wood grown in sustainable forests.
The logging and manufacturing processes are expected to conform
to the environmental regulations of the country of origin.

Hodder & Stoughton Limited
Carmelite House
50 Victoria Embankment
London EC4Y 0DZ

The authorised representative in the EEA is Hachette Ireland, 8 Castlecourt
Centre, Dublin 15, D15 XTP3, Ireland (email: info@hbgi.ie)

www.hodderpress.co.uk

To my teachers, who have shaped me and opened my mind:

Vic, Jill, Hannah, Colin, Andrew, Bill, Michael,
Peter, Anthony, David, and many others.

Contents

Part Four: East

Introduction

On the British mainland, we don't have borders.

The last international boundary that we could walk to – the line between Scotland and England – ceased to exist with the 1707 Act of Union, and although it wondered about reappearing in 2014 and may yet do so, we have experienced more than 300 years of feeling as if we are pretty much the same country. We export our efforts at drawing boundary lines, whether the recipients (from Ireland to Belgium to India) like it or not.

The concept of getting directly to a foreign country by driving, or getting a train you don't have to go through security to board, or even more radically just walking, is an unfamiliar one to the English imagination. The first time I crossed an international land boundary was in the bleary early morning one day in summer 1984. I was with my parents and my sister on a coach that had set out from London the previous evening. I had slept fitfully as it drove from Calais through the battlefield zone of northern France and then via Reims and Metz to reach Strasbourg. Perhaps to discourage the passengers from wandering off at rural pit stops, *Rambo: First Blood* was playing on the communal video screen, and after it finished we drifted into uneasy sleep. I was hoping to witness the moment of transition and my parents woke me up just in time. The coach powered through empty, brightly lit roads in the industrial part of Strasbourg. Over the Rhine bridge . . . and POW! I was in Kehl, Germany. Germany! A whole new country. In an instant, from France into Germany, without getting on a ferry or even getting out of my increasingly uncomfortable bus seat. I took my first steps on German territory at a service area off an autobahn near Baden-Baden, whose very name was a talisman of Teutonic logic and literalness. My parents and sister seemed less thrilled.

A few hours later – quite a few hours, during which the driver switched the video to *The Sound of Music* to get us in the right mood

– we pulled off the trick again. The landscape got hillier and hillier, and at some point the hills became mountains and we crossed through a checkpoint from Bavaria into Austria. A few years after the Austrian journey, my parents told me that travelling by coach had been part of the plan because they thought I would like it.

I was a student when the Iron Curtain came down; my first Interrail journey took me to post-communist Prague and Bratislava in 1990, the other side of what had been a forbidding frontier in the mind as well as on the map. Europe was a lot bigger than I had imagined. I became conscious that huge political changes were still possible in my time – that 'big history' was still being made. Some of that – in Czechoslovakia, the former USSR and former Yugoslavia – meant that those apparently fixed lines in the atlas could move after all.

A fair bit of my professional life as an election expert has involved analysing, commenting on and recommending boundaries; nearly every electoral system involves drawing some lines on the map to determine political representation. But I have never lost my fascination with national boundaries, and with central and eastern Europe. When eight countries in the region joined the European Union in 2004, and the cheap flights began, I was able to explore in person in a way I could never have imagined before 1989. The distinct qualities of places like Latvia and Slovakia revealed themselves to me as I travelled, and I enjoyed that transgressive pleasure of crossing land borders more frequently.

The genesis of this book was in that traumatic period of political life when Brexit and Trump reared their heads. The events of 2016 left me bereft of political enthusiasm and encouraged me to try to find a way of looking, indirectly, at what was happening and fitting it into a larger context. I looked first to my own country's land border in Ireland, which had been fading into the background since the Good Friday Agreement in 1998. We had experienced the victory of a campaign largely devoted to the generalised merits of putting up border controls; what would be the consequences for our actual border? I walked the fields and hedgerows of Fermanagh and Armagh, looking for answers. But I realised that the question was more general, and tied into my own lifelong curiosity about land borders and ambiguous areas. One of the problems of how I, through no fault of my brilliant teachers, learned history was that 'our' national history was put aside from European concerns. As I read about places like Silesia and the Sudetenland, and the conflicts there in the early 1920s, the parallels with Ireland jump from the page. While the British Empire did not collapse with other European empires in 1917–18, it was still never the same again. Nor is Britain's economic history an island story. Britain, try as it might, cannot escape its European context. So I embarked on a series of journeys of discovery that took me to and often across all the borders that I write about in this book – from the Russia–Finland border near Vyborg to Ukraine's southern plains, from Ireland to Croatia. I travelled even further, but in writing a book about boundaries one has to draw the line somewhere.

I have never forgotten my feeling of awe on crossing that national border line from France to Germany that day in 1984. Reginald Maudling, the amiable, flawed politician I once served as posthumous biographer, was fond of saying that the start of philosophical wisdom was a simple sense of wonder and surprise, and that is the kernel of this book. I have been waiting a long time to explore that sense of an abrupt transition that comes with crossing over a line that, however concrete, owes its existence to the human imagination and its limitations.

One frequently comes across two metaphors about borders and border zones: the bridge and the door. The idea of the bridge celebrates the role of the border as an open place of interchange, while the door implies the ability to keep the border shut, to admit others to one's home selectively or not at all. Both ideas are valid, to different degrees in different circumstances; Estonian border guards regard the Russian frontier very much as the external door of their home, to be kept secure, while the Latvian border is entirely open. There's even a playground in the border town of Valga-Valka where a swing will take a child back and forth between Estonia and Latvia. The Ukrainian writer Victoria Amelina (1986–2023) wrote of the border as defining where 'home' started. In saying that, she was not talking necessarily of a national border, but a broader community of fellow-feeling that could span some national borders but not others, and was not necessarily easy to identify. Are we, as Amelina lamented, 'doomed to constantly make mistakes about where our home, the safe space of trust, ends and which of its borders should be especially well-guarded'?

In the Europe of empires before 1914, there were few controls over the movement of people other than those that the market imposed through the affordability of travel. Migration was relatively free, even – before the Aliens Act 1905 – to Britain. Passports were not usually necessary, and as well as migration there was an extensive system of tourist travel to seaside resorts, spas, antiquities and even 'dark tourism' to battlefields. Travel guides such as Baedeker went through frequent editions for the hot spots such as Switzerland and Italy, and were branching out to more adventurous tourist destinations such as Egypt and Russia ('with a side trip to Peking') on the eve of the Great War. But there were barriers to the transportation of goods. International rail travel could involve painstaking customs inspections, and the amount that an individual could carry across an international boundary free of duty was very limited.

Borders themselves are not as old as we tend to believe. What we imagine as 'states' in the world before changes such as the Peace of Westphalia in 1648 and the French revolutionary wars were often not in exclusive charge of their territory; they had to look up to imperial and religious obligations and down to the rights of lords and cities, and the edges of their sovereignty were blurred in both political and geographical senses. However, while most of the lines we draw on historic maps are imaginary, there were a few ancient boundaries that were meaningful on the ground. China and the Roman Empire both built border fortifications two thousand years ago, although even these were not quite the same as modern borders. The empires did not usually recognise the sovereignty of entities the other side of the line; there was a hazy border zone beyond the Roman Limes in Europe in which there was trade and urban settlement. Borderlanders have therefore existed for longer than legal borders. The Limes* stretched across what is now Germany and central Europe, and its purpose seems to have been regulation of trade and small-scale migration rather than imperial defence; it proved inadequate when the great age of European migration began in the fourth and fifth centuries. The British possibly have an exaggerated idea of how formidable the external frontiers of the Roman Empire were because one of the most militarised, Hadrian's Wall, runs in a straight line across northern England.

Less known to the British reader is the Military Frontier that divided Austrian Christendom from the Islamic Ottoman Empire. It formally lasted for nearly three centuries until 1881, but it was the successor to the unstable borderlands that stretched across Croatia, Hungary and Transylvania for another two centuries before that. In some ways, the

---

*A Latin word giving rise to the English 'limit'.

psychological impact of the Military Frontier has been deeper than that of the Iron Curtain; the imagery of the fault line between the 'West' and Islam is still powerful. The psychological crossing point between 'Europe' and 'the Balkans' was fixed for two centuries at Belgrade, just across the Sava and the Danube from the last town in Croatia/Hungary, Semlin (which is now the Belgrade suburb of Zemun). The Islamic presence had been longer established and ran deeper in Belgrade than it had in the territory to its north, and there was a Turkish garrison in the otherwise de facto independent Serbian city until 1867.

The Military Frontier was a place where new forms of society began, not so much because of contact with the other side as because the Habsburg authorities encouraged the settlement of the territory by farmers who, in exchange for obligations to serve in a militia to defend the border, were free of feudal ties to landlords or aristocrats. Free peasants had the task of walking along the border to guard it, prevent it from being encroached upon and to help traders and travellers get through the border territory safely despite the dangers of banditry. Everywhere in border country in Europe I noticed that people often had large, fierce dogs; they had to rely on their own protection. The Bohemian Shepherd dog was originally bred to assist the free peasants who patrolled the borders. Over the centuries, different ethnic groups were settled in border regions, creating places like the Serb-inhabited Krajina of Croatia and the scattering of German and Croat communities across central Europe. The Russian imperial conquests such as southern Ukraine in the 1790s were variants on the same pattern of annexation, fortification and settlement. The Military Frontier's historical legacy of mixing and sorting the various peoples of central and south-eastern Europe has been important well beyond the borders of the region – never more so than with the assassination of Franz Ferdinand in 1914.

The paradoxical freedom of the Military Frontier resembled the colonial frontier, which was a formative influence on the United States. The idea of the independent smallholder serving in the militia to guard his family, and the frontier as a space where freedom reigned and people could reinvent themselves, was a European one before it was an American one. The concept of the frontier was re-imported under the Nazis, who dreamed of a tribe of yeoman farmers securing the eastern frontier of the new German empire. Boundary changes after 1945 produced little Wild Wests in communist Poland and Czechoslovakia, where the property of the expelled Germans was up for grabs and there was a need for reliable elements to put down roots and guard their side of the Iron Curtain.

Borders are both sinister and liberating; their dual aspect is not confined to the truism that there is a country on both sides of the line. The sinister aspect is hard-wired in some languages, including English. The old English-language version of the Lord's Prayer puzzled me as a child – why is trespass singled out as something to forgive as opposed to every other misdeed? But trespass encompasses all other wrongs – it means crossing over, unasked, into someone else's legitimate sphere of interest. Similarly, 'transgress', 'overstep the mark', 'cross the line' . . . all link the idea of crossing a boundary with being in the wrong in a legal, social or moral sense. The connection is not just an English language quirk, either, as I found out when I read *Crime and Punishment* and discovered that the Russian word for 'crime' (prestupléniye) came from the idea of crossing a boundary as well (пре meaning across, ступление meaning step). The Polish word for crime, przestępstwo, has identical roots, and it is the same story in Bulgarian, but not in the Romance languages or in German. To eastern Slavs and the English, at least, our language suggests to us that a boundary is generally a bad place.

Our psychology is affected by the presence of these imaginary lines; at first glance they seem to forbid. The 'bad stuff' is always on the far side of the border, as I discovered again and again throughout the research for this book. Unacceptable ideas and urges are projected onto the people across the border, and – for those living away from the borderlands – might seep across unless the border is locked down and the people living near it are brought to heel. People whose relationship with borders is unsettled, like Jews and Roma, are particularly at risk.

Crossing a border, or settling a frontier, also gives permission for us to leave the normal social and even moral constraints behind us at 'home'. The border may be a hard line on a map dividing jurisdictions, but it is surrounded by a fuzzy zone in which national law is bent or broken before it reaches its geographical limit. Even when one passes through the border itself, there is a sense of having gone through the mirror to a place where what has just been illegal is now trumpeted from the roof-tops. Welcome to the land of liberty where you are allowed to go to a casino, or drink at the age of 19, buy alcohol, shop on a Sunday, buy fireworks! You're not really supposed to take the goods back over the border with you, but we won't tell if you don't . . . The freedom of the border can often have a more sinister side, as it did for instance on the Czech–German frontier, where the sex industry exploded after the fall of the Iron Curtain. At its height in 2000, there were 50 brothels and 400 sex workers in the Czech village of Dubí, often working in dangerous and involuntary conditions. At its most serious, soldiers in invading armies feel they are permitted to behave in bestial ways once they throw those border gates open and violate (the linguistic relationship between rape and invasion is no coincidence) the territory of others.

The boundaries of the nation, the state, are important. Despite the European Union and freedom of movement across borders, people seem to need nations, and with nations come the boundary lines that separate them from each other. Although this has often been treated as a natural phenomenon, it is a recent historical development. Before the early 19th century, nations, nationalism and borders mostly worked in different ways than they do now. The last couple of centuries, in which these borders have been tightly defined and policed, have been an experiment.

One can produce maps that purport to set out national or imperial territories in, say, the year 1500, but the boundaries don't mean the same thing as the lines on a modern political map of Europe. If you physically went to a border, the chances are that there would be no checkpoints or guards. There would be nothing to stop you crossing it and probably no immediate way of knowing when you had crossed it, although you might be fortunate and come across a stone marker. The influence of the state will have faded out some time before you reached the actual border. Much of what states now do at borders was then transacted by different sorts of authority. The city gate, not the largely notional national border, was the prime location for the taxation of goods and the regulation of the movement of people. The division between urban and rural is older and stronger than most national distinctions.

We tend now to think of states as exclusive; that if you – or a piece of land – are in one, you can't be in another. But this is not how things have worked in Europe for most of its history; the rough equivalent of the state – historians tend to shy away from calling them states, as opposed to polities – often did not have a freehold on sovereignty. The ruler had to look both up, to complex supranational institutions like the Holy Roman Empire and the web of constitutional and hereditary rules, and down, to the cities, margravates and cantons, which all had their own jealously guarded powers and privileges. There were wide bands of territory whose allegiance was mixed between what we now call France and Germany, and Germany and Poland. The first time a clear border was drawn between France and Germany was in 1814 (and it was revised a year later).

The philosophy of nationalism has always had problems with the lands near the borders, and, given that nationalism is the dominant way in which we organise states, this is a significant flaw. Dividing land into states is going to be a problem if there are areas where people with different languages, religions and identities live mingled together. Putting ethnically mixed areas into nation states creates national minorities, as happened in many areas of Europe after 1918. A 'Europe of nations' in the pure sense only existed for a couple of decades after 1918, and it was a political and economic disaster. Its scars are still apparent on the land and in people's minds.

Between 1938 and 1947, European boundaries were redrawn again and again; many of the minorities were violently uprooted; the logic of nationalism, including the communist variant of nationalism, produced ethnic cleansing. The legacy of these years embittered relationships between people and states, and the hand across the lands depopulated and despoiled by the bitterness of border conflict is still offered only tentatively in some places. Is there any peaceful, acceptable way of reconciling the way we organise ourselves into states with the interests of border people in living their lives and conserving their diverse identities? Is Europe's past and present, of overlapping and shared sovereignty, the best solution available? And can Britain really stand aloof, given that it too has a border drawn amid the violence of the years immediately after the Great War?

If we decide that borders really are necessary, are they a necessary evil? National boundaries and the maps that illustrate them are not neutral facts. They are the legacies of violent imperial power, in Europe and across the world. The maps of the places where most of the people of the world live were drawn by the European colonial empires – in the scramble for Africa in the late 19th century, in the Middle East shaped by Sykes and Picot in 1916, in the Indian subcontinent divided by Radcliffe and Mountbatten in just over a month in 1947. Successive powers have used their dominance over Europe to redraw the map of the continent, with varying degrees of success: the fingerprints of Napoleon, Alexander I, Castlereagh, Napoleon III and Bismarck are all there. But the present shape of Europe is mostly the work of Woodrow Wilson and the Allies in 1919 and Joseph Stalin in 1945. Each round of changes was progressively more disruptive, culminating in the rapidly changing blood-soaked lines on the map that were imposed in central and eastern Europe between 1938 and 1945. Another memory I have from the 1980s was learning about the Treaty of Versailles in the history classroom, and a key part of that was labelling a duplicated, narcotically fragranced purple outline map of the bits of territory that changed hands in 1919. By contrast, there was a map of Hitler's Reich as it was at the start of 1941, a big blob in central Europe looking like an organ afflicted by gross tumours.

Throughout history, there have been times when lines on the map that had been hugely important a few years earlier were no longer of much significance, while new ones appeared in places where people had crossed freely not so long ago. Sometimes the language of daily life changed as well. If the lines could change, what justified putting the lines here rather than there, and who was a legitimate authority to decide? How much should any of them really matter? What did it actually feel like when the line moved and people found themselves somewhere essentially different without having moved anywhere themselves? What is the relationship between home (in the sense the Germans call 'Heimat', a locality where one feels a sense of belonging) and nation, and who are 'we' as defined against 'them'?

Border people may speak different languages, or non-standard dialects, and however hard authoritarian regimes have tried they have never entirely expunged this diversity. In our times, there is kinship between the cosmopolitan big cities, where multiple groups of people mix and mingle, and the provincial cosmopolitanism of the two faces of the border town. Borderers often have a tense relationship with their own national authorities, especially those whose capitals are based a long way physically and psychologically from the border, and who skimp on public services and economic development for border towns while swamping them with customs officers and military barracks. Sometimes the very territory is evacuated or destroyed to create secure areas or troop exercise grounds, and the Czech borderlands became notorious for polluting industries. Nor does the central state like borderers very much; they may be regarded as dubious in terms of national loyalty and suspected of perennial borderland criminal-economic activity such as smuggling. In a world integrated by trade and technology, perhaps we are all borderlanders now; what can we learn from the people who have lived with duality and ambiguity all their lives?

The present period of European history involves healing some of the scar tissue left by Europe's traumatic 20th century. Nationalism, war, fascism and communism all left deep wounds on the map of Europe. People were severed from each other by national boundaries and by the status of being the basis of a nation state or a minority within a nation state that would never allow them full membership. Under the Nazis, and in the immediate post-war period, people were forced to conform to the lines drawn on the map, rather than the lines of the map being drawn in the interests of people (which, whatever the faults of the Treaty of Versailles, the peacemakers of 1919 had tried to respect). Millions were moved from their homes to fit racial or strategic convenience, like Cinderella's sisters bloodily chopping bits off their feet to fit in the glass slipper. After this brutal phase, the Iron Curtain descended and became a harder border than had previously existed anywhere in peacetime. It is an emotional shock to get close to places that have been sterilised of much of what had made them special – particularly the Jewish border-lands, most of whose people were murdered, but also the blankness left by the co-option of nationalistic hatred by communist regimes. The ambiguity, the connective tissue between places like Vienna and Prague or Bratislava or Budapest was severed. It is growing back, and part of the joy of my journey across Europe while writing this book was in seeing that regrowth and reconciliation as some of the damage of the 20th century was undone. Perhaps Europe's borderline personality disorder can be managed, even treated.

Europe is the location for ambitious projects to do borders better – to stabilise them so that they do not move again, to soften their impact for people crossing them and to repair the damage done by the borders of the past. People often distinguish between hard and soft borders. This is a spectrum rather than a binary division. The Berlin Wall is an example of a very hard border – a literal concrete barrier policed by armed guards through which access was only possible at certain places with the right paperwork. The physical barrier and the administrative requirements for people and goods are elements of hardness.

At the other end of the spectrum from the Berlin Wall there are some borders so soft that they barely exist, marked by signs similar to those welcoming you to the next county. Internal borders within the Schengen zone and customs union are the softest of all. After more than a decade of Schengen, people will sometimes give you local directions without specifying which country the place is in, as I experienced when looking for a restaurant near Ostritz on the German–Polish border. When controls were temporarily reimposed because of COVID in 2020, people experienced them as an unnatural obstacle. Take the divided town of Cieszyn (Poland) and Česky Tešin (Czechia), where the border runs along the Olza river: people on each bank of the river held up banners saying, 'I miss you, Pole' and 'I miss you, Czech' when their bridge closed. In 1918–20 Poland and Czechoslovakia had fought a small war here, and in 1938 Poland seized some Czech territory. But the soft border has brought out the softest of feelings.

The soft border is an ideal that, mostly, works on the European mainland and on the island of Ireland. But the economic and social benefits come at a cost. Physically open borders transfer the burden of border enforcement inland, so that identity checks for housing, employment and dealings with the state involve checking residency status. The greatest burden is borne by those outside the Garden of Schengen; with the open internal borders comes a very hard external border. Local treaties can make this less onerous for people immediately across the line in, say, Ukraine or Serbia, but border enforcement in the Mediterranean and the Spanish enclaves in North Africa is ferocious. Nor is this a temporary problem. As climate change and population growth strain the resources of the Sahel and other poor regions, the widening gap in living standards is going to make even the most dangerous crossing more attractive than staying in an uninhabitable home. When does border control become passively, or actively, genocidal? And can Britain, thanks to an accident of geography, really disclaim responsibility for what is happening in its neighbourhood?

In *Borderlines*, I have discovered a secret history of Europe, told from the edges rather than the imperial capitals, from the places where people of different countries are neighbours, friends, lovers and enemies rather than diplomatic colleagues. Let us follow the lines on the map, and love the imperfect places we find along them, for, as Leonard Cohen tells us, the light only gets in because there is a crack in everything.

Place Names

A book on changing borders is bound to mention places that have names in more than one language, and that will lead to controversy. My general approach has been to use English names where these are familiar – it would be pretentious to refer to 'Praha' and 'Warszawa' all the time in an English text. But there are many places that are not amenable to this treatment, and in those I have tried to use the name that is most appropriate for the time and context – so the city we now know as L'viv in Ukraine is Lwów between the wars and when discussing the Polish community, and Lemberg in the context of the Habsburg empire.

There are at least nine different systems of diacritical marks in use in the places that are discussed in this book, a challenge to even the best intentions of author and copy-editor. There are also two alphabets; I have used transliterations of Ukrainian and Russian names and words in what should be a familiar and approachable form.

Part One

German	French		Dutch
Elsass-Lothringen	**Alsace-Lorraine or Alsace-Moselle**		
Diedenhofen	**Thionville**		
	Louvain		**Leuven**
Lüttich	**Liège**		Luik
Mainz	Mayence		
Mühlhausen	**Mulhouse**		
Saarbrücken	Sarrebrouck		
Strassburg	**Strasbourg**		

Part Two

German	Polish	Lithuanian	Yiddish	Russian
Danzig	**Gdańsk**			
Goldap	**Gołdap**			
Hirschberg	**Jelenia Góra**			
Königsberg	Królewiec	Karaliaučius		**Kaliningrad**
Küstrin	**Kostrzyn**			

Mohrungen	**Morąg**				
Nimmersatt		**Nemirseta**			
Posen	**Poznań**				
Swinemünde	**Świnoujście**				
Stettin	**Szczecin**				
	Wilno	**Vilnius**	Vilna		
Waldenburg	**Wałbrzych**				
Breslau	**Wrocław**				
Frankenstein	**Ząbkowice Śląskie**				

Part Three

German	Czech	Slovak	Serbian	Romanian	Hungarian
Pressburg		**Bratislava**			Pozsony
		Čachtice			Csejthe
Eger	**Cheb**				
Komotau	**Chomutov**				
		Košice			Kassa
Karlsbad	**Karlovy Vary**				
Erzgebirge	**Krušnohory**				
Brüx	**Most**				
Grosswardein				**Oradea**	Nagyvárad
Ödenburg					**Sopron**
			Subotica		Szabadka
				Timişoara	Temesvar
Aussig	**Ústí nad Labem**				

Part Four

German	Polish	Ukrainian	Romanian	Hungarian
Czernowitz		**Chernivtsi**	Cernăuți	
		Khust		Huszt
Lemberg	Lwów	**L'viv**		
			Sighetu Marmatiei	Maramaros Sziget
		Uzhhorod		Ungvár
	Żółkiew	**Zhovkva**		

NORTH
SEA

DENMARK

NORTHERN
IRELAND

Derry /
Londonderry

Monaghan

Dublin

IRELAND

UNITED
KINGDOM

London

NETHERLANDS

BELGIUM

R. Rhine

GERMANY

Baarle

Brussels

Koln

N

Lille
LUXEMBOURG

Paris

R. Moselle

SAARLAND

Schengen

Metz

Frankfurt

Mainz

Saarbrucken

Strasbourg

ALSACE-
MOSELLE

Mulhouse

Basel

Stuttgart

Hohenems

FRANCE

Zurich
SWITZERLAND

Geneva

Campione
d'Italia

ITALY

Western borders

⎯O⎯ Belgian language border

Flanders

Wallonia

PART ONE
West

I

Where the checkpoint used to be

(Ireland/United Kingdom)

The United Kingdom's land border in Ireland has a certain bleak quality for much of its length. International boundaries often run through the hills, along lonely rivers or across empty heaths, and the border landscape in Ireland has all these desolate features. Boundaries are neglected spaces, not valued by the governments on either side of the imaginary line; they are not loved even as much as the border town, that strange but often lucrative interzone where people and cultures meet. While the land-scapes of the Irish border may be reminiscent of other borderlands in Europe, the history of this twisting line is in a class of its own. During the 'Troubles' between 1969 and 1998, the border was a septic scar where violence and fear seeped from the hedgerows.

The Irish border's tragic history is inextricably linked with its absurdity. For example, if you're in the Irish town of Monaghan and want to drive to Cavan, the next county town to the south and west, something weird happens on the N54 just past the town of Clones.* The paint on the road flips to white, signs start being in miles per hour and you're suddenly on the A3. It doesn't last long: on this short stretch of road, the motorist crosses an international border four times in about four miles (6 or 7km), ending up back south of the border at the end of it. However, ascribing a compass point to the border at this point is misleading, because it weaves crazily around what geographers call the 'Drummully Polyp' – Ireland having a surplus of place names, it is also 'Coleman's Island' and 'Connons'. It is a whorl of County Monaghan intruding into County Fermanagh, connected to the rest of the county only at a few unbridged yards of the Finn river. Its shape is so irregular that it also creates a de facto exclave of Fermanagh only accessible from Monaghan. The Polyp is one of many anomalies along

---

* Clones is pronounced Clow-Ness, not as the plural of clone.

3

a border line that was created in haste in the 1920s and has been repented at leisure ever since.

The Irish border stretches between Carlingford Lough in the south-east to Lough Foyle in the north-west. It is about 300 miles long, the imprecision of the number reflecting the irrational, fractal nature of the border line, which, like a coastline, has more jagged edges and odd corners the closer one looks at the detail. Much of the country through which it runs is, like the environs of the Polyp, farmland, meaning that there is a dense network of lanes, paths and tracks, and fields that straddle the border. When the Irish and Northern Ireland governments got round to mapping the number of crossings in 2018, they agreed on a total of 208, which is more than the total number of crossings between the EU and its neighbours to the east (137).[1] There may well be more; the writer and map-maker Garrett Carr, who walked the line in 2016, found 71 informal crossings that didn't appear on any maps. The Irish border is a messy greenstick fracture rather than a clean break.

The Irish border did not have deep historical roots, nor did it reflect the wishes of the population at a fine-grained local level, and it was not drawn with economics, transport or hydrology in mind either. This neglect put Ireland out of step with the borders being drawn at the same time in mainland Europe, where the experts at the Paris Peace Conference paid attention to detail about the proper boundaries of small nations, what they needed to function economically, and the protection of minorities on each side.

The Act of Union 1800 abolished the Irish Parliament and incorporated Ireland into the United Kingdom, with 100 MPs in the House of Commons. In theory it was part of the metropolitan territory but this, like the similar status of Algeria in France or Posen (Wielkopolska) in Germany, was forgotten by governments when it was convenient to treat it differently; Ireland's suffering in the famine of the 1840s is unique in Europe's modern demographic history. The pattern of land ownership was bitterly resented by the majority of the population, as it was the product of past expropriation.

Ireland was majority Catholic, but with a Protestant minority of around 23 per cent (in 1881) that comprised several different strands, from 'planters' who had colonised the land from Tudor times, to Dublin professionals, to the industrial working class around the city of Belfast. Nationality in Ireland was not directly related to religion – for instance,

Wolfe Tone, who led the United Irishmen in 1798, was Protestant – but issues of land, religion and nation increasingly ran in harness during the 19th century. As voting rights grew in the UK, the demands of the Irish majority were reflected in the growth of a pro-devolution 'Home Rule' party after 1874, political and social unrest on the land and, in 1885–86, the conversion of Gladstone, the British Liberal leader, to the Home Rule cause. At that stage, opposition to Home Rule was based on all-Ireland arguments, but by the third attempt at Home Rule in 1912–14 counter-arguments increasingly revolved around the interests of the local Protestant Unionist majority in the north-east of Ireland around Belfast. The 'Ulster' conflict – on national lines and on the different interests of industrial and agricultural areas – anticipated other national disputes in post-1918 Europe, notably the German–Polish borderland fighting in Upper Silesia.

Once the idea of partitioning Ireland had taken hold in 1914, one of the inevitable questions was where the border between the two units would be drawn. Ireland had four historic provinces, the northernmost being Ulster, which was comprised of nine counties. But there was only a narrow Unionist majority in Ulster as a whole, so, while it was the largest unit that would be compatible with a majority for the British connection, that majority would be vulnerable to demographic trends. Three of the counties – Monaghan, Cavan and Donegal – had large Nationalist majorities and the northern Unionists had been ready since 1914 to keep them out of their political entity in the interests of having a 65/35 rather than 55/45 majority. The counties of Fermanagh and Tyrone, and the city of Londonderry, had small Nationalist majorities but were successfully claimed by the northern Unionists anyway. Curiously, many of the Fermanagh Protestants had origins among the 'Border Reivers', who had lived on the England–Scotland border but owed loyalty to neither. The Reivers were feared for banditry and violence until the Union of the Crowns of England and Scotland in 1603 and their pacification and resettlement in western Ulster.[2]

In a failed attempt to solve the problem on the old 'Home Rule' basis, the British government's Government of Ireland Act 1920 provided for parliaments for Northern Ireland and Southern Ireland within the British Empire. The six-county Northern Ireland entity produced a Unionist majority in its first election in May 1921 and rapidly took over effective police and political power, while Southern Ireland never functioned – all but four of the members elected in its first election in May 1921 regarded themselves as serving in an independent Irish Dáil. The border came into existence as a frontier, subject to later review, between two units established by the UK government, one of which was a legal fiction.* It was not clear in 1914, nor in 1920–21, that it was going to be a permanent international border. Northern Ireland was supposedly only temporarily excluded from Home Rule, and Home Rule did not mean that Ireland would leave the UK. The 1922 solution, with Northern Ireland gaining Home Rule in the UK and the Free State becoming de facto independent, was much more radical than had been envisaged in 1914.

Living with a bad border was therefore supposed to be a temporary state of affairs, even when the Anglo-Irish Treaty was signed in December 1921. It included a review of the border under a Boundary Commission representing the Free State and Northern Ireland, with a neutral chair. The British government had sent what can, with an excess of charity, be called mixed signals – the Free State hoped for significant changes such as the transfer of Fermanagh and Tyrone, while the Unionists were told that it would involve tweaks to reassign a few villages and iron out the anomalies, what was called 'rectification' in mainland Europe under the Paris treaties.

The northern Unionists had already gone cold on border revision and refused to appoint a commissioner (the British government imposed one in 1924), and the chair, Richard Feetham, a South African judge, proved sympathetic to the Unionist idea of what the commission should do. The Free State devoted great effort towards organising representations to the commission, but the proposed outcome was gravely disappointing. Not only did it recommend only small rectifications – the largest to take Crossmaglen and its surroundings into the South – but it also suggested the cession of some Free State land to the North. To those in the Free State, the idea of surrendering any 'liberated' Irish soil to the British was anathema, and border revision would not solve the central problem, which was the partition itself – perhaps, they considered, future unity would be easier to achieve if the North were more than a small

*Under the 1921 Anglo-Irish Treaty, the whole of Ireland was to be the Free State and the existing Northern Ireland Parliament was given the right to opt out of the six-county territory, which as universally expected it exercised a day after the transfer of UK legal power to the Provisional Government of Ireland.

north-eastern Protestant enclave. The Irish and British governments agreed to suppress the commission and its report, and in exchange the Free State would no longer have a share of the UK government debt. Both sides turned away from the border, and followed their separate paths.

An unusual feature of the Irish border was the limited impact it had on migration. In mainland Europe there were large movements of population out of areas that changed hands after the First World War, even in the absence of violent ethnic cleansing of the sort that had been happening in south-east Europe for a century already as the Ottoman Empire crumbled. Over half a million Germans left Pomerania and the Posen region in 1919–21; by 1926, 85 per cent of the German urban population and 55 per cent of the rural had left.[3] Hungarian populations were more inclined to stay where they were, but the demographics of Slovakia, for instance, shifted somewhat every year, particularly in the cities. Professionals and businessmen were more able to pack up and move 'back' to within their country's new borders than farmers, who were tied to the land. Rural populations had the choice of sticking it out as a minority in the new country or taking the ungenerous compensation available and leaving to start a new life (something not helped by the closing of the US frontier).

In Ireland, very few Catholics left the North for nationalist reasons, while the Protestant population in the South did dwindle. Big landowners, whose lives were half in London and half in the Irish estate anyway, could write off or cash out of what had been increasingly unprofitable land holdings. Professionals could move but a significant number around Dublin decided not to, and made their peace with their inevitable minority status in an age of democracy and nationalism. Living in a predominantly Catholic society, there was gradual assimilation by marriage. Except on the border and around Dublin, the Protestant minority was very small even in 1911; the sort of 5–10 per cent population that even the most ambitious Poles would forego claiming, were it in early 1920s Ukraine. Smaller farming communities along the border stayed with their land; the Free State was not a bad place to be a farmer. The fading away of the Protestant population in the South has latterly led to self-criticism in Ireland, for failing to accommodate them more comfortably; but, in the context of what happened to similar minorities in mainland Europe, Ireland's experience is mild.

The border and the Big House

Europe's borderlands were full of twilight ascendancies at the turn of the 20th century. The power that came from land was fading, as industrialisation created new and better-paid – if dangerous – work and personal freedom in the cities. Britain imagined that it was different, as it always does, but it was not. The Anglo-Irish landlords, the German Junkers, the Austrian aristocrats of Bohemia, the Szlachta of the eastern Polish lands and the haughty Hungarian lords of Slovakia and Transylvania all had a reckoning coming too, because their rule was incompatible with the demographic trends and the growing 19th-century ideologies of nationalism and democracy. The British government had started to buy out the landlords in 1879, and after 1903 their era was clearly ending; the German government was still trying to promote settlement in Posen as late as 1908.

The consequence of these social and national relationships can be seen in the landscape of the countries that asserted their independence in the years around 1918. In Ireland and Poland, for example, people have childhood memories of playing among the ruins of stately homes that were destroyed in traumas that happened to people long since gone. The memory of the 'Big House' is ambivalent; to the generations who lived in their shadows they were places that were associated with extreme inequality but also with employment. Some were made into political symbols of oppression and decadence, as Irish historian Vincent Comerford wrote of Mitchelstown Castle in County Cork.[4] Mitchelstown's symbolism to the aristocracy was crystallised in August 1914, when there was one last garden party, self-consciously the end of an era, on the day that war was declared. It is a scene echoed at the end of the first season of Julian Fellowes's *Downton Abbey*.

A handful of the Big House dwellers embraced the revolution. Constance Gore-Booth of Lissadell House in County Sligo ran with an artistic circle in 1890s Paris, where she met Casimir Markievicz, who hailed from a minor Polish aristocratic family from the east of the Vinnytsia oblast in what is now Ukraine. They married in 1900 and moved to Dublin in 1903, though Casimir went back to Warsaw in 1913. Constance embraced the radical chic of the day, advising young ladies to 'dress suitably in short skirts and strong boots, leave your jewels in the bank and buy a revolver'.[5] She fought in the Easter Rising in 1916 and was elected to parliament for Dublin St Patrick's in December 1918 – the first woman elected to the British House of Commons, but as a Sinn Féin representative she took her seat in the First Dáil of Ireland.

The burnt Big House and the ruin at the end of the long drive was a phenomenon of Ireland as borderland in the extended sense, in which the power of the landed minority was retreating, rather than the literal border that appeared in 1920–22. More of the border and Ulster Big Houses survived than their southern counterparts; the owners were more likely to be able to call upon people with paramilitary Ulster Volunteer Force or British Army experience to defend the house. The use of southern houses as bases for the Black and Tans, the ill-disciplined British equivalent of the German Freikorps who fought their border wars in Silesia and the Baltic in the same period, attracted Republican arson. The Civil War of 1922–23 led to a new round of burnings to keep the houses out of the hands of the rival forces. By the end of the burnings in 1923, over 300 in total had been destroyed.

Many of the attacks were more agrarian than political, part of a broader social revolution. There were occasional gestures of respect; a house spared because its occupants had bought the land fair and square rather than being planters, or where the family had been generous with famine relief in 1846 or were known as good employers. There was more restraint in the Irish revolution than in many of its mainland counterparts.

The redundant Big House that escaped the flames usually succumbed to the forces of economics and history. When the demesnes around the houses were bought up after Irish independence, the house itself was often assessed as having very little value and commonly demolished. They survived a bit longer north of the border, but there too the inexorable economics of land, inheritance tax and upkeep took their toll. The 1925 agreement on the border passed the costs of restitution of war damage, including Big Houses, to the Free State government. Payment was usually only partial, and was most likely to be generous if used to rebuild the house, although many former landlords accepted pennies on the pound and abandoned the sites, as their counterparts did in Poland and Ukraine.

The hardening border 1922–69

The stitches that bound the Free State (which formally acquired the title of Republic in 1949) to Northern Ireland pulled apart over the next decades. The leaders of the two polities, Michael Collins and James Craig, concluded a non-aggression pact in March 1922 as independence beckoned. The border became a customs frontier on 1 April 1923. The last vestiges of constitutional connection were definitively expunged in 1949. However, a liberal informal arrangement for individual travel remained in place. The Common Travel Area (CTA) allowed British and Irish citizens (and those of the Channel Islands and the Isle of Man) to live and work in each other's countries. The British Parliament affirmed that Irish citizens were not categorised as aliens in Britain, although despite this legal tolerance there was widespread prejudice ('no dogs, no blacks, no Irish') – another common feature between Ireland and other recently liberated nationalities such as Poles. Irish citizenship was open to all of those born on the island. The CTA was suspended in 1939–45 but has otherwise been continuously in place since the 1920s, a precursor to the Benelux and Schengen free travel areas. It was a work of improvisation and default, partly because constitutional disconnection took several steps, partly because the countries' economies and labour markets were still deeply connected, to say nothing of families, and partly because it was nearly impossible to stop people crossing the Northern Ireland border.

For most of its length, the Irish border runs across open country, and there were many small connections between each side that threatened to make the customs border unenforceable. The governments agreed a system in which there were three types of road crossing. The simplest were the Approved Roads, where there were Irish and UK customs posts along the main roads linking North and South. The innumerable lanes and footpaths were 'unapproved' and did not have customs huts. It was initially forbidden to cross these in motor vehicles, and using unapproved routes was a very local business – farmers whose land straddled the border, vets, doctors, and the occasional priest would go back and forward. The other crossing type was the Concession Road, which was for when the border weaved around the road and journeys between places in the same country (Cavan to Clones, or Monaghan to Dundalk) meant clipping the corner of the other side. Ordinary people were allowed to cross without stopping, and commercial vehicles could carry sealed compartments across.

This permeable border, running through poor agricultural country where people on both sides knew each other well and distrusted the authorities, was a hotbed of smuggling. Borders everywhere reflect one aspect of human nature – the desire to draw a limit around one's tribe – but are confounded by another, the desire of border neighbours to live their lives and get a little richer while cocking a snook at those in power. Goods were generally cheaper in the North, and most people who were children at the time remember sharing the car with smuggled groceries, or sitting on the disassembled cushions of a new sofa as their parents drove through the customs checkpoint. Where there were anomalies, such as a farm whose fields straddled the line, anything went. There are country ballads about pigs that crossed the border several times a day to pick up agricultural subsidies from North and South, and less charming stories from the fields of South Armagh where Thomas 'Slab' Murphy had a fuel tank with access on both sides and could arbitrage the difference in duty.* Murphy's scam – enabled by the border – was a major source of funds for the IRA, whose purpose was to abolish it.

Ireland's railway network had been built with no regard for county boundaries, and was therefore arbitrarily divided by partition – in the Paris treaties on the borders of mainland Europe, railway infrastructure caused several adjustments to traditional borders, but this did not apply in Ireland. For many border country lines, it only took one government – North or South – to decide that the route was uneconomic to make closure inevitable. From a dense network, there is now only one cross-border railway line (the Dublin to Belfast line crosses near Newry) and one other line that even approaches the border (Belfast to Derry/Londonderry).

The IRA concentrated on the border in their armed campaign of 1956–62, hoping to create areas under their effective control in majority-Nationalist parts of the border counties in the North. Their campaign was not widely supported by northern Nationalists, and the Northern

---

* Murphy was imprisoned in Ireland from 2016 to 2018 for tax evasion.

Ireland police and Irish security forces squashed it by interning IRA suspects. The Northern Ireland government also counteracted the campaign by closing smaller border roads to stop IRA men moving between jurisdictions, which disrupted local life along the border until the last 'spiked' road was reopened in 1963.

The UK–Ireland border softened a little for commercial purposes in 1965, with a new trade treaty, and again in 1973 when both countries joined the European Economic Community. While trade became easier, other sorts of crossing became harder with the conflict that began in 1969. The legal right to cross remained in place for British and Irish citizens, but in practice the border got much tighter.

Crossing the border on approved roads now involved a British Army checkpoint at which people could be questioned and their vehicles examined. The border was far from the only place where there were checkpoints; it happened in cities and country roads across Northern Ireland. Customs controls could sometimes be treated as a joke, but the checkpoints were serious and unpleasant. People wanting to cross the border – mostly Nationalists – did not want the army there, resented the intrusion and feared the soldiers. Being stopped near the border by armed men was always frightening; in 1975 Loyalist terrorists used this method to kill the musicians of the Miami Showband, in 1976 the IRA killed Protestant workmen in a sectarian atrocity at Kingsmill in County Armagh. You might be the next victim. The British soldiers were in the grip of boredom and fear – fear that the passengers in the next car wanted to kill them, or that they would miss an IRA bomb being delivered to somewhere where it could kill civilians. In South Armagh, soldiers travelled around only in helicopters from their isolated fortress of Bessbrook. All along the border, RUC police stations were armoured compounds, regularly under attack – even in the quaint little border village of Belleek, the police station was behind massive metal gates and high walls, and was targeted by dissident Republican mortars in 1998.

From summer 1970 onwards, the British Army policy on unapproved roads across the border was to close them if possible. Army engineers followed the same techniques as their police predecessors in the late 1950s, spiking the minor roads and putting up concrete blocks, or 'cratering' them with explosives. In this side campaign, the army was mostly up against border country farmers rather than the IRA; the weapons the other side used were mechanical diggers to fill up the holes and fork-lift trucks to take away concrete blocks. Margaret Thatcher wondered about boundary revision to reduce the length of the border and make it easier to control, but she was dissuaded.

The peace agreement in 1998 was swiftly followed by the dismantling of the border security infrastructure (the customs huts had already disappeared on the last day of 1992 with the coming of the European Single Market). The erasure was quick and complete; there are fewer traces of it than you will find along a Schengen border on the mainland of Europe. Bessbrook was abandoned, as were many of the fortified police stations. Belleek's is deserted, down a side lane that crosses the border a little further on – a superfluous notice in the bushes on the border reminds the visitor to drive on the left when in Ireland, the advice given in English, French and German.

The lanes near the border in Ireland are still lonely places, particularly in the North. Twenty-five years of peace has not quite dissipated the sinister, vulnerable aspect of the border country. I came to recognise the defensive style of building of the isolated houses. There is usually a wall or a sturdy fence around the edge of the plot, and a gate across the drive. The gardens are basic, offering no cover for intruders. There is usually a 'beware of the dog' sign, and often loud, grumpy barking from the resident Alsatian or wolfhound when one passes by. During the Troubles, these houses and farms were frightening places after dark. Former First Minister of Northern Ireland Arlene Foster grew up in such a place, at Dernawilt in the Fermanagh borderlands. In 1979, when she was eight years old, the IRA shot her father, John Kelly, when he had gone out of the house after dark to feed the animals on their farm. Kelly survived the attack but the family had to move out of the area.

Writers Colm Tóibín and Garrett Carr, who walked the border in 1986 and 2016 respectively, felt that the borderers were guarded, closed-mouthed people. When I spent some time in Fermanagh in 2017 my experience was a little different, and I enjoyed the company of the regulars at the pub I was staying at in Belleek; perhaps my expectations as a southern Englishman were different. But many stories of violence along the border start with loose talk, or the intimate betrayal of neighbour against neighbour, so it is unsurprising that people are still wary of giving away too much about themselves.

The life and death of the Irish politician Billy Fox (1939–74)[6] embody the universal paradoxes of the borderland. Fox was the only parliamentarian of the Republic of Ireland to be killed in the 'Troubles' of 1969–98. He was a Protestant, a County Monaghan farmer whose family had stayed with their land after independence and who identified as an Irish patriot; he was elected the Fine Gael TD for Monaghan in 1969, narrowly lost his seat in 1973 and then became a senator. He was a hands-on politician with a 'devil may care' attitude according to his friend, future Taoiseach (1994–97) John Bruton: Fox personally took part in filling up craters and reopening border roads.[7] As a border country politician, he was vocal in condemning the British Army's actions such as closing roads and using rubber bullets and CS gas. He was once suspended from the Dáil chamber in 1971 for brandishing examples of these weapons, which he said had ended up on the wrong side of the border. He was criticised by some of his rivals as a Republican, but by others as a 'B Special' (a reference to the notoriously sectarian police reserve in Northern Ireland).

Fox's fiancée, Marjorie Coulson, came from very near the border, a tiny place called Tircooney just off the N54 north-east of Clones. He tended to visit her on Monday evenings, when she was home from her cross-border commuting job as a matron in a hospital in Belfast, but when Fox arrived on 11 March 1974 there was an IRA raid in progress and he was shot dead after being stopped on his way to the Coulson house. The IRA, apparently, had been told that the Coulsons had been storing weapons for Loyalist paramilitaries but this information – possibly supplied by the Coulsons' neighbours – was untrue. It might have been invented after the fact as an excuse for sectarian violence. The IRA subsequently ordered the Coulsons out of their house, and burned it down,[8] a gesture to identify their modest dwelling with the Big Houses that had burned in the 1920s.

The murder of Fox had a traumatic impact in Ireland; his Senate election campaign had meant meeting people all over the country. John Bruton told reporter Aaron McElroy forty years later that 'the death of Billy Fox imprints on my mind and on my heart'. Border stories are always complicated; that line on the map is never clean. Five southern IRA men were imprisoned for Fox's murder, but it was put about that someone from north of the border had fired the fatal shot. Particularly shameful murders in the northern border areas were, likewise, often attributed to people from the South. The 1981 murders of former Northern Ireland Parliament Speaker Norman Stronge and his son, James, and the burning of their home at Tynan Abbey in County Armagh, are said to have been the work of an IRA unit from Monaghan. The destruction of the centre of the border town of Strabane in the early 1970s was supposed to have been the work of IRA men from across the river in Lifford. Projecting the unacceptable onto the other side of the border is a way of cushioning the blow from realising that sometimes the man in the balaclava is the neighbour to whom one nods in recognition when you meet him in daylight.

Stroke City

When I arrived in the city by the Foyle river in the north-west of Ireland, I went into a newsagent and bought a street map. It's an occasion for

The unofficial border within Derry/Londonderry, August 2016.

local humour that is fading with the ubiquity of electronic maps, so people take the chance when they can. 'Map of Londonderry? I'll tell you what, I'll throw in a map of Derry for free as well. Two for the price of one, that's got to be a bargain.'

Derry is a border city, both in its literal geography and in its personality. It always had a hinterland the other side of the line in County Donegal, with village pubs supplied by its whiskey wholesalers (a cause for complaint about the new border in the 1920s), and people coming for the big shop in the city's stores. Derry's politics is even now divided between Sinn Féin and the constitutional nationalists of the SDLP, and a handful of smaller splinters. Its people are Irish, in a different and easier way than the people of the Falls Road in West Belfast. The wind blows Atlantic air around the old city walls, and you are in non-prefixed Ireland before you cross the actual border.

Londonderry, though, has a heroic role in the iconography of Ulster unionism. The addition to its name reflects the role of the Guilds of the City of London in promoting settlement in Ulster, and the story of its Apprentice Boys and their resistance to the siege of 1689 is retold every year. The symbolic importance that unionism invests in Londonderry, despite its population being largely nationalist, resembles the nostalgic nationalism one finds about lost cities elsewhere. Londonderry's secret twin cities are Polish Wilno, Finnish Viipuri and German Königsberg. At least Londonderry is still in the country its admirers want it to be in, and its people avoided the summary expulsions that mean the other cities exist only in the memories of a departing generation.

But Derry/Londonderry is three cities superimposed on each other, not two. The third city is the line in the middle, 'Stroke City' in the name popularised by local broadcaster Gerry Anderson (1944–2014). Stroke City started as a wry nod in the direction of its divided personality and a way for a radio presenter to avoid constantly having to use both contested names. But since the Good Friday Agreement/Belfast Agreement in 1998, Stroke City as a deliberate creation of a shared, borderland community has started to exist on the ground as well. The Peace Bridge has only one name; it was opened in 2011 as a crossing between the mainly Catholic cityside and the mainly Protestant waterside at the former British base of Ebrington, its light, curved suspension span symbolising reconciliation and unity. The European Union chipped in £14.6m as part of its PEACE-III Shared Space Initiative funding; projects along the Irish border have always been generously treated. The city was the inaugural UK City of Culture in 2013, the same year that David Cameron hosted the G8 summit in peaceful Fermanagh to the delight of many of the travelling officials who discovered this beautiful green countryside and the fishing possibilities of Lough Erne. At long last, it seemed that everything had settled down.

Former prime ministers John Major and Tony Blair, architects from the British side of the peace agreement, came to Stroke City just before the Brexit referendum in June 2016 to point out how important the EU had been in peace and reconciliation. Derry, and part of Londonderry, was listening – the city constituency (diplomatically named Foyle) voted 78 per cent Remain, exceeded only by parts of inner London and the other UK border territory, Gibraltar.

Since the referendum, there has been a cloud over Stroke City. Can its carefully constructed ambiguity survive? Derry's recent history is explored in the popular comedy series *Derry Girls* (2018), set in 1993–98, days of fear and hope as the peace process made its faltering but ultimately triumphant progress. Like all period drama, *Derry Girls* has nostalgic pleasures, but it is a nuanced piece of work with an implied warning – do we *really* want to go back to this? There are dark undercurrents in Derry; the city is a centre for dissident Republicanism and it was where reporter Lyra McKee was murdered during disorder in April 2019. Londonderry, too, has its problems with alienation, poverty and apathy among young working-class Protestants. As in the 1920s, the threat of a hard border is felt particularly strongly in the city by the Foyle, regardless of community.

The Irish border has become a frontier between two occasionally divided and shaky Unions. The EU was a hidden bit of machinery in the complex arrangements that made the invisible border work in Ireland as it did on the European mainland. To take an example, it finally abolished roaming charges for mobile phone data and calls in June 2017, having driven down charges for a decade before that. For people living well within the borders of a country, roaming charges may not impinge much. But for border residents it is a much more serious matter. Even without crossing the border oneself, phones frequently lock on to the signal from a mast on the other side, particularly if – like the Irish border and many others — the landscape is rugged and rural. Your phone will enter Poland while you are physically still in Frankfurt an der Oder in Germany, which is a mere curiosity now, but I have also been for a walk in Polish woods and been 'welcomed' to Russia by Vodafone, which is potentially costly as well as menacing. Brexit has meant the revival of roaming charges at the Irish border, with all the complication and expense that entails.

Despite the efforts of Major and Blair, the UK's referendum on 'controlling our borders' took place without much consideration of what would happen at the country's actual land border. Arguments were made with reference to people crossing borders, but it turned out that the real consequences were more about goods. Under the CTA and the Good Friday Agreement, the border would have to be kept open for people to cross freely, but after 2016 there was a choice between a customs border in Ireland, a customs border in the Irish Sea or — and this option was hastily ruled out by Theresa May in 2016 — the UK remaining compliant with European arrangements. The border itself developed a persona on Twitter (@BorderIrish) during the Brexit years of 2018–20, commenting to its 100,000 followers in a wry tone of voice. Ultimately, Boris Johnson conceded that there would be checks between Northern Ireland and Great Britain. The hard edges of the Brexit border trilemma could be softened somewhat with facilities for trusted traders, inspections away from the border, labelling and classification of goods, but there was no getting around the essential problem.

There is only one product for which the border does not seem to pose much of a trading issue — the humble potato crisp. Crisps were boring in the 1950s, with salt and oil being the principal tastes available. A Dublin entrepreneur, Joe 'Spud' Murphy (trust me, this is true — I would have made up less stereotypical names), had the bright idea of making flavoured crisps and so production of the savoury delight that is the Tayto crisp began in the Republic in 1954. Murphy sold the UK rights to the Tayto brand to Thomas Hutchinson, a Northern Ireland businessman, who set up production in a castle (as I said, I would have tried harder if I were making it up), and the first Northern Tayto was bagged up in 1956. Each has their own slightly different Mr Tayto on the packet. Perhaps it's just me, but I can imagine the southern one as being genial Joe Murphy and the northern one being salt of the earth Tam Hutchinson.

There are not many loyalties that unite the entire population of Northern Ireland, but the Northern Tayto is one of them. One can start an entirely non-sectarian North–South argument about which Tayto is better. The northern identity is bolstered by school trips to the factory at Tandragee Castle in County Armagh. The existence of a rival southern version, and the incomprehension in Britain about the importance of the Tayto, make it symbolic of the province; it's an all-Ireland phenomenon but with the northern difference recognised thanks to a complex legal arrangement. Academic Ciaran Martin was joking when he suggested that there should be a statue of the northern Mr Tayto outside the parliament building at Stormont, but there have been worse ideas.

You're not supposed to sell Taytos on the other side of the border. It's a breach of the licensing agreement between the two firms, although customers' strong preference for their own version of the Tayto does most of the work. But people travel, and there are rumours about places in the border country where you can get hold of the 'wrong' Taytos. I would hate to get anyone into trouble by saying any more.

The Irish border illustrates several general truths about European borders. Its combination of absurdity and tragedy will find many echoes. So too will its complex psychological and social impact on those who live with and around it. The border literally divides Fermanagh from Monaghan, but it is also a feature that unites the two counties because they have to cope with its drawbacks and anomalies.

Whether a border is hard or soft is the product of the decisions of the authorities on both sides. Once a border is drawn, however negligently, defending it (or sometimes the ambition to move it) becomes a symbol of national sovereignty. The paradox is that this attitude makes managing the border so much more difficult, as Ireland experienced in the 1920s and in a different form in the period since the UK's 'Brexit'. In many countries across Europe, the interests of border people in freedom of movement and trade are opposed to the priorities of national governments. Soft borders, such as the free-movement Schengen borders of mainland Europe and the complex post-Brexit open border in Ireland, reconcile these edges of national sovereignty with the practicalities of border life – working, shopping and socialising across these artificial lines. But the soft border, fixed in place but permeable, is a more ambitious project than just to make life easier for border people. It is part of a philosophy of international co-operation that developed along one of Europe's violent historical fault lines, the Rhine frontier between France and Germany.

2

The watch on the Rhine

(France/Germany)

The Gare de l'Est is my favourite station in Paris. It is a short walk from the Gare du Nord, the insanely complex, busy and somewhat sleazy terminal where the Eurostar trains from London arrive, but it has a very different atmosphere. Sunlight streams in through the glass ceiling but the air feels cool and fresh, and even the shops seem a bit more upmarket. It's a lovely piece of Parisian architecture, elegant and thoroughly suitable for its purpose. Since 2007 it has been the terminus for the TGV-Est train service, the fastest in Europe, which can carry you to Luxembourg in two hours and Stuttgart in a little over three.

Look around the station a little, though, and there are bitter memories of dark historical chapters and the deep wounds that borders and border revisions inflict. I remember that it was considered a little embarrassing for the first direct trains from France to Britain to arrive at the London terminal named after the Battle of Waterloo. However, in Paris trains from Germany terminate at the Place du 11 Novembre 1918, which gives out onto the Rue du 8 Mai 1945. Inside the station there are several well-tended plaques commemorating the prisoners of war and Resistance fighters deported from here, and the transports to Auschwitz that left from the depot at Bobigny, a short distance down the line. On the roof of the east wing there is a stern memorial to the 1916 Battle of Verdun, dedicated in 1931 – the Métro station is also named after Verdun.

One memorial, however, did not start off as a reminder of war but acquired that meaning a couple of decades after the grand station first opened in 1849 as the 'embarcadère de Strasbourg' (Strasbourg landing stage). Capping the central arch there is a statue representing the city of Strasbourg as a queen, holding a key (to the Rhine? To France's destiny?). But in 1871 the journey from Paris to what was now the German city of Strassburg became international rather than domestic. Part of the price for France's loss in the Franco-Prussian war was the transfer of the province of Alsace, containing Strasbourg, and parts of Lorraine around the River Moselle. The Strasbourg statue became a painful symbol of the amputation of a 'lost province', a reminder to Parisians of a humiliating moment for France and the unsatisfactory state of its national borders. France suffered a psychological blow, whose impact was peculiarly strong given that Alsace was a culturally distinct province and parts of Lorraine had also not been French territory for very long in historic time. The lost provinces, greyed out on many a map of France after 1871, were a 'pays perdu' and their eventual recovery was a dream common to nearly everyone in the country:

> La Croix de Lorraine est brisée,
> mais ce n'est pas pour toujours
> (The Cross of Lorraine is broken.
> But it is not forever.)

Revanchism – the desire to reclaim the lost provinces – was not just an extreme right demand in France. The loss of Alsace and the Moselle section of Lorraine was a physical manifestation of the humiliation that France had suffered at the hands of the rising power of Germany. Building a huge colonial empire, as Third Republic France did, did not fill the void. The German annexation of Alsace-Lorraine (including Strassburg) lasted until 1918, but the bitterness and division within France lasted nearly until the present day, and the imprint of the boundaries of 1871 is still there in law, administration and culture.

If one is looking for stereotypically German-looking place names, Alsace might be a better hunting ground than anywhere actually in Germany – Pfaffenhoffen, Hilsenheim and Oberhausbergen are all in France. I think I was puzzled by this even before I travelled through Alsace on the way to my first international land border that day in 1984. I knew that people there were French in terms of their national allegiance and spoke French, but also that they spoke a dialect that was closer to German. I knew that a lot of French beer came from around Strasbourg – Kronenbourg, for instance – but that the Germans on the other side of the line produced white wine and smelly cheeses. I knew that the sovereignty of the area had changed repeatedly throughout history, and also understood that this process had stopped and that the lines on the map wouldn't move again. Maybe the idea of a 'nation' and somebody being part of it was a bit more complicated than one is led to believe.

In 1871, the French and Germans had different ideas about what constituted a nation; to the Germans, the culture of Alsace made it part of the German nation, recently unified under the Hohenzollern crown, while to the French its history and its civic political culture made the region part of *their* nation. While Germany could make a claim to Alsace on the grounds that the people there were culturally German and belonged in a German nation state, the same was not true in most of the section of Lorraine that was annexed. The rationale there was strategic, albeit via a circular version of military logic – Germany needed the fortresses of Metz in order to defend herself from France, who would be permanently alienated by the annexation. The coal and iron deposits of Lorraine were also worth having, although the industry was in its infancy in 1871.

The Treaty of Frankfurt was innovative in the way it treated the inhabitants of the transferred territory. When territories were moved about by the 1815 Congress of Vienna after the final defeat of Napoleon's France, there had been little consideration for the interests and national feelings of the populations who lived there. But by 1871 it had to be acknowledged that there were some people in the region who experienced it as an affront to their identity. Instead of automatically acquiring German nationality, the citizens of Alsace-Moselle were given the option of retaining French nationality instead. Most of the people who did so were already resident in the rest of France or in French colonies, but 160,878 people living in what was now Germany went through the bureaucratic process to stay French.[9] Around 50,000 exiled themselves from Alsace-Moselle. Among them was a patriotic Jewish Frenchman from Mulhouse, Raphael Dreyfus, and his son Alfred. A few years later Alfred joined the army, but he was the victim of prejudice against him as a Jew and as a borderlander and unjustly accused of spying for Germany. The resulting scandal polarised France at the turn of the century.

The Franco-German border in Lorraine and the Vosges was a soft boundary for nearly all its existence. People could cross it freely. As well as the old ties uniting Lorraine, there were new bonds with people who had relocated to the other side, particularly to Nancy. Patriotic occasions in France such as 14 July celebrations were augmented by people coming from across the new border. Both Nancy and Belfort benefited from an influx of exiles from the German territory, and the relocation of some of the most patriotic industrial concerns. Nancy became the unchallenged capital of the French east and the recipient of official favour and supportive public sentiment. It became an intellectual and artistic city, and a distinctive variant on Art Nouveau was born in its artists' studios, with a strong contribution from the Alsatian exiles.

This tense frontier was, as the historian Benoit Vaillot has written, a prototype of modern border enforcement. The rules were not strict by today's standards, but the level of official surveillance of travellers was experienced then as an infringement of human rights of movement, particularly in 1888-90 when the Germans imposed a passport and visa requirement. Like other borders in the late 19th and early 20th centuries, the Franco-German frontier was of interest to border tourists. Postcards of border posts and officials, and of curiosities created by the border line, were published. For example, two brothers in military uniform – one French, one German, both sporting splendid moustaches – were depicted meeting at the frontier post near Metz.

The border also attracted war-related tourism and remembrance; my Baedeker's *Rhine* of 1903 has a detailed map of the 1870 Gravelotte battlefield and instructions on how to get there. The area was studded with small war memorials, mostly German, put up by their regiments near where they fell. This era came abruptly to an end in July 1914; as Europe stumbled towards war, the border was suddenly closed.

The annexed territories did not stand still during the German period. People move around within big countries, particularly as they industrialise. In the east of the German Empire, nationalists fretted about the erosion of the German presence in the Polish lands, but the same westward drift had Germanised the areas acquired from France. The growth of heavy industry in northern Lorraine, adjacent to Luxembourg, pulled in industrial workers from all over Germany and by 1914 towns like Diedenhofen (now Thionville) had large German majorities.

The German years in Elsass-Lothringen – as the province was now known – were an example of the phenomenon that Norman Angell, in

Two brothers standing on the Franco-German border.

his 1909 book *The Great Illusion*, took to illustrate the futility of territorial conquest and therefore of war. Germany had acquired a province, but it had also acquired a reluctant people who were constantly sensitive about slights to their interests and identity, such as the Saverne affair of 1913, a furious scandal that began when a Prussian officer was rude to the locals in the town of Zabern (Saverne) near the border with France. Germany had also made an enemy of France, whose resentment then had to be considered in all of Germany's diplomacy and military planning. The reparations demanded in the Treaty of Frankfurt invited retaliation in kind should the tables ever be turned.

When war began in 1914, France's emotions were expressed in the straightforward plan of attack – the French army would launch a frontal assault on the border in Lorraine and the Vosges and drive the Germans out. The attack was mostly unsuccessful and the desperate need to hold off the German attack in the north meant that it could not be pressed. The French briefly captured Mühlhausen (Mulhouse) but lost it again, and their Alsace offensive only gained a few sparsely populated valleys. However, the Germans were perturbed at the welcome given to French troops where they appeared and exercised ever tighter military control over the border province. The high command prudently directed army units from Alsace-Lorraine away from having to fight their French brethren, and sent them mostly to the eastern front. As the war developed, they wandered ever further into imperial Russia, to Vilnius and beyond. For most of the duration of the war, their home front south of Verdun was a quiet stretch.

The outbreak of war added to a tendency that already existed for both sides to regard Alsace-Lorraine as a child custody battle. French nationalist art depicted the two as innocent little girls, torn away from their mother's bosom. The Germans saw their role as being protectors and guides of the two little ones. Nationalism infantilised and sentimentalised the provinces.

The November 1918 Armistice agreement stipulated that Alsace-Lorraine would be transferred to French control within 15 days, along with all the occupied territory. Unlike elsewhere in the emerging borderlands of the new Europe, no plebiscite was offered to the inhabitants to determine which country they would like to be in. Having won the war at such high cost, France could not settle for less than the entirety of the lost provinces, and the risk of a plebiscite was that some areas had become sufficiently Germanised since 1871 that they might produce a pro-German majority. President Poincaré, looking out from the balcony of Strasbourg City Hall when visiting in December 1918 and seeing a vast cheering crowd, claimed that his reception was mandate enough: 'the vote has been cast'.

The French army took over Metz on 19 November and Strasbourg on 22 November and were given a rapturous welcome in the streets. The French tricolour was everywhere – borderland people often have more than one flag in the attic to provide for such occasions. But the joy was genuine enough. As well as national feeling, there were other reasons to celebrate. Alsace-Moselle was free from war, hunger and military dictatorship and with one bound its people had gone from being citizens of a defeated power to being on the winning side.

The return to France of Alsace-Moselle was a change of a historic nature; the first time an 'advanced' industrial territory went from one nation state with a well-developed welfare state and rule of law to another. Taking no chances, the new French authorities severed many of the German Rhine rail bridges.

As with the annexation by Germany in 1871, there was a long hangover after the return of Alsace-Moselle to France. There was public recrimination between people in the territory, often spiteful and hypocritical, and a vengeful official attitude to Germans from the other side of the Rhine who had settled in the province. The French authorities oversaw a process of classification of the population according to their national characteristics and family background. There were four categories, A to D, decided by military-dominated selection committees, and 120,000 of the lowest ranked 'Reichsdeutsche' were expelled into Germany proper. About another 90,000 felt sufficiently unwelcome as to leave with various degrees of reluctance but without legal compulsion. It was a much more severe regime than the Germans imposed in 1871.

In hindsight, the sorting of the population of Alsace-Lorraine seems a chilling precedent for organised, bureaucratic discrimination and ethnic cleansing in conquered territory. It was one of the first such exercises to take place in Europe outside the Balkans, although colonial powers had frequently classified and relocated populations. The Nazi authorities in the areas of Poland incorporated directly into the Reich in 1939 would go on to have their own fourfold classification system. However, the differences are important as well as the similarities. The classification programme in France was devoid of the racial pseudo-science that lay behind the Nazi programme in Poland, the criteria were much less haphazard and severe, and the consequences of a failing grade were much lighter. The 1919 Reichsdeutsche were expelled in a reasonably orderly way into a state with which they could identify, as opposed to the 1939 Poles who were reduced to slave status or sent to the grisly colonial regime in Hans Frank's Generalgouvernement.

Fitting the lost provinces back into France was a complex business, in which the future architect of European unity Robert Schuman played a part. There is to this day a faint imprint from the German period on the map of France. The pre-1871 map of the subdivisions of France was not restored in 1918.* The main stumbling block for reintegration after 1918 was the relationship between church and state. The French state had

---

*Hence the oddly shaped départements of Meurthe-et-Moselle and Territoire de Belfort, which were the bits of Alsace-Lorraine that had stayed in France in 1871.

become completely secular in 1905 but German Alsace-Lorraine had continued to be under the French rules as they had been in 1870. While the French state now kept completely away from religious matters, except for legal ownership of church buildings, the main religions and denominations were officially recognised in Alsace-Lorraine. This meant that public funding goes towards the churches and there are still religious schools in the reattached provinces.

The French government was willing to relax its anti-clerical principles in the interests of conciliating the returned provinces and accepted that they could keep the old rules, and the three eastern départements of Haut-Rhin, Bas-Rhin and Moselle are treated differently to this day. The provinces also kept their favourable German legislation on social insurance and pensions, for an unspecified but long transitional period. Not all the work of harmonising Alsace-Moselle to French standards and law had been completed even when the German army came back in June 1940.

Despite all this solicitude to the peculiarities of Alsace-Moselle, there were still resentments that continued throughout the interwar period, particularly over language and education. The province had missed out on French centralisation and assimilation and the Alsatian dialect had more status than other French regional variants. The deportation of key German workers left a skills gap in industry, and their replacements who travelled east from Paris needed phrase books to communicate with the locals despite them all supposedly being French.

For many of the French, the sentimental idea of the two lost children was more appealing than the reality of these culturally mixed, complicated provinces where not everything German was perceived as bad. For many of the Alsatians, France was experienced as patronising and dominating and a movement for greater regional autonomy gathered steam in the 1920s and 1930s. The nationalist yearning, both sides found, was more about an idealised image frozen in 1870 than the contemporary reality.

When France was conquered in 1940, the German desire for territory did not stop at Alsace-Lorraine. France was divided into several pieces after the armistice, with varying degrees of German control. Germany did not annex Alsace-Lorraine or Luxembourg outright after the defeat of France. Part of the reason for this restraint was to make the armistice easier to swallow for the French. It was also that the Nazis hoped to wrap up the war in the west shortly with a comprehensive peace treaty in which all the territorial issues would be addressed. In the meantime, these areas were placed under German civil administration while still being outside the Reich – in contrast to Poland, where large areas were claimed as integral German territory in 1939. In parallel, the Nazi party organisation was extended to the newly occupied border areas and racial classification began; racial hierarchy was more important in the New Order than legal national boundaries. The more ambitious and ideological Nazis hoped for the permanent fragmentation of France beyond the Germanised zone into small states that would not challenge German dominance of Europe.[10]

The de facto annexation was a much more abrupt transition than the changes of 1871 and 1918. The Nazi authorities treated the local culture with contempt, laying down the law as to what was proper German culture and what was 'Welsch' – i.e. strange western Celtic ways. A French political mentality had survived under the Second Reich but the Third was going to try to stamp it out.

In 1942, the men of regions under German civil administration like Alsace-Lorraine and Luxembourg became subject to conscription into the Wehrmacht. Fighting in German uniform was deeply uncomfortable for most of them, and sometimes compelled only by coercive measures against their families, and they became known as the malgré-nous (despite ourselves). Despite the risks, as many as 40,000 of those conscripted deserted, some of them joining the Resistance. But there were also a few thousand volunteers and enthusiasts who had enlisted in the Waffen-SS. While most of the malgré-nous served in the east, some of them were deployed in the west, including as part of the Das Reich SS division that committed the massacre at Oradour-sur-Glane in Limousin in the west of France in which 642 people were murdered and six escaped. Thirteen were found guilty of the crime in a military trial in 1953, but after an outraged public response in Alsace the National Assembly legislated for an amnesty for the malgrés-nous, to another round of protest from people in Limousin. The extent of willing collaboration, and implication in war crimes, was too hot an issue for post-war France to look at directly, and the history became nearly taboo.

War memorials in Alsace-Moselle are different from those in the rest of France. They are discreet about for which side the fallen soldier died; the vast majority of casualties from 1914–18 will have been serving in the German armed forces, and post-war France did not ask their neighbours and families to disown them or forget their existence. The list of names from 1939–45 reflects anguished divided loyalties and impossible dilemmas too complex to capture in a stone inscription. The memorials emphasise mourning the loss of human life rather than patriotic ideals or celebrating victory. In Schirmeck, near Strasbourg, the casualties belong to the village rather than a country. The casualties of colonial wars in Indochina and Algeria are added to the bottom of the memorial, objects of ambivalent memory for another set of reasons. In the borderlands, it is impossible to maintain one's illusions about war for very long.

Schirmeck war memorial, May 2019.

The shrine of Robert Schuman

If you take a brisk walk east across country from the 1870 battlefield at Gravelotte, you will come across the village of Scy-Chazelles, on the edge of the urban area of Metz. There is a little fortified village church that has become a shrine to the European idea. The European flag has pride of place, and the national flags of the EU member states are displayed on the west wall of the church. The mixing of religious and supranational symbolism forms something from a Brexiter's nightmares. Even as a convinced British European, it made me wince a little on first encounter. But if one understands how such a place could exist, one understands a lot about Europe and its borders.

Scy-Chazelles is the final resting place of Robert Schuman, a man whose life is a borderlands story – born in 1886 to a Luxembourger mother and a father who was a German citizen but born French. Even his name was part French, part German, like those of many people in these middle lands. Schuman died a French European in 1963, rejecting the binary divides that had created Gravelotte, Verdun and Oradour. In 2021 the Catholic Church declared this founder of the European Union 'venerable', the second of four steps between ordinary layman and saint.

Schuman embodied the borderland's mixture of the cosmopolitan sophisticate and the provincial bourgeois. He commuted from Scy-Chazelles to Paris – a considerably harder journey in his time than in the era of TGV-Est – and was never fully content away from his manor house and the church in the little village he regarded as home. Schuman was devoutly serious about his faith and his political ideas, which he saw as aspects of the same calling – a Christian Democrat even before that title formally existed. The trail of his semi-secular sainthood at Scy-Chazelles continues to the museum at his house, where the room in which he wrote the Schuman Declaration speech on the future unification of Europe in May 1950 is preserved as a shrine. The draft text lies on the table, as if he were making a few last-minute amendments before catching the train to Paris.

The first moves towards European unity reflected the concerns of Schuman and the Rhine borderland. The subject of his Declaration was co-operation in coal and steel, in the interests of economic rationality and the breaking of national military-industrial complexes that divided the heavy industrial regions of the Saar, Lorraine and southern Luxembourg. But Schuman's first European venture was in law, in the form of the Council of Europe, which in 1949, with heavy British involvement, established European standards on human rights and international law.

These two initiatives marked the determination of Europe's post-war leaders to move past the destructive competition for industrial resources and territorial jealousy that had led to disaster in 1870, 1914 and 1939. The cycle could have begun again, but thanks to Schuman and his colleagues it did not. Europe was not just a technocratic collaboration, it was an ambitious geopolitical project that – 70 years of history has proved – turned a previously violent corner of the globe into a realm of peace and prosperity.

The idea of European unity was not invented from nothing at Schuman's desk. There has hardly ever been a moment in the continent's history in which unfettered, wholly independent states have dominated, and the moments that have come closest to this state have been everybody's nightmares. Schuman was struggling with the same issues as others had before him and have done since. How can we reconcile nation states with the interdependence that modern economics produces, and the tendency of people to choose to move across borders? How can national sovereignty co-exist with countries behaving respectfully to each other and towards their own minorities? How can national competition be regulated so that it does not turn violent? Schuman's Rhineland, western European perspective formed the EU. It was easy in the divided Europe of the Cold War era to forget that others had been pondering it all for a while – from Prussian Gottfried Herder's ambiguous celebration of nationalism, to Polish-Jewish Ludwik Zamenhof's invention of Esperanto in borderland Białystok, to the Austrian Franz Ferdinand's Slovak adjutant devising a way of transforming the Habsburg empire into a federation of peoples, the idea of a Europe that was more than competing nation states had a lot of intellectual and political power.

The Saar borderland

The Saar's main city of Saarbrücken looks like a typical West German city. Most of the buildings in the centre were put up in the 1950s and 1960s; its shopping centre is a ribbon of pedestrianised main street leading from the railway station to St Johann square. A concrete highway follows the south bank of the Saar, running below the old castle and the Saarland's parliament building. There is very little bilingual signage – normally an indicator of borderland status – in the city. It is cross-border in the sense that it has suburbs such as Forbach on the French side, and its trams run as far as the French town of Sarreguemines; there is a commuting population from an area of France otherwise without a large city. It takes an hour and fifty minutes on the non-stop train to Paris – a shorter journey time than it is to Frankfurt, let alone Berlin. Here is a clue to that slight air of ambiguity about the place – a German city, but one that feels the gravitational pull of France. France has tried to woo the Saarland, roughly and smoothly, on several occasions, but despite these efforts the Saar has remained dourly faithful to Germany.

The re-annexation of Alsace and Moselle reversed the French losses of 1871, but French ambitions went further than that during and after the First World War, because 1871 was not the first territorial loss that rankled with French nationalists. The argument went back to the Congress of Vienna in 1815, when France's boundaries agreed in 1814 were clipped back after the series of unfortunate events that ended in Waterloo. Desiring to see monarchist France readmitted to reputable international society, the treaties had initially been generous to the defeated foe and given France some parts of what are now Germany, around Saarlouis, Saarbrücken and Landau.

France's British allies were unwilling in 1919 to see Waterloo as the first manifestation of Teutonic aggression, but on other issues the Allies were willing to admit that France had a point. During the German Empire, an industrial area had grown up in the Saar alongside Lorraine, which had become part of Germany in 1871. Saar coal and Lorraine iron ore created a third German heavy industrial region in competition with the Ruhr basin and Upper Silesia. People came from all over Germany to the Saar and Lorraine, which were effectively a single economic unit. Lorraine was returning to France, so leaving the Saar area in Germany would split the region with a customs barrier. France had been dependent on coal imports before the war, making it vulnerable to Germany, and the domestic French coal industry in the north-east had been trashed during the German occupation. Leaving Lorraine's steel dependent on yet more imports from the Saar would be a grave economic disadvantage. In these circumstances, the British and the Americans were prepared to agree that, although France could not annex the Saar and Luxembourg, there could be some special arrangements for an interim period. The newly defined Saar became a League of Nations protectorate separated from Germany. The mines, state-owned under Germany, would become the property of France. The protectorate would be subject to a vote in

15 years' time on whether it should continue or whether people wanted to join France or Germany.

The German identity of the Saar region proved stubbornly indifferent to the economic calculations and the influence of the Allies. The population of the protectorate looked forward to rejoining Germany. When the Nazis took power in 1933, German activities in the Saar were 'co-ordinated' as they were in the Reich. Anti-Nazis were free in the Saar, but there were episodes of Nazi bullying and sinister reminders that when the vote came in 1935, the jackboot would kick down the doors of those who had opposed the new Germany. Even so, surprisingly few Jews and socialists left the Saar in 1933–35.[11] Although the socialists wanted the plebiscite postponed until Germany was democratic again, they faced a painful conflict of loyalty that most of the anti-Nazi German Saarlanders resolved into 'my country right or wrong'. As the British historian Margaret Lambert (1906–95) wrote, 'flags run riot in the Saar, and on the slightest provocation the towns are decked' – with a motley range of German decorations from swastikas to the blue and white flag of Bavaria to the red flag of socialism.[12]

The January 1935 Saar plebiscite was one of the grimmest exercises in democracy that can be imagined. The electorate were given a free choice between joining Germany, staying as they were, or joining France. National sentiment made the second two options palatable only to a small minority, and the knowledge that they would be joining Nazi Germany inhibited the expression of contrary views. For the sake of form, the Nazi movement promised moderation although the true face of its rule was apparent just across the border, where it held massive nationalist rallies from August 1933 onwards. On a 98 per cent turnout, 91 per cent voted for Germany, 9 per cent for the League of Nations and 0.4 per cent for France. It was Hitler's first victory in his quest to revise the Versailles boundaries of Germany.

The same economic and strategic problems for France that led to the interwar Saar protectorate were still there after 1945, and the Allies went for a similar solution. A slightly larger Saarland would be detached again from Germany to assist in France's economic recovery and take some heavy industrial power away from Germany. This time, it would be ruled as a French protectorate but from 1947 to 1957 it was a semi-independent state with its own 'national' sports teams and postage stamps. But, realising the unwillingness of the Saar to become French and the interdependence of heavy industry across the borders of France, Germany, the Saar, Luxembourg and Belgium, French policymakers opted for longer-term solutions.

This detached Saarland also had a date with destiny in a plebiscite, this time in October 1955. The vote was on the proposition that the Saar should become the first piece of European sovereign territory, its parliament functioning under a commissioner appointed by the West European Union and its economy part of a customs union with France. Unlike the League mandate, there was a positive case for the European option, in that the Saar would become a leader in a bigger process of European integration. The offer was supported by 32 per cent of voters on a 97 per cent turnout, one of the highest shares of the vote ever anywhere for a radical and explicit post-nationalist proposal – but still less than half the number of opponents, whose votes were nearly all signalling that they wished to be in West Germany. The transfer took place in 1957. But by then, the issues that had led to the Saar problem were being solved at a higher level, with the European Coal and Steel Community (ECSC) in operation since 1952 and the more ambitious Treaty of Rome establishing the European Economic Community signed by six nations, including France and West Germany, in 1957. It still took until the Schengen Agreement of 1985 and the single market of 1992 before formal borders were lifted.

Schengen

The Germans have a compound word for it: *Dreiländereck*; 'three nations' corner'. There's something even more liminal about a tri-point border than there is with a regular one, although in topological terms they are simpler, being a point as opposed to a line; people mark them in ceremonial ways with obelisks and flags rather than the functional clutter that often surrounds border places. My travels have taken me to tri-points such as the highest mountain in the Netherlands, a sculpture park in a field near the Danube, and a contentious memorial that has been shuffled a few metres south of Viktor Orbán's fence, but few of these points are as famous as the one in the far south-east of Luxembourg.

As the Moselle flows north and slightly east towards Koblenz and the Rhine, through a green landscape of hills and vineyards, its right bank meets the boundary between France and Germany at a large lock gate between the French village of Apach and the small German town of Perl. The Dreiländereck is in the centre of the Moselle (Mosel to the Germans, d'Musel to the Luxembourgers), as the other bank of the river is in Luxembourg; one passes the duchy down the left-hand side. The Luxembourg vertex of the triangle is a small village whose name is known across the world, for we have come to Schengen.

Road sign by the Musel bridge in Schengen, August 2018.

The Saar in 1957 was the last significant territorial alteration in western Europe, but borders altered in western Europe in the 1980s and 1990s. They did not shift around on the map, but they became steadily less and less significant. The sense of a border as barrier started to disappear. First money, then goods, then people were able to move between countries without interference.

Back in 1984, a few weeks after I crossed that bridge at Kehl, other less naïve minds were turning their attention to the question of Europe's borders. President Mitterrand and Chancellor Kohl were chatting over a drink after a European summit meeting and the Rhine bridge came up in their conversation; they concluded that it would be a fine idea if that border crossing could be thrown open and people could move between Strasbourg and Kehl without official hindrance. Kohl and Mitterrand's speculative proposal took flight and in June 1985 five European leaders met at Schengen. It was not widely noticed at the time, but it was the start of something radical and historic. Within Europe, the world of 'hard borders' – arc-lit no-man's lands of tarmac and traffic jams, gruff officials in peaked caps, passport stamps – was on the way out, although it was difficult to discern given that one of the hardest borders of all still ran through the middle of Kohl's own country and, in the form of an ugly, lethal concrete ribbon, through its largest city.

After 1995, Schengen gave an old freedom of movement – which had been enjoyed in the pre-1914 Europe of empires if one was rich enough to travel – to ever-increasing numbers of people. The present Schengen zone covers 400 million people – the second largest free movement zone in the world after India.* Schengen creates the conditions for a steadily denser web of connections in cross-border regions – people shopping, working and forming relationships without the need for official permission to travel to the next village or town across the artificial line.

The freedom of Schengen is not without its harsher aspects. Borders have not dissolved entirely. The treaty allows countries to reimpose border controls if they have one of a wide range of permitted reasons. France has exercised this right, arguing counter-terrorism; Sweden has imposed controls, and the policies of the German border guard on the edges of Poland and Czechia sometimes push the discretion under the treaty beyond tolerance. The COVID epidemic in 2020–21 saw borders temporarily slam shut again, and countries have argued since 2022 about how best to respond to would-be Russian travellers. At the edge of the Schengen zone, particularly in the Mediterranean Sea off Greece and Italy and the Spanish enclaves of Ceuta and Melilla in North Africa, the borders are more forbidding than ever. Frontex, the European external borders agency, is no soft touch with migration from outside the zone.

Schengen is underpinned by an expansion of law enforcement. Border and customs control has never just been about what happens at the line on the map, but also in everyday encounters requiring ID and the person's

* In a legal sense, the internal passport system means that China is not a free movement zone, although in practice there is unauthorised inter-province movement.

proof of approved status. With registration of population and the technology of surveillance, everywhere is the border. With Schengen came a new sort of cross-border policing with its own new police language, 'Schenglish', and new powers for police to operate across borders.

Schengen created an archipelago of redundant official buildings across the continent, some of which have been put to various uses. Old customs offices are hotels or houses, old checkpoints in the roads are sometimes converted to imaginative uses. On the road from Aachen in Germany to Eupen in the German-speaking region of Belgium, one has become a florist catering mainly to Belgian commuters working in Germany. On the older road running parallel to the motorway from Austria and Slovakia into Hungary, there is a derelict border control station amid the cornfields, redundant since the latter countries joined Schengen in 2007. I always enjoy coming across these; my heart lifts as I see these authoritarian impediments to free movement and neighbours visiting each other rotting away as another European winter does its work on the concrete structure.

Disused border control post on the frontier of
Slovakia and Hungary, December 2018.

The Europe of Schengen, the single market and a supranational Union has meant the end of the long tug of war over Alsace-Lorraine and the Saarland. The Rhine frontier has, as Robert Schuman and his contemporaries hoped, become a prime example of reconciliation and peaceful, co-operative interdependence. War has become unthinkable along this battle-scarred borderland. On a deeper level, the feelings that lead to war have disappeared; old ideas of the German destiny of Alsace or the French frontier belonging at Mainz are mere historical curiosities with no contemporary resonance. This is the difference between the Rhine and some other boundaries in Europe, including those in Ireland and Poland – while inter-state war is unthinkable there too, the idea that the boundary is in the wrong place is still capable of arousing passions. But the Rhine's historical baggage as the fault line between French and German worlds means that it will remain a visible borderland for the indefinite future. The same is less true of the even longer-established mutual soft borders of Belgium, the Netherlands and Luxembourg, where history and simple practicality have created extraordinarily close relationships across these imaginary lines.

3

United by borders

(Netherlands/Belgium)

House in Loveren, Baarle-Nassau and Baarle-Hertog, January 2023.

International boundaries separate countries on the map, but in the places through which they are drawn they are local. Sometimes they are even domestic. There is a small housing block on Chaamseweg in the town of Baarle on the border of Belgium and the Netherlands, and in 1995 the two countries were finally getting round to drawing the border line in detail. Before the surveyors started work it had been believed that house number 10 was in Belgium, but according to the ancient land ownership documents it was actually in the Netherlands. This did not go down well with the occupant, a lady of 84 years, who insisted that she was a Belgian, had always been Belgian, and wasn't going to suddenly become Dutch against her will at her stage of life.

The situation seemed impossible until someone had a bright idea. The lady's door was only just in the Netherlands, and her lobby spanned both countries because there were windows next to the door. Why not swap the door and the windows around, and put her back in Belgium where she belonged? A little bit of building work later, and everyone was happy.

10 Chaamseweg Baarle-Hertog, January 2023,
after the door and window were swapped.

The block on Chaamseweg might not even be the weirdest border-based predicament in Baarle. There are several houses where the border line runs right through the front door. The very strangest situation is probably a building on Desirée Geeraertstraat, where, to comply with planning regulations on the Dutch side, two of the flats are in the Netherlands and one, because of the arrangement of the flats' doors, is in Belgium. The result is the international equivalent of a flying freehold, where a piece of Belgium is sandwiched vertically between two Dutch apartments. There are two doors in from the street, one Dutch and one Belgian, leading to the same entrance lobby. It is a very Dutch solution, a pragmatic working around that is not quite against the law although one would struggle to think of it as being entirely *with* the law.

At first glance, Baarle doesn't look particularly odd. Its red-brick centre, small shops and hedge-lined suburbs look very much like those of other small towns in the region. Regular people go about their lives in comfortable north European prosperity. But look a bit closer and you will see lines of white painted crosses on the pavements, which mark out the boundary between the two conjoined towns of Baarle-Nassau and Baarle-Hertog and therefore the international border between the Netherlands and Belgium. Look further, and it becomes apparent that there are a lot more crosses than there would be if the border ran through the town in a straight line. Baarle is actually a little north of the main frontier between the two countries and Belgian Baarle-Hertog is an irregularly shaped patch of land enclosed by the Netherlands. It is not even a single patch; the Belgian town is a scatter of 21 small enclaves, not joined to each other, and encompasses seven 'counter-enclaves' of Dutch territory surrounded by Belgium.*

These crazed boundaries were established over eight hundred years ago in 1198 when Godfried, the Lord of Breda, ceded some parcels of his land to Duke Hendrik of Brabant in exchange for his protection. A very long time later, Breda is in the Netherlands, and therefore so is most of Baarle, while the duke's territories, including a number of enclaves of Baarle, ended up in Belgium. The understanding of exactly where the boundaries were had drifted over the centuries, and as the town had grown its street plan did not correspond to the borders of the irregular groups of fields and cottages that had been marked out in 1198. Successive international treaties had dodged the question of

---

*There are two more exclaves in rural areas, one on each side of the principal border. Geographers tend to prefer the term 'exclave' as being more descriptive, but 'enclave' is more popular in Baarle. I shall flit between the two.

where, to the centimetre, Baarle-Hertog stopped and Baarle-Nassau started until the Dutch and Belgian governments finally decided to bring certainty to the town in the 1990s. The surveyors consulted old maps and took measurements, and reset the border to its legal course. Baarle's strange status is not so much the original creation of the enclaves in 1198; complex feudal land transactions were not unusual and the whole of what is now Germany and some neighbouring areas was a patchwork of statelets and enclaves for centuries. The odd thing about Baarle is that, unlike nearly every other enclave situation, the boundaries were never rationalised at times of international upheaval. The area around Baarle was a frequent battleground in the long wars between Habsburg Spain and the breakaway provinces of the Netherlands until the Peace of Münster (part of the Westphalian Treaties) in 1648 in which Baarle-Nassau became part of the United Provinces of the Netherlands and Baarle-Hertog was put in the Spanish (southern) Netherlands. There were at least fifteen more occasions between 1648 and 1945 when rationalising the border was attempted or considered, but Baarle either remained divided or reverted to that state as part of a wider reset of international boundaries.

Perhaps the best opportunity to straighten the border was in the 1830s when Belgium became independent of the short-lived United Netherlands, which had included what is now the Netherlands, Luxembourg and nearly all of Belgium. But the Treaty of London, drafted in 1831 and finally signed by the Netherlands in 1839, that settled the matter was a slapdash piece of boundary-making and after a decade of strife there was no appetite to unpick historical boundaries.

When Belgium and the Netherlands worked out the detail of the border in the Maastricht Treaty of 1843, the question of Baarle was left to one side as being too complicated. The surveyors mapped the frontier from the coast as far as obelisk number 214 west of Baarle, skipped around 50km and then started again with marker number 215 as they worked eastward, promising to get around to the middle bit sometime. It took until 1974 for the main line of the border to be mapped, and 1995 for all the exclaves to be fully defined using cadastral (land survey) maps. Each of them has a code number, so it is possible, for instance, to travel from H8 to N7, as if one were a knight in a peculiar game of chess.

The people of Baarle are proud to have baffled the surveyors. In the middle of the town there is a monument in the form of a large border obelisk bearing coats of arms and '1198' on one side, and '214.215' on the other. The three numbers have become part of Baarle's identity; its apparently chaotic status is centuries old and part of tradition, and the town and its enclaves are a complex interpolation in what was supposed to be an orderly, methodical process of creating nation states with logical borders.

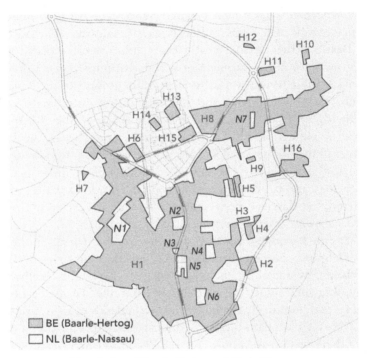

Boundaries of Baarle-Hertog and Barle-Nassau.

There are some discreet visual cues as to which country one is in, as it is easy to forget. The house numbering system is very complicated and buildings in the town have plates by the door in one of two national styles. There is one 'wrong' door plate at the time of writing, and Baarle people such as Willem van Gool, the civic activist who showed me around, will challenge the visitor to find it.

People on both sides of the town get irritated by national and regional governments, which often seem not to understand or even know about the special local circumstances. This is a familiar story along the edges of countries, particularly where the borders don't make a great deal of sense. Baarle-Nassau understands Baarle-Hertog much better than Amsterdam or Brussels understand either place. The Dutch government proposed to reorganise local government in 1997 and merge Baarle-Nassau with five other municipalities; fearing that they would become a minority within the municipality, the people of the border town organised an informal referendum and formed a political party that swept the local elections. *'Baarle moet Baarle blijven'* – let Baarle stay Baarle – was the slogan. When a delegation from the regional government came to visit Baarle, the activists encouraged people to hang out their national flags to give a visual sense of the complexity of Baarle, and staged a mock border inspection for the visitors' bus. The plan to merge the local councils was dropped.

Baarle-Nassau instead entered a partnership across the international border with Baarle-Hertog, a joint municipal body known by its Dutch acronym 'GOB'. Baarle-Hertog's new town hall in 2010 was nudged slightly from its original site so that the border ran through the boardroom; council members have to make sure that they are not sitting on the Dutch side when they cast votes on Belgian-only issues. A growing number of services are jointly operated, enabled by the Benelux Treaty and its updates, lately the BGTS Agreement of 2014 that created special rules for Baarle and some port regions allowing international public services. The fire brigade was the first of the public services to go cross-border; fires do not recognise international borders and it was obvious that there were economies to be made in having a single fire station for the town. Because Nassau is over twice the size of Hertog (7,000 inhabitants to 3,000 in the Belgian blocks), it had the resources to pay for professional firefighters while the Belgian side relied more on volunteers; there were initial cultural differences, but they were the same sort that one would get if two private companies merged. On the other hand, the library – housed in a cross-border building – is technically Belgian because that gets superior funding and staffing. People in Baarle are wily at navigating the system and their unique situation to get the best of both worlds; it is a contrast with the neglect that is often the fate of the border town.

Baarle is an unusual posting for police officers. There is a joint police station in the Baarle-Hertog town hall and it is normal for officers to go out on patrol in pairs, one Dutch and one Belgian, because they have no powers of arrest when they are out of territory. Policing Baarle would be farcical if people could run away over a line of crosses in the street and challenge the police to extradite them back again. There are powers of pursuit under the Schengen system, but that involves filling out a lot of forms, and Baarle has its own way. 'We're normal, practical cops. It's a small town and everyone in the community knows each other,' as officer Ad van Boxel put it to me when I popped in. Nobody pushes the technicalities to their limits, even in the courts. How it works is a mystery to police elsewhere – as Ad puts it, 'you speak to people in Amsterdam about this, and they think it's a fairy tale'.

There are some rules that are just too complicated to enforce in Baarle. One is about parking – in Belgium you are supposed to park facing in line with the direction of traffic, but in the Netherlands there is no rule; Baarle-Hertog piggybacks on this Dutch freedom because it is quite possible for motorists not to know which country their parking space is in, or indeed to park straddling a border. However, there are some rules that can be followed; Belgium switches off its streetlights in the small hours, while they are dimmed in the Netherlands. By the means of some intricate wiring, Baarle complies.

The worst time to be a border town, particularly one as complicated as Baarle, is when there is a national crisis and the central government feels the need to act quickly. The wrinkles that make up border life are fixed later at best, ignored completely at worst. For instance, implementing a ban on transferring agricultural or food products across borders is practically impossible in Baarle. A delegation from the central government came down to see what people in Baarle-Nassau were complaining about when moving meat products was banned as a health precaution, and only really got the point at lunchtime. The meeting sent out for sandwiches and sausage rolls, which were carried from the bakery across the street, and the visitors were told that they had connived in an infringement of the ban because the bakery was in Belgium.

When the COVID lockdowns began in March 2020, the national authorities on each side did not give much thought to what would happen to little Baarle, where it was impossible to close the borders. Restrictions in Belgium were generally tighter than those in the Netherlands. In the Zeeman clothes store, which straddles the border, the Belgian end of the shop was shut and items on display there were not for sale, while business went on across the line in the Netherlands. The local authorities in Baarle decided to follow the most restrictive combination of mask and lockdown rules from each side. There was no legal force to this, no way of imposing a fine for someone following Dutch law in streets and houses in Baarle-Nassau if they insisted, but most people complied voluntarily. As lockdown was lifted there were some tensions between libertarian Dutch and cautious Belgians about mask wearing, but Baarle weathered the pandemic.

There are a few occasions when nationality does divide Baarle. Belgium is a more religious society than the Netherlands, and Catholic festivals and parades are regarded as 'ours' in Baarle-Hertog; their Nassau neighbours are friends and guests rather than the keepers of the tradition. When the Netherlands plays Belgium at football, locals support their national side as passionately as anyone else – although perhaps with less needle towards the other side than most of their compatriots. Locally, some sports such as football and tennis have different clubs on each side, but it is not unusual for someone to join the other nation's club if their friends are already there or it's on the right side of town. There are two school systems in Baarle but it is possible for parents to choose to send their children across the border. The main flow is from the Netherlands to Belgium, as children start school earlier there and Dutch childcare is expensive; some parents also like the stricter style of teaching on the Belgian side. Given that people meet and mingle so much, it is not surprising that there are a lot of people on both sides – particularly Nassau – who have both passports. Nationality exists in Baarle, but it doesn't structure everything around it.

One sign of Baarle's careful management of its odd position is that there is none of the usual border zone clutter of heavily advertised retail outlets for cigarettes and alcohol, there are no sex shops, a normal number of petrol stations and it seems a wholesome if unusual small town. Because there are so many border crossings in a densely populated area and Baarle is off the main trade routes, there is no purpose for organised smuggling there – why not simply drive a van along the motorway from Antwerp to Rotterdam? You cross the border once, rather than a dozen times, and it is more anonymous than operating in a small town where drivers stop and chat to friends they pass in the street and everyone knows everyone.

The relaxed treatment of cannabis in the Netherlands has caused border friction with Belgium, whose police and government resented the way that their citizens could buy weed in Dutch coffeeshops and bring it back across a border that was open and impossible to police. While the Dutch authorities have rolled back some of the toleration extended to cannabis across the country, there have been special measures for the south near the Belgian border. The first was the unpopular Weed Pass, requiring coffeeshops to register as members' clubs, introduced in 2012 and scrapped in 2013 because people did not like being on an official register of weed smokers and the illegal street trade returned. The current Dutch system is that in towns that opt to do so – including most places near the border – buyers need to prove residence in the Netherlands. There has never been a coffeeshop in Baarle-Nassau, part of the give and take that makes the place work, but no punitive enforcement of Belgian drug law in Baarle-Hertog either. If anything, there is more trouble in the other direction. Belgium lowered the age at which people could buy beer or wine to 16 in 2009, while it remained at 18 in the Netherlands. There is an informal system operating where the Belgian beer shops are supposed to make rigorous checks on Dutch IDs, but there is little anyone can do in practice because Dutch youth can usually find a Belgian friend to buy the beer for them. It is a familiar story in border zones across the world.

Baarle's transnational tourist office in the Baarle-Nassau town hall promotes it as a destination for the curious. The focus is on the borders themselves as a tourist attraction, not the possibilities that borders create. 'Buiten in Binnenland' is its slogan – hard to translate into idiomatic English but 'abroad at home' is close. It conveys Baarle's atmosphere of exotic cosiness, both provincial and cosmopolitan. Baarle has nominated itself the World Capital of Enclaves. Depending on one's precise definition the total number will vary, but Baarle reckons there are 64 fully credentialled international enclaves of which 30 are in its own neighbourhood. Baarle cornered the world market in 2015 when India and Bangladesh implemented an exchange of enclaves in the even more complex Cooch Behar area – 111 parcels of Indian territory went to Bangladesh and 51 went in the other direction. Baarle recognises four others in Europe – Llivia (an island of Spanish territory within France), Campione d'Italia, Büsingen am Hochrhein and Jungholz. I might allow a few more, but they're the experts. They are introducing an enclave passport, listing all of them and allowing the determined enthusiast to tick them off, and perhaps, in the more popular ones like Baarle and Campione, getting an official stamp from the tourist office.

The joy of Baarle is in the absurdity of the borders. At some point, whatever the visitor's high-minded intentions, he or she will see a particularly peculiar line of border markings in the street and be unable to resist the temptation to step back and forward a few times between Belgium and the Netherlands, and straddle the line with a foot on each side. I capered happily for a minute in the street called Loveren, by the smallest of the Belgian exclaves, under Willem's tolerant, amused gaze. One enjoys being free to be frivolous, to hopscotch across a line that is supposed to be serious and important and treated with respect. Baarle is permissive of this transgressive pleasure.

On the second day in Baarle, one needs a harder dose of border strangeness to feel the same hit of unfamiliarity; the Zeeman shop with the boundary down the middle, the door that was moved to make its owner officially a Belgian, the suburban street with three separate national territories marked out by the ubiquitous crosses on the pavement and metal studs in the road. It's impossible to keep count of how many times you have crossed the border. For the border enthusiast, Baarle is like eating a whole box of chocolates in one sitting. You get used to it, perhaps even jaded. It's not a big thing to cross from one country to another. You realise that people in Baarle come in two categories – those who are only vaguely aware of which country they're in, and the people like Willem who carry a mental map of the chessboard of enclaves and have an instinctive sense of where they are at any moment, even if the national divide isn't that important. If I lived in Baarle, I know I would be in the second category, because the little differences between even 'normal' localities always catch my eye.

This is when the other joy of Baarle strikes you. You realise that it's a satire, a metaphor for all the imaginary lines that divide us. It's one of those edge cases that reveal a general truth. Other national boundaries are only a little less absurd; we are only slightly more independent of each other than Baarle-Nassau and Baarle-Hertog. Sharing waste disposal and a fire brigade makes sense at the municipal level in Baarle, and they make it work despite the bemusement of the national authorities in Amsterdam or Brussels. So, is it really impossible for larger governments to come to sensible arrangements to govern trade, employment, human rights and the environment and trust each other to act in good faith? Life in Baarle would be completely impossible if people decided to be bloody-minded about national sovereignty and the letter of the law, but the same is true of Europe, as we are perhaps discovering.

The deeper truth about Baarle is that, while it is fun to visit, that first impression that it is an ordinary town is not entirely wrong. It looks uniformly prosperous, with none of the differences in income and quality of the public realm that are obvious at many borders. This – to create a liveable, regular town, in a place where borders are ridiculous and it would be easy to divide people – is an achievement indeed. Cross-border working is sometimes slow and frustrating, as it requires a consensus not only between the two sides but sometimes between a wide spread of political opinion on each side. Major projects like the ring road take longer than they should, but that is not a problem unique to complex border towns. Things tend to get done more slowly and a bit more expensively than they might do, but they get done eventually. Baarle demonstrates that the opposition between cosmopolitan liberties like freedom of movement and multilingualism, versus the locally rooted virtues of the provincial bourgeois, is profoundly false.

To be sure, Baarle is a favourable location to test the co-operative approach to borders. There is no language barrier, the countries have similar legal systems and are founder members of the European Union and have shared a deeper level of co-operation since the 1958 Benelux Treaty that dismantled barriers and co-ordinated economic policies long before the EU entered those areas. The border at Baarle has been one of the world's softest for a long time now.

However, relations between Belgium and the Netherlands are not smooth by some rule of nature. They were spiky for a long time and the present harmony is the result of a shared trauma and a lot of effort from generations of political leaders at national and local level. Belgium fought a war of independence to secede from the United Netherlands in the 1830s and the outcome was messy, with borders that did not please either side and a situation where shipping access to the Belgian port of Antwerp depended on the Scheldt river, which had Dutch territory on both banks. The Belgians always suspected the Dutch of trying to strangle Antwerp in the commercial interest of mighty Rotterdam.

The First World War drove another wedge between the two countries. Germany invaded Belgium in summer 1914 but decided to amend their plan of attack, the Schlieffen Plan, to avoid violating Dutch neutrality. Nearly all of Belgium was occupied but the Netherlands remained neutral, continuing to trade between their ports and the German industrial heartland around the Ruhr and Rhine.

Dutch neutrality meant that Belgian Baarle-Hertog was spared from German occupation and remained – along with the far north-west corner of Belgium bordering on Dunkerque – free Belgian territory throughout the war. Its post office handled large numbers of clandestine letters and packages in both directions. The Dutch military, twitchy about anything that could be seen as a breach of neutrality, locked down the Baarle area. But somehow the components for a radio mast arrived in Baarle-Hertog and people there started transmitting Belgian Resistance messages.

The 1914–18 German occupation of Belgium was harsh. Men were conscripted into working in factories in Germany in order to help the war effort and, not surprisingly, around a million people took the chance to escape into the Netherlands across the long meandering border. Some of them, particularly those from the defeated military, promptly took the boat from Dutch ports to Britain and then were able to rejoin the war on the Western Front. Smuggling also ran rampant along the border. The response of the German military in 1915 was to run an electric wire to seal off Belgium from the Netherlands. This was relatively new technology; the first successful experiment in long-distance electricity transmission had only come in 1882 and the first use of electric fences in wartime was on the front between Russia and Japan at Port Arthur in 1905.

The 'Wire of Death' (Dodendraad), as the Belgian border fortification was known, was a two-stage barrier, with a barbed-wire inner defence and the outer line being the electrified section. There were combined guard post and switching stations in wooden huts every 4–5km along the line and at a few roads where soldiers guarded traditional border gates. The wire was crude but extremely powerful, running at 2,000 volts. For many people in the rural area where it ran, particularly older people who had grown up without electricity, this humming metal thread must have seemed infernal. The Belgian Resistance devised a wooden frame that could be locked into place along the wire and widened to allow a person to squeeze through, but it was a perilous enterprise. The death toll from the wire is put at 37 from the Baarle section alone. One can visit a couple of reconstructed sections in the countryside near Baarle. It is a glimpse of the beginning of the 20th-century European nightmare. The forbidding wires and the neat little huts with their black-on-white instruction boards in German look like unheeded visual warnings about the future horrors of concentration camps and the wall through Berlin.

When the war ended, the electricity was switched off and the wire was immediately torn down. Farmers still sometimes dig up fragments of the wire, mostly curved pieces of ceramic from the insulators along it. People wanted to bury the deadly border as quickly as they could, but the bitterness of the war years lingered. Belgians resented comfortable Dutch neutrality, forgetting for a while that the Netherlands had sheltered so many refugees.

Belgium came to the Paris Peace Conference in 1919 with ambitious demands for annexations as compensation for the losses suffered during the war and to make the country easier to defend. The furthest claims reached the Rhine at Köln and took in Luxembourg as well as German territory. But Belgium also had ambitions against the Netherlands, whose neutrality in the war was perceived by many in Belgium as having been rather sympathetic to Germany. The Allies lost patience with the Belgian demands and decided that they would not alter the Dutch border at all – not even to sort out the Baarle enclaves – and would transfer only a small area around Eupen from Germany to Belgium.

Relations between Belgium and the Netherlands remained poor during the interwar period – a failed land grab at the expense of one's neighbour does make for a chilly atmosphere. But in 1940 Germany invaded and occupied both countries. Most of Belgium was liberated in September 1944 but the Netherlands suffered a bleak, hungry winter under Nazi control in 1944–45. The experience encouraged the leadership of both countries, and Luxembourg, to find common ground and put the contentious history behind them, and the governments-in-exile agreed to peg their currencies against each other in 1943 and introduce a tariff union in 1944. From these beginnings the post-war countries grew closer, leading to the Benelux economic union treaty signed in 1958. As well as the economic benefits, the countries also believed that they would be stronger together and more able to stand up for their interests against larger states. It made the situation in Baarle more manageable, although this surely did not rank high on the agenda.

The Benelux countries are a particularly close unit within Europe, with nearly invisible borders even before the Schengen treaty. Their economies are tied to each other, and to Germany, by geography; the open trading border with their neighbour up the Rhine has fuelled the enormous growth of both Rotterdam and Antwerp, the first and second ports of Europe and the tenth and fourteenth worldwide. The Netherlands and Belgium, particularly Flanders where Dutch is spoken, are tied together by sentiment as well as practicality, but it is the sort of closeness that is often expressed as sibling rivalry. The Dutch cliché about Belgians is that they are stupid; the Belgian cliché about the Dutch is that they are rude and mean with money. But the giveaway is that Dutch people generalise about Belgium, while the Belgians themselves tend not to, because the real border around here is in the middle of their country.

The language barrier

Belgium is a larger version of the house in Baarle where a boundary runs through the front door. The Belgian language border – Dutch to the north, French to the south – is probably the most serious internal border in Europe.* It is obvious even to the casual visitor who strays outside Brussels. If you are on a train in Belgium, the language in which the announcements are made will change when the train crosses the linguistic border. Your outward journey, for instance, will be described at the start of your trip as being from Leuven to Luik, but you will return from Liège on the train heading towards Louvain.

The language border runs in a fairly straight line east–west across the country. Because things are always complicated in Belgium, there are a couple of exclaves at each end of the country – a Francophone one on the French border near Ypres (Ieper) and a Dutch-speaking one at Voeren (Les Fourons) on the Netherlands border. In addition, there are some patches where one community is a protected minority. The Brussels metropolitan area is bilingual for official purposes but majority Francophone; it has its own parliament. In the east, around Eupen, there is a region where German is the majority language. There are separate parliaments for the French and German language communities and the Wallonia region, while the Flemish language community and the Flanders region are consolidated into one parliament. Belgium packs a lot of complexity into a small area. In recent decades, powers have flowed

---

* Excluding places such as eastern Ukraine and northern Cyprus where one section is under occupation.

towards the regional units, leaving the central government more of a holding company than a directing authority; it was this that enabled Belgium to carry on regardless for over a year in 2018–20 under a caretaker government.

The language border was fixed once and for all in 1962. Although some villages shifted composition in the years before the language border was finally fixed, and Brussels is a special case, the location of the line has been consistent for a very long time. Setting the line metaphorically in stone, as if it were a national border, was intended to avoid sterile territorial arguments and it has basically worked. Sterile arguments take place on other Belgian intercommunal issues instead, but the frontier is not going to move even if there are demographic changes. When there is strife, it tends to revolve around the 'facility' municipalities – areas that are part of one community but have a recognised minority from another. Government services are supposed to be provided in the minority language, but there is always wrangling about whether this is being provided to the proper extent. Like other big cities, Brussels has been growing and its suburbs are spilling out beyond its administrative area, but this has caused cross-border friction as it is surrounded by Flemish territory and many of the new suburbanites speak French or a third language. From the Flemish point of view the fixed border means that, if you choose to live within the borders of Flanders, you are accepting that Dutch will be the language of state and everyday life beyond your own household.

The European Union and NATO bring many people to Brussels who are fluent in English but have difficulty in French or Dutch; while English is widespread in professional use even beyond the big international institutions, people have to communicate with the authorities in one of the two traditional Belgian languages. In Flanders, many people are highly competent in English; while a stab at conducting pleasantries in Dutch is appreciated, interactions with visitors switch rapidly into English. The historic, local hegemony of French is resented more than the growing global role of English and people tolerate someone launching straight into English more than they would French.

Belgium is a shared house rather than a family. People have structures in common such as citizenship, religious tradition, the monarchy, a discreditable colonial history and the international metropolis of Brussels, but they have their own well-defined areas. Not all of the rooms in the house are shared. Neither side really wants to break up the house share, despite their differences. Belgium is a pleasant house in a nice neighbourhood and trying to sort out how to divide Brussels while keeping it functioning would give everyone a headache. Better to live parallel lives in the shared house. Being able to sort out one's parts of the house as one wants, function comfortably in the common areas and mend the roof together when required is not that bad a deal. A soft border, as the people of Baarle will tell you, is much better than a hard border, and occasionally better than no border at all.

4

Switzerland and its neighbours

(Italy, France, Germany, Austria)

When you board the pleasure boat across the lake from Lugano to Campione d'Italia, you pass a notice from the Italian customs agency reminding people to declare movements of cash that total more than 10,000 euros when they get to the other side. I don't think anyone was violating the rule the day I travelled – it was raining and there weren't many people on the boat. It is unusual nowadays to travel with that much cash, but Lugano to Campione is one of the most likely places in Europe for it to happen. You can smell the dirty money, despite the clean

View of Campione d'Italia, August 2020.

alpine air. As you get closer to Campione, you notice a hulking out-of-scale building, a yellow-brick cybernetic-looking helmet that dominates the skyline of the village. This is the casino of Campione d'Italia, a small Italian enclave within Switzerland.

Campione is in Italy but is directly accessible only by boat – or helicopter – from the rest of Italy, and even then you cross Swiss waters or airspace. But the Swiss authorities have been reluctant to interdict any traffic, so Campione has become a honeypot of semi-licit and illicit border activities. It is raffish where its fellow enclave of Baarle is conservative. In 1917 the Italian government set up a publicly owned casino whose purpose was at least in part to gather intelligence from allies and enemies alike. It was dubbed 'Campione d'Italia' as a piece of fascist grandstanding in the 1930s (its people had shown interest in joining Switzerland in 1919), and the nationalistic name stuck. During the post-war economic boom, there was a steady flow of people seeking to evade Italian exchange controls or launder dirty money via Campione, and the lakeside village became known to a new generation of dubious characters. Howard Marks (1945–2016), the international cannabis wholesaler, was particularly fond of it and its piquant atmosphere. His favourite restaurant, La Taverna, was in the village ('criminals are very discerning'):

> On my first visit in 1973, an impeccably clad waiter ushered me to an al fresco table covered with gleaming glass, cutlery, and porcelain. A London taxi drew up outside the restaurant. A handsome, bespectacled fifty-year-old German came in accompanied by a garishly dressed Rastafarian, a rich cockney businessman, a Sophia Loren look-alike, and a blonde Teutonic beauty. I used the public telephone. It was Swiss. Outside, a fully uniformed Italian policeman sat in his car, which had Swiss number plates.[13]

Marks had many identities in his criminal career, but the one he had to abandon by burying a passport in Campione, Mr Nice, gave him the title of his autobiography.[14]

The casino was rebuilt in 2007 on its present obtrusive scale, just in time for the global financial crisis. It was scandal-hit and had difficulty paying its way, declaring bankruptcy in 2018. The collapse took down the municipal council, which owned the casino, and most local government services in Campione. When I visited in August 2020 it was a subdued place, a shadow of its former shady magnificence. Campione was also more overtly Italian than it had been in Marks's day, as the Italian government decided to bring it back into Italy's customs territory from 1 January 2020 in a sort of miniature Brexit.

Switzerland's current national borders are the ones that were decided at the Congress of Vienna in 1815, although even then it was arguable whether the confederation of largely independent cantons qualified as a single country. Its constitution dates from 1848, which can, despite the air of time-honoured antiquity about Swiss arrangements, be regarded as the foundation of the modern state. Switzerland was one of the few permanent successes of the European revolutions of 1848, the springtime of nations, but it is a paradoxically unlikely formula for a cohesive nation. The country has four languages, three of them shared with neighbouring nation states, and internal divisions between Catholic and Protestant and industrial and agricultural. Switzerland's exception makes it a seductive model to others. The founders of Czechoslovakia talked about creating a central European Switzerland, and nearly every peace plan for Bosnia in the 1990s had 'cantons' on the map, vaguely implying harmonious confederation. The Swiss model, as it turns out, is an example rather than a reproducible blueprint. Switzerland's unique arrangements – confederation, international neutrality, a citizen military and direct democracy – make the whole thing stable, although it has wobbled more and existed for a shorter time than Orson Welles and Graham Greene would have you believe.

> 'You know what the fellow said – in Italy, for thirty years under the Borgias, they had warfare, terror, murder and bloodshed, but they produced Michelangelo, Leonardo da Vinci and the Renaissance. In Switzerland, they had brotherly love, they had five hundred years of democracy and peace – and what did that produce? The cuckoo clock.'[15]

Switzerland has some very peculiar borders to match its other idiosyncrasies. They were finalised in pre-nationalist times and neutrality set them in stone, so the oddities the modern state inherited have been preserved. There are two enclaves recognised by the authorities in Baarle – Campione d'Italia and Büsingen am Hochrhein. Büsingen is a little piece of Germany adjacent to the Swiss city of Schaffhausen; the village has been within Swiss customs territory since 1967 and remains so, despite Campione's withdrawal. People there have both German and Swiss postal addresses and land telephone numbers. Although it is not technically an exclave, the town of Konstanz is situated in a pocket of German territory across the Rhine from the neighbouring parts of Germany; it was a small enough scrap of territory that the Second World War Allies did not dare to attack it for fear of bombs falling accidentally on the Swiss side of the border.

The cities of Geneva and Basel generate brain-bending border phenomena. Basel's trams are even more cosmopolitan than Strasbourg's, venturing into three different countries. There is even a bridge where the trams along the top are in French territory but the buses running underneath are in 'Zone 13', a peculiar bit of the map whether you look at it from the public transport or international legal point of view. The lower road is a special route under Swiss customs rules from Basel to the EuroAirport of Mulhouse-Basel-Freiburg, which is sited on French land. It was held up, dubiously, by British minister Chris Philp as being an example of how smooth a border crossing between the EU and a non-EU neighbour could be. Philp seemed unembarrassed when it was pointed out that in customs terms the road was not a border at all, and the neighbouring highway has a customs checkpoint and is frequently congested.

The Basel triangle can only work with an exceptionally law-abiding population, and even then the authorities have to put up with a certain amount of smuggling. People often drive into Germany to do their supermarket shopping because it is cheaper there; duty is technically payable on the way back and this is sometimes enforced when cars are stopped. The same applies on public transport.

Geneva has even more peculiar liminal qualities. Its history as a head-quarters for international organisations, and Switzerland's neutrality, helped with the bid for the peaceful exploration of the outer limits of atomic science. The proposal to establish CERN at Meyrin, a suburb of Geneva hard by the French border, was passed by referendum in 1953 and the first accelerator, the synchrocyclotron, was switched on in 1957. For the first two decades CERN was entirely on Swiss territory but, as the particles studied got smaller, the accelerators and the site got larger. The Super Proton Synchrotron, switched on in 1976, was the first accelerator to cross the border as there was not enough room in Switzerland. The SPS had a circumference of 7km, which was huge when it was built but small compared to the 27km Large Hadron Collide, which went live in 2008. During a spin in the LHC, a proton will cross the Franco-Swiss border 20,000 times a second.

There is no visible border within the CERN complex; there is a customs post on the road that runs alongside the site but the frontier seems to end at the CERN fence. CERN is a rare particle existing at an oblique angle to normal national space. Its security fence is more powerful than the national border. Within CERN, Schrödinger's stray cat is both Swiss and French until someone adopts it. Particle physics is a liminal discipline by its nature, breaking down apparently solid objects into ever more splintered parts, flipping matter and energy between states, so there is something fitting about these frontiers of science being pushed in a place that straddles the mundane border of Switzerland and France.

Geneva and Basel are leaders in cross-border commuting for work. Not counting internationals such as CERN and Red Cross employees, 35 per cent of the Geneva workforce comes across the border from France, and 30,000 cross in the other direction. In French, they are known by the stylish title of 'frontaliers'. Cross-border working can become a thicket of bureaucracy, and here as in the region around Luxembourg the EU has been trying to make it easier. The local authorities are also keen to ease the burdens, and this involves complex agreements between Geneva and the French municipalities. A chunk of local payroll taxation is remitted across the border, and the Swiss funded the construction of a new commuter railway line within France. The local economy is complicated by the huge differences in pay and taxation on each side of the international border, and the growth of home working. How fair is it for two people sitting at adjacent tables in the same café in Ferney-Voltaire in France to be paid disparate salaries because for one of them the office they hardly ever visit is in Switzerland rather than France?

Neutrality was part of the formula for Switzerland in 1815 because the country was seen as being at risk of splitting apart on nationalistic issues if there were to be another large-scale European war. There could be no consensus within Switzerland to go to war on the side of France, but equally there could be no consensus to fight against France either. The solution was guaranteed neutrality.

Switzerland adopted the hedgehog strategy to keep out of the First World War – to be so well defended that the costs of invading it would outweigh the strategic benefit to any of the belligerents. Swiss defence concentrated on Porrentruy, at the corner of France, Germany and Switzerland, to discourage ideas of taking a short cut in either direction between German Mühlhausen (Mulhouse) and French Besançon. Before the war, the Dreiländereck by the Largue river had been a peaceful object of curiosity, but now it became Kilometre Zero, the end point of the trenches of the Western Front.[16] It was a surreal place, the two muddy rainbows of parallel misery coming to a sudden stop. The front in the region was one of the quietest battlefields of the First World War. After seeing the first shots fired in the west on 2 August when French and German patrols blundered into each other, an initial French assault was repulsed in August 1914 and there was little movement until the German forces were obliged to pack up and retreat across the Rhine by the Armistice of November 1918. There were a few border incidents here, and on the Swiss–Italian frontier after 1915, most of them involving attempts to overfly Swiss territory or errors in the heat of battle.

In the Second World War there were more threats to Swiss neutrality, particularly in late 1940 when Europe was largely under Axis control and Nazi Germany and its allies surrounded Switzerland. Switzerland had to bend in order to survive, and the compromises that it made – like those in Sweden – were a difficult subject for decades after 1945. In the later stages of the war, the role of neutral banker, and meeting place for spies and back channels, proved a convenient one, and Switzerland emerged from the war ready for an economic miracle that made it the prosperous enclave it is today.

During the Cold War, this fortress of capitalism was protected by geography. But neutrality has also made aspects of life difficult. Adhering to long-term treaties requires ratification in a referendum, and that – as we know – can be troublesome. Switzerland only joined the United Nations in 2002, despite its long record as host country for international organisations including the UN's predecessor, the League of Nations. Switzerland rejected joining the European Economic Area (the outer part of the EU's economic union) in 1992, and the EU itself in 2001, but did approve the Schengen treaty in 2005. In 2020 another referendum attempted to revoke free movement, but was defeated by a large margin as the Swiss realised the benefits of the 320,000 frontaliers who kept their economy working.

Switzerland's arrangements with the EU are complex and bureaucratic, and the burdensome nature of their rules made the EU unwilling to grant the UK anything remotely similar following Brexit. It would be less trouble for Switzerland to join, particularly as all its neighbours bar Liechtenstein are members and it would not be taking sides in that sense, but the commitment to neutrality runs deep. In the modern world, in which the concepts of international law and human rights are to the forefront, neutrality can seem less relevant than in the days of nationalist squabbles or ideological confrontation. To its critics it can seem little more than selling weapons to both sides while maintaining an air of smug moral authority, and there are still debates over how well Switzerland managed to combine its historic role as a bastion of liberty and human rights with neutrality in the face of Nazi aggression in the years around 1940.

When Austria became part of the Greater German Reich in March 1938, the Swiss border at Vorarlberg became a lifeline for the country's Jewish population, who were instantly pitched into a nightmare world of racial laws and street thuggery. Many Jews unsurprisingly wanted to leave immediately and headed westward for safety, as did anti-Nazi Austrians and Germans who had sought refuge in Austria. Among them was the writer Carl Zuckmayer, author of the screenplay of the 1930 Marlene Dietrich film *The Blue Angel*, who wrote about his frightening train ride to the border in his memoirs:

> It was a three-hour journey [from Innsbruck to the border] in the middle of the night, and the closer we came to the border the weirder, more hectic and frenzied the mood in the train became. Patrols kept pushing through the crowded aisles, entering the compartments, checking individuals, asking for names, destinations and the sums of money the passengers carried.[17]

The train halted at Feldkirch in Vorarlberg, right by the Swiss border, in the early hours for yet another intimidating inspection. People and luggage were prodded and poked by uniformed SS and SA men rather than the regular border guard, whose Nazi loyalties were in question. Zuckmayer himself escaped the worst because of his air of confidence and because some of the Nazis secretly rather liked his banned plays. He reflected later that he was acting out the moral of one of his works, *The Captain of Köpenick*, a satirical telling of a true story in which a fraudster had turned up at a Prussian army barracks pretending to be an officer and was unquestioningly obeyed. But only when all the people on the train had been subjected to humiliating inspections and the confiscation of any goods worth more than 10 marks – being caught smuggling meant disappearing into Nazi custody and perhaps never returning – could the train continue from Feldkirch:

> As the train crossed the border, the sky was a glassy green, and cloudless. The perpetual snow glittered in the early-morning sun. The Swiss customs officials entered the car and uttered friendly gutturals. It was all over. I was in a train, and it was not headed toward Dachau.[18]

The real Von Trapp family escaped Austria in a similar fashion, on a train to Italy with their musical instruments on the way to play in America; Zuckmayer had a meeting in London with Alexander Korda. Technically, they were not refugees. *The Sound of Music* – the film version of *The Story of the Trapp Family Singers* – in which the Von Trapps flee across the mountains into Switzerland is both historically and geographically inaccurate; starting from Salzburg, it was a very long way to any place of safety.

In the early stages, the Nazis were happy to see refugees and opponents leave, provided they had been stripped of as much of their property as the authorities could find. Zuckmayer vividly remembered the sweaty panic of a man who had tried to carry banknotes on his body, before – wisely, as it turned out – he snapped and threw the money out of the window somewhere in Tyrol. The Nazi guards on the Austrian side were more interested in searching people for hidden valuables than stopping them; it was the Swiss authorities, anxious about the prospect of thousands of penniless refugees arriving, who were more of an obstacle to people entering. As spring turned to summer, the number of people fleeing rose steadily and the efficiency with which Adolf Eichmann's Central Office for Jewish Emigration was depriving them of their property increased. The Swiss federal authorities responded by encouraging the Nazis to manage the situation and staunch the flow of people at the border. One of the methods adopted as a result of these discussions in October 1938 was the overprinting of 'J' (*Jude*) on German-Jewish passports.

When controls started to tighten, people realised that the border at Hohenems, a little north of Feldkirch, had an anomalous, almost magical property. The historic border between Switzerland and Austria ran along the upper Rhine, upriver of Lake Constance. But the curving, shallow river was unsuitable in places for modern ships and in the early 20th century several new cuts were carved to improve its navigability. One of these, opened in 1923, replaced the long bend around the Swiss town of Diepoldsau with a shorter straight channel, creating a half-moon-shaped island between the new and the old river. Although rivers may seem like good borders, they are problematic because they move around, both naturally and as a result of human intervention, and people on both sides use them and can come into conflict over them. After 1923 the border at Hohenems ran along the old course of the Rhine, which was a shallow, tranquil backwater lined with trees. Even larger children could wade across it, and small-time local smugglers had established stepping-stone routes across the old Rhine.

Hohenems, certainly by Austrian standards at the time, also seems not to have been a very anti-Semitic town. It had a significant Jewish history and community of its own, although by 1939 nearly all its members had left. To the people of the town, particularly its young men, helping Jews into Switzerland was just a continuation of the border-town demi-monde way of life – cigarettes yesterday, families today. They already knew the routes across the shallow river, the places where trees obscured the view from the border hut, the times (8 p.m.) when the shift changed and the officers were distracted, but each time they refined their know-ledge. It was a way of earning pocket money while doing a bit of good. It appears not to have been difficult for refugees to find willing helpers once they arrived in Hohenems; it was generally known that the guest house 'Habsburg' was the place to go to make a connection. Informal crossings like this worked because the general official attitude in Switzerland was that, although they would try to control the border, they considered deporting people back across it inhumane. Once the refugees had planted their wet footprints on the far side of the old course of the Rhine, they were through.

The other magical thing about the Hohenems–Diepoldsau frontier was the presence of some Swiss officials of exceptional courage and conscience; quiet, strong heroes whose story is still little known. There was a clandestine escape network in the area run by Paul Grüninger, the chief of police of the St Gallen canton, who was in charge of the border posts in the region. Several other officials, such as Ernst Kamm, who managed the refugee reception camp in Diepoldsau, and border officer Eigenmann, were also in on it. Their motivation was a simple sense of right and wrong, although decades later officers like Kamm were still troubled by having brazenly broken the rules, even at the insistence of a vindicated conscience.[19] They backdated arrival stamps so that people could be processed as if they had arrived before the tightening of the border in March 1938, and produced and recognised documents such as bogus Mexican permits to travel that would not have passed even cursory inspection. Kamm would massage the statistics and integrate newcomers into the Diepoldsau camp as if they had been there for months.

The officers took their clandestine role even further in the next few months. As more people made it across, they tried to get their families across as well. Refugees also wanted to avoid having their property seized by the Nazis on the way out. The solution was sometimes for the Swiss officers to cross into Austria to pick people up and to transport valuables. Grüninger and his colleagues, at great risk, personally carried money across the border and on one occasion Ernst Kamm returned to Switzerland with a gold watch hidden up his backside. Nor did the officers gain any personal benefit from their work – they passed on all the valuables and would buy warm clothes for refugees out of their own money. Grüninger rescued around 3,600 people.

It could not last forever, and Grüninger was exposed and summarily sacked in March 1939. He was deprived of his pension and lived in obscurity, and some measure of ill-repute from his neighbours, for the rest of his life until he died in 1972. He always said, quite simply, that he regretted nothing and would do the same again. He was recognised as one of the Righteous Among the Nations in 1971[20] but it took until 1995 for his conviction for abuse of office to be set aside and for his family to receive compensation for the removal of his pension. In 2012, the bridge across the Alter Rhein at Diepoldsau was renamed and dedicated to Paul Grüninger.

Although the Grüninger network was exceptional, there were other instances of the Swiss border police taking a liberal attitude to refugees. The frontier in Basel was also more porous than it 'should' have been, although there were fewer loopholes to exploit there than along the Austrian border. The role of the Swiss federal government was less heroic. The overall head of the police, Heinrich Rothmund, consistently argued to restrict the number of refugees coming across the border and collaborated with his German opposite numbers to achieve this aim. In August 1942 the border was completely closed to 'racial' refugees (but not 'political' ones), even though it was clear by then that turning people back was a death sentence. The official inquiry found that about 25,000 people were turned away between 1940 and 1945, although this might be an overestimate.[21]

After a long period of silence and forgetting, the Swiss refugee policy was the subject of debate and an official independent inquiry in the 1990s and 2000s. Even at the time there was an argument within Switzerland about whether the policy was right – some Swiss felt that it was a betrayal of the national tradition of democracy and giving asylum for dissenters. Some, such as Rothmund, had prejudices about Jews. Others were acutely conscious of the precarious position Switzerland was in, particularly after the fall of France in June 1940 when it was surrounded. There was a limit to how far it could go against the Nazis without bringing down retribution. Nor could Switzerland serve as a transit point any more – refugees who made it to the country could probably not go any further and would stay in Switzerland for an indefinite time, increasing the risks of a nativist reaction within Switzerland. The costs for the Swiss of letting people in increased, even as the dreadful consequences of not doing so rose so steeply after 1941. Grüninger's moral clarity in 1938, his quick recognition – before Kristallnacht, even – of the evil direction in which Greater Germany was heading, is therefore all the more important a service to humanity.

Although we celebrate Grüninger, we need to recognise that in the present day he would be sacked at least, probably imprisoned, if he forged papers and used his office to save people from death by smuggling them across the UK or US – or Schengen – border against the rules. Perhaps it does take 50 years to recognise those occasions when someone is right to break the law in a good cause. For all that one can regard people like Rothmund with refined distaste, his attitudes and policies were not very different from those of many people in safer places at the time. American and Canadian politicians and officials who turned the 900 or so Jewish refugees on the MS *St Louis* back to Europe in 1939 are certainly in no position to comment. There will always be more Rothmunds than Grüningers, everywhere.

The British do not have strong perceptions of the role of border guards, partly because of the relatively small number of British who had anything to do with the UK's land border in Ireland before it became invisible, and the thoroughly routine encounters most British people have with customs and immigration officials at ports and airports. We don't get the importance of the places where the UK state bumps up against other states. It's a majoritarian bias that erases the experience of the minorities who feel the sharper end of 'controlling our borders' – the Irish people either side of the border, and the many people whose status is in any way irregular or non-standard who feel a shiver of fear at encountering potentially arbitrary authority. Majorities tend to want border guards to keep the barriers up, minorities want them to interpret the restrictions in a humane way. Even I, with my white native-born English privilege, felt alarm and helplessness when I was taken aside by Special Branch at Heathrow one time on returning from an unusual destination, penned in a little enclosure with baffled Ghanaians and stoic Iraqis. The police officers were perfectly affable and reasonable, but it was a little experience of my time and my dignity not mattering, and of being in an airport limbo trapped behind the Border Force perimeter. But for most people, the humiliating encounter usually takes place away from the border, in correspondence and interviews with an obdurate Home Office or an unsympathetic consular official.

A new generation of continental Europeans are growing up without much experience of border guards, thanks to the huge zone covered by the Schengen Agreement. But along the edges of the Schengen area, and in the recent past, the border guard is an important symbolic figure. He, or she, helps to define the nation itself, as in Finland or in Czechoslovakia, particularly against larger neighbours. The heroic aspect of the idea of a border guard is about preventing external threats from penetrating the national body. In societies where there are deemed to be 'enemies within', like Cold War Czechoslovakia, the basic idea of protecting the nation from threats can be turned inward towards making the border guard a sort of prison warder. It is perhaps significant that, in the transition in spring 1938, the Austrian border guards – legacy of a more humane state – were not trusted by the new Nazi authorities and the SS and SA were unleashed to enjoy pushing the refugees around and steal their property as they tried to leave.

Borderlanders – whether their work is to uphold or subvert the dividing line – are sensitive to the ways in which states become oppressive. They are the canaries in the mine. Grüninger, from the vantage point of his border post, could see the Holocaust coming, while in Czechoslovakia a border guard called Josef Hasil saw the Iron Curtain becoming a reality on the ground right in front of him and took action. The border post can be a rampart against tyranny as well as a place where people are controlled.

Western Europe has some of the most intricate borders in the world, with more than its share of anomalies from Ireland to Switzerland to the crosses on the pavements of Baarle. National boundaries have been disputed, diplomatically and violently, for centuries, and have varied between vague lines on the map and fortified barriers upheld by deadly force. The present state of peaceful, porous borders exists not because western Europe is somehow more advanced than other places, but because it has suffered so much in the past. France and Germany were victims and perpetrators of wars over borders, and experienced the violent feelings and deeds arising from the combination of nationalism and the existence of mixed, disputed borderlands. A lot of other options were exhausted before Robert Schuman's solution of leaving borders unalterable but increasingly permeable took hold. The lure of open borders – at least on this regional, negotiated scale – is such that countries such as Norway, Switzerland and the United Kingdom want to participate to some extent in the systems that make land borders invisible even if they resist full membership of the European Union.

The European Union is defined by its soft internal borders, but also by its hard external border. Frontex, the EU's external border control agency, tries to assuage the anxieties of the Schengen zone's population by its rigorous approach to its job. It is a back-handed demonstration of the existence of that often-disputed body, the European *demos*. The paradox, which we shall meet at frontiers such as Hungary's with Serbia, is that tight external control co-exists with an ambition to extend the Union to other countries in Europe (and therefore convert hard external borders into soft internal ones).

National sovereignty comes at a price. A hard border reduces trade and well-being, and closes off choices for people. Border disputes were exercises in futility, even in the world of the industrial age. How much more futile is ambition for territory in a world where services, technology and creativity are nearly impossible to pen into national frontiers. The trade-offs are at their most obvious for smaller states like Luxembourg or Ireland; membership of the political and economic union gives them a measure of influence over a common set of rules and added muscle in relations with outside powers. For many of the smaller states of central and eastern Europe, historically caught in the crossfire of empires, it seemed a matter of national survival to become part of such an entity. The idea that national independence meant a measure of interdependence was part of the idealistic legacy of the dissident movement but also served hard-headed purposes of security and economic growth.

Poland's rebirth and relocation

	Poland's gains in 1916–22
	A Austria-Hungary
	B Russia
	C Germany

Poland's losses to the
USSR in 1939–45

Poland's gains from
Germany in 1945

Free City of Danzig
(part of Poland in 1945)

From Germany to Russia
in 1945

PART TWO
North

5

The very hungry empires

(Lithuania, Russia, Poland)

Postcard of the pre-1914 Germany–Russia border post at Nimmersatt.

Nimmersatt, now called Nemirseta, is hardly even a village, but for a century it was famous as the furthest frontier of Prussia and therefore Germany. In a clearing in a forest, the impeccably uniformed officials of the German and Russian empires faced each other either side of a wooden barrier across a country road. Fascinated by border posts, 19th-century travellers could send postcards of this little scene of state power and its limits to their friends. Nimmersatt was celebrated in a German children's rhyme: 'Nimmersatt, Nimmersatt, Wo das Reich eine Ende hat' (where the empire comes to a stop). But the name itself raises questions.

Nimmersatt means 'never satisfied' – German children now hear the word as the description of the translation of *The Very Hungry Caterpillar*, 'Die kleine Raupe Nimmersatt'. What sort of border can satisfy and pacify an empire, or a nation state? Twice in the 20th century, Germany's frontiers went way beyond Nimmersatt. But then the Soviet Union struck back, pushing its state frontier past Nimmersatt and the old Prussian city of Königsberg and its political influence far to the west, almost to the western German city of Lübeck. Will states always be hungry? Perhaps looking at Nemirseta now, within the borders of the small, peaceable republic of Lithuania and the European Union, one can be hopeful that there is a cure for the lethal hunger for land.

Germany is now a long way from Nemirseta, and has given up any ambition to gobble up more territory – abandoning any claim on places that were legitimately German for centuries. Russia is still close. The largest country in the world is greedy for more; in Ukraine to the south, its forces brutalise another part of its former empire. The Baltic states and even Finland fear for their own security.

The clash between Russia and the European community is embodied in ideas about borders. Since 1945 western Europe, and most of central Europe, has built a political community around the idea that borders within that community are fixed but fading. Altering boundaries by force is the ultimate taboo. But it is the other way round for Russia: borders are the temporary result of the balance of power and are to be rewritten when that balance changes – but while they exist, the places through which they run will bristle with military power, paranoia and repression.

Just as the French world collides with the German along the Rhine, the north-east of Europe is a crossing point of cultures and empires. Sweden, Germany, Poland and Russia have contended for power and influence over the centuries, the smaller nationalities of the region coping as they could. The Cold War created a line between the Scandinavian social democratic north and the Soviet east, with Finland positioned uneasily on the edge. While boundaries in western Europe were little altered in 1945, those in the east were radically changed. Stalin's Soviet Union swallowed up the Baltic states and took chunks of Poland, Germany and Finland, and Poland was shunted westwards, annexing a large swathe of eastern Germany.

★   ★   ★

The Dreiländereck (three nations' corner) between Poland, Russia and Lithuania in a forest north of the Polish town of Suwałki is the successor to Nimmersatt. It is one of the most charged border points in Europe. The Russian–Lithuanian border here is a perhaps unique anomaly; it is the same line as in 1914 but Russia has switched sides. In 1914, East Prussia was in Germany and the Russian Empire ruled Lithuania; in 2023 Lithuania is independent but Russia has taken over what used to be the German side of the border.

Obelisk at the tri-point of Poland, Lithuania and Russia, May 2022.

Two entirely different sorts of border meet at this pink marble obelisk. The one between Poland and Lithuania is marked by a groove on the monument and some marble tiles on the ground. There are no controls, because both countries are members of the Schengen partnership and there is free movement across the line. The main difference is that it is an hour later in Lithuania than it is in Poland. It is good country for a cross-border walk among gentle hills, placid lakes and deep forests; as with some other border zones, a lack of human activity has made it a haven for nature. There are marshes that sing with birdsong and the croaks of frogs and toads, and there are wolves somewhere deep in the forest – about 30 per cent of Poland's wolves are cross-border commuters.

You can't cross legally into Russia for 30km from the obelisk in either direction. On the Lithuanian side it is nearly physically impossible, as the border itself lies behind layers of fencing and barbed wire; on the Polish side at the time of my visit in May 2022 there was a strip running through the forest that was covered by watchtowers and cameras; farm tracks and abandoned roads trailed unconvincingly towards the border line. The Poles built a barbed wire barrier in 2022–23. At the obelisk itself, fences obstruct attempts to step even for a moment into Russian territory. It is physically possible to clamber over the fence, but it is not recommended. You are being watched – certainly from the Polish side, and surely also by the Russians. The Polish border guards will fine you 500 zloty (about £92) for the privilege. I felt the temptation – it is only human to feel some bravado and defiance at a border – but even more than the cost I was deterred by a feeling that I would be letting down the polite Polish border guards I had spoken to earlier in the day. They don't see many British passports around Lake Wiżajny, and I think it was more than the language barrier that made my presence seem baffling to them. But I promised I had no intention of trying to enter Russia, and they smiled, and I was going to keep my promise.

It is also illegal to throw things at Russia, and here I had more difficulty – this was May 2022 and Russia was conducting its vile war well within the borders of Ukraine. I even had a banana skin and an apple core with me. But again, I resisted. I remembered what a Finnish border guard had told me, that borders were shared spaces and even where the countries are as hostile as Poland and Russia there is mutual respect between the border guards and a common interest in avoiding 'incidents'. It is also forbidden to take pictures of the Russian side of the border, but this was one transgression I allowed myself.

The peaceful Polish–Lithuanian border country east and south from here is known to military planners as the Suwałki Gap. It separates the Kaliningrad oblast, a small western exclave of Russia, from Belarus, Russia's partner in the 'Union State', while connecting Poland with fellow NATO member Lithuania – and therefore also to the other two Baltic states of Latvia and Estonia.

Part of the reason why Suwałki is militarily vulnerable is that it is a rural backwater with – even now, despite Poland's ever-improving infrastructure – poor links westwards. But that is part of its charm. It is dairy country, renowned for its cheeses and butter; away from the emptiness of the border strip itself, one walks among glossy, contemplative cows. As I did, I felt the obscenity of the idea that it was a 'gap' to be overcome by violence. Suwałki itself is a slow-paced market town. It has a partnership arrangement with the Ukrainian city of Ternopil, which (as Tarnopol) was also part of interwar Poland, and the blue and yellow Ukrainian flag was everywhere in town. Ukrainian refugees seemed to be on every bus and train. It felt like an unwelcome revival of the Europe of the 1930s, when lawless states used borders to ratchet up tension and then launch murderous invasions.

The Suwałki region has been border territory for centuries; a four-way contest between German and Russian empires and the recently more modest ambitions of Poland and Lithuania. Suwałki, like the bulk of Poland, was part of the Russian Empire in 1914. The buildings in the town centre are mostly low-slung Russian neoclassical edifices, like pastel-shaded wedding cakes, from its 19th-century role as an administrative centre for soldiers and officials trying to cudgel the region's Poles, Jews and Lithuanians into a semblance of conformity to the tsar's empire. The town is built from the same flat, yellowish bricks that one finds in Kyiv, or Kars; on one or two buildings on the edge of the older part of town you can see Cyrillic lettering in the brickwork. But go just a little bit to the west, into apparently similar countryside of lakes and forests, and the buildings are taller, spikily Gothic and built of red bricks, indicating that towns such as Gołdap were once in East Prussia, on the eastern edge of Germany.

For all the beauty of the lakes and forests, the settlements of Polish East Prussia are often a little bleak and disjointed, an encouragement to put on one's hiking boots and head out into nature if you are there at the right time of year. A typical vista will feature some well-restored red-brick Prussian buildings, including the main church and the town hall and a stretch of town wall with a gateway in it. There is likely to be a castle of some sort, either a turreted Teutonic edifice or a stately home once occupied by the Prussian aristocracy. There will be humbler older buildings too, but a lot of the centre is heavily reconstructed into plain, unadorned concrete versions of Polish or Prussian architectural forms. There are grassy open spaces between buildings in the older part of town, scars from the destruction the Soviet army wrought across the province in 1944–45. Look closely, and you will probably see burn marks and bullet holes. Most of the town will consist of low-rise concrete blocks of flats. There may be strange reminders of the 'German time' in the countryside as well – weathered stone memorials, old railways disappearing amid the lakes, red-brick stately homes crumbling into the earth and military remnants – above all, Hitler's ruined Wolf's Lair complex near Kętrzyn, forbidding concrete bunkers standing like a lost Mayan city in the forest.

The Germans captured Suwałki from Russia in 1915; after they were in turn defeated in 1918, Suwałki was claimed and fought over by Poland and Lithuania. The struggle, a side issue to the bigger contest between the two over control of Vilnius (Wilno), was unknown to me before I visited. My ignorance was an example of the common misunderstanding that the post-1919 boundaries of Europe were all devised by technocrats and diplomats at the Paris Peace Conference ('Versailles'), when many of them were actually settled on the ground in bitter little wars between successor states that dragged on into the mid-1920s.[1] Suwałki's time in independent Poland was interrupted in September 1939 when the area was occupied by the Soviet Union and handed over after a few days to Nazi Germany who, ludicrously, incorporated it into the Reich as 'Sudauen'. In 1945, it was returned to Poland.

The old boundaries are written in the land or in the buildings, and even in people's psychology. Look at many modern political or demographic maps of Poland and the ghostly lines of the pre-1939 or pre-1914 boundaries are still visible. Every time there is an election in Poland, people point out the difference between the liberal-voting ex-German territory in the west and the conservative-voting ex-Russian and ex-Austrian east. The continuity is despite years of Nazi tyranny, ethnic cleansing, resettlement and communist conformity. Poland's complex history has made it a palimpsest of boundaries; old European borders are overwritten but hardly ever completely erased.

Changing borders have meant disaster for Poland and its neighbours: moving the lines on the map meant a country was partitioned, recreated, made the victim of multiple acts of genocide and imperialism, and then relocated from one place to another by cynical great powers. International civilisation says, but does not always mean, 'Never Again' to genocide. Legally it should also mean 'Never Again' to changing borders by force. Can we escape from the facts of borders as lines drawn, mostly through violence and the urge for conquest, manifestations of distrust and exclusion? Or can places like Nimmersatt and Suwałki be locations where such ambitions are abandoned and people learn once again to live alongside each other, and find what they have in common and what is interestingly different?

6

Exit, pursued by a bear

(Finland, Estonia, Russia)

I was waiting in the dark and the cold at the edge of Russia. It was February 2019 and I, normally a creature that thrives in cold temperatures, was wearing a thick jacket, boots, gloves and a furry Russian hat as I stood on the cold platform in front of the grand hall of the railway station in Vyborg at the end of a brief visit to some of Russia's westernmost outposts. The building impressed me and I held up my iPhone to take a picture of the central arch. 'No photographs please,' said a stern official, so I put the phone down again. I had already been stamped out of Russia by a border official who took a painstakingly detailed look at my passport and cleared me through customs, but I didn't want to risk being called back. My visa conditions meant that I had to be out of Russia by midnight. I had missed the previous train thanks to a misunderstanding, and this was the last chance.

A sleek white and blue train* appeared in the distance, slowing down to approach the arc-lit platforms and finally stopping. Half an hour later it stopped again, at a snowy halt in a railway yard in Vainikkala, Finland, so that the Finnish customs and border guard could board the train and do their checks.

All hard borders have potential energy embodied in them; they are lines that stop things happening. They reassure people who live a long way from them who like to keep their towns and villages as they are, but at the cost of suppressing the natural inclinations of others – young people and borderland residents, for instance – to move where they choose and not to feel trapped. The Russian–Finnish border is a particularly extreme instance of a line that divides two very different sorts of country: a wealthy, democratic, egalitarian state on one side and a violent

---

*The Allegro train service between Helsinki and St Petersburg ceased in spring 2022, following the Russian attack on Ukraine.

kleptocracy a few metres on the other side of the fence. In terms of concrete outcomes – life expectancy, education, health, income and so on – the gap between Finland and Russia is enormous. It is also a cultural frontier, between the eastern Orthodox world and the north European Protestant world; between Cyrillic and Latin, between a big and almost endless country and one that knows it is small, and above all between a low-trust and a high-trust sort of society. I was interested in how the two countries on either side of this line managed to insulate this crackling, high-voltage border.

The Russia–Finland border stretches for 1,340km from its northern point, well inside the Arctic Circle, down to its southern terminus at the Gulf of Finland, a little over halfway between Helsinki and St Petersburg. Most of its length is an arbitrary series of straight lines and zigzags through a primal landscape of forbidding dark forests. The physical border itself is a thin strip of cleared land, a literal line in the snow between the trees. It dodges madly through and between lakes, slicing its way across peninsulas and natural features. One can imagine the moment when Stalin, sitting in Moscow with a map, slashed a line across this distant wilderness with a stroke of his pen. It is a border with a grim history that few people outside Finland know very much about, but which reveals a lot about what national boundaries mean in central and eastern Europe.

Like most hard borders, the Finland–Russia boundary can be crossed legally at a limited number of points – in this case, eight permanent and two temporary posts on the roads plus the railway crossing by which I entered Finland (reversing the last leg of Lenin's 1917 journey across Europe from exile in Switzerland to what was then Petrograd). The bulk of the traffic crosses at the three southern road checkpoints where the border shears south-west to take a bite out of historic Finland. This is where the roads run between the populated southern part of Finland and St Petersburg, with the smaller northern crossings more for the convenience of locals than for long-distance travel.

About three-quarters of the roughly nine million annual crossings of the border in the late 2010s involved Russian citizens coming over to Finland, mostly for the same reasons that people have for crossing any border. Russians went on shopping trips to Finland to buy white goods, and indeed consumer produce, in the belief that the articles available in Finland are of superior quality to the Russian variants, even if they have the same brand name. This arose because of both counterfeiting and the idea that multinationals palm off inferior products on the Russian market while the production lines for northern and western Europe are run to higher standards.

For Finns going in the other direction, the main draws were some of the usual ones that attract people from wealthy high-taxed societies to poorer countries – cheaper alcohol, tobacco and fuel. Alcohol has a peculiar role in Finnish culture and the authorities' fear of alcoholism means that supply is limited, taxes are high and most sales are through the official monopoly. The same restrictions do not apply in northern Russia. Particularly at the northern end of the border, locals on both sides have multiple-entrance visas to allow them to shuttle back and forward to buy products on the other side.

The border also attracts more serious international criminal activity. There is a Finnish television crime series, *Bordertown*, set in Lappeenranta, about the culture clash between a cop from Helsinki and the locals, and the shadowy presence of the even bigger metropolis of St Petersburg only a couple of hours away across the border. One story, 'Dragonflies', features toxic party drugs being trafficked from St Petersburg to small-town Finland, and this is based on reality in the area. The drugs are more likely to be toxic or adulterated, and the gangs involved in trading them more likely to be murderously violent, than one finds further west. Some parents in Finland even advise their children that if they do want to try drugs, they should do it in London or Amsterdam rather than in Finland because the risks are so much lower.

There are a few incidents every year when people cross the border illegally, away from the authorised points. The wildness of the terrain in the north and the lack of roads makes unauthorised crossings difficult and dangerous. Many of these incidents are mishaps that arise when fishermen drift over the wrong side of a border lake. Others tend to involve stupidity rather than malice, often on the part of foreign tourists who wander over the border during outdoor sports in rural Finland. Sometimes this is inadvertent, but the border has a mysterious pull on the imagination that virtually compels people to try to pop over to Russia just for the sake of it, drawn to the striped Russian border marker like moths to a flame. Eight of the forty cases during 2017 came in one week in June, when border bravado overtook one British and one German group. The British men, flushed with their success in completing an orienteering event, wandered over equipped with a bag of cans to enjoy a quick beer in Russia. They were picked up by the Finnish Border Guard when they crossed back and charged with illegal crossing of the border, an offence that usually carries a fine. It could have been worse. If they had been picked up on the Russian side, they would have caused an international incident and suffered detention in unpleasant conditions.

The low number of illegal crossings also indicates that the Border Guard are good at stopping them. There is a sophisticated system, which starts up to 3km away from the border on the Finnish side of the line. Entering the border zone requires a permit from the Guard, which in turn requires some form-filling and a convincing reason. The guards are familiar with local residents and frequent visitors to the border strip. The most populated stretch of border in the south is bristling with cameras that detect motion and gather evidence, there is monitoring from the air from aircraft and drones, and the Guard go out on patrol. In winter they speed along the border line in snowmobiles and the Guard employs around 200 dogs to assist in detecting illegal activity. The distribution of cameras and the patrol rota are frequently changed to prevent blind spots developing. As of 2023, the Finns had started building a steel mesh fence along the southern 200km of the line. There is also a secure zone on the Russian side, for most of its length rather deeper than on the Finnish side, and their own system of checks and patrols.

Part of managing such a high-voltage, politically significant border has been to create a system that takes the drama out of potential problems before they escalate. There is a reporting system where incidents are registered and reported to local border delegations on which the Finnish and Russian border guards are represented. When evidence of an illegal crossing such as footprints in the snow or a scent trail is discovered, there is a joint investigation. At local level, there is day-to-day co-operation. For instance, if a reindeer wanders across the border the Finns and Russians tell each other, and at the end of the day the reindeer is recaptured by the herder under the supervision of the border guards. This system keeps working even when relations between the two governments are poor. When I visited in 2019, there seemed to be a sense of professional respect and courtesy between the Finnish and Russian border guards, even if the Russian state was regarded with suspicion.

Line of control

The Finnish border in February 2019, while indisputably chilly, was much warmer than the climate at the Russia–Estonia border in October 2022. The full-scale invasion of Ukraine in February 2022 had resulted in EU sanctions against Russia, including the withdrawal of short-term visas, and a huge drop in traffic. Relations between Estonia and Russia were cool anyway, and that was reflected in the everyday relationships between the border guards on each side, which were very distant. Back in the 2000s there had been joint seminars – starting, when Russia was hosting, with a 10 a.m. vodka – but, these fell away. Before COVID there had been co-ordination meetings but when health restrictions ended, the meetings did not resume. When I visited the border zone at the line of control in the south-east in 2022, the Russian and Estonian officers and contract workers did not acknowledge each other, although the Estonians were constantly aware that they were being watched by the other side. The Estonian police were open about their suspicion that people on the Russian side were complicit in some of the smuggling and criminal activity that took place around the border – that the FSB would allow criminal organisations to do their business if they supplied intelligence.

To my surprise, visiting the line of control with the calm, cool Estonian border guards in 2022 was one of the more emotional moments of my journey. There was something viscerally frightening about the unfenced line between Estonia and Russia. A vast state, run by a cruel regime that did not respect this imaginary line, lay over there, stretching all the way to the north Pacific. Estonia, with its population of 1.4 million people and its liberal society, felt very little and vulnerable. I felt glad that a fence was going up. Rationally, I know that a bit of barbed wire is not going to stop an aggressive power's military, but I understood the emotional consolations of a physical barrier in a way that I had not done before.

Most of the business of the Estonia–Russia border takes place at the city of Narva, in the far north-east of Estonia and closer to St Petersburg than it is to Estonia's capital of Tallinn. The bridge across the Narva river is one of the most border-ish looking places I have been – a span stretching between two castles, Narva on the Estonian side and Ivangorod in Russia – but it has actually not been on an international boundary for very long. Both banks of the river were in Estonia as it existed in 1920, but when the Estonian SSR was re-established within the USSR in 1945 the east bank was transferred to Russia and became the nominally separate town of Ivangorod. It made little difference until 1991, when the river became an international boundary and in 2004 when it became part of the EU's external frontier.

Before the Second World War Narva was majority-Estonian, but following its destruction in a Soviet–German battle in 1944 it was repopulated with people from elsewhere in the USSR, principally Russia. After 1991 Narva became an Estonian city with a large majority of its population being Russian by language and ethnicity; in the first few unsettled years of the 1990s there was speculation about a Russian-controlled breakaway statelet, such as the one that was established in Transnistria in 1992, but this came to nothing. An initiative in 1998 by people in Ivangorod to join Estonia also fizzled out.

People in Narva have one of three sorts of passport. Estonian (and therefore EU) passports are available to people who can trace their ancestry to pre-1940 Estonia, people born since 1992 and people who can pass a citizenship exam involving competence in the Estonian language. There are foreign passports, principally Russian. The third category is the 'grey passport' – a document for resident non-citizens who for whatever reason do not take the citizenship exam path to a full Estonian passport and remain technically stateless. Grey passport holders have Estonian ID cards and most civil rights, including voting in local but not national elections, but the document does not give them European citizen rights such as freedom of movement.

I had an interesting chat with a fellow in Narva whom I'll call Sergei. He was about 30, and like nearly everyone else there was 'Russian'. But he told me he didn't feel like a Russian: he said just that 'my parents had a Russian background' and if pushed he would be an Estonian of Russian heritage. He felt loyal to Estonia, working in one of its public services, and to Europe; he was looking forward to visiting London before long. The language issue was fading because Estonia, with a small state's consciousness of the world beyond its borders, is extremely good at educating people in different languages. Nearly everyone under 35 is proficient in Estonian and English, and often Russian and German as well. While there are older people with Russian or grey passports who live in a Russian bubble and are vulnerable to Kremlin propaganda, younger people with Russian heritage are often like Sergei, grateful that they were born on the Estonian side of the line with the human rights, living standards and freedom to travel that it brings.

It is possible therefore to live in Narva and feel optimistic about the future, but Narva has its share of problems and did so before it became a dead end rather than a bridge from St Petersburg to the EU. Its population has shrunk by a third since 1991 – though it is still Estonia's third city after Tallinn and the university city of Tartu. It was, like some cities along the eastern border of Germany, a textile and manufacturing town that has weathered economic transition badly. One of the only parts of Narva that was not destroyed in 1944 was the huge textile mill of Kreenholm, situated on an island on the Estonian side of the riverine international boundary but almost literally within spitting distance of a larger, Russian island. Before it became a border town, Narva was a factory town. Kreenholm chugged along as a state-owned enterprise under the USSR, and for a while after privatisation, but shed thousands of jobs and declared bankruptcy in 2010. The mills are derelict, used sometimes as an eerie industrial backdrop for concerts, and nobody seems to know what to do with them. The population of the 19th-century red-brick blocks of flats of workers' housing near Kreenholm is thinning out, as retired workers die or move on. It is the sort of vista that has produced hateful populist politics in western countries, but – particularly given the Russian dimension – the politics of Narva could be a lot worse than it is.

By its fingertips, Narva remains part of a unique urban area with parts in both the EU and Russia. Even with frosty international relations, the governments of Estonia and Russia recognised that Narva and Ivangorod were closely linked by economic and family ties; prior to 1991, people had settled on either side of the river without much regard to which Soviet subdivision they lived in. Nearly everyone had some valid human reason for crossing the border frequently – a Narva resident with parents in Ivangorod, an Ivangorodnik with a job in the mills at Kreenholm – and the authorities were prepared to let it continue for people with all three sorts of passport.

As well as the main bridge between the castles, there used to be a more intimate footbridge crossing between a suburban Narva square of weatherboarded wooden houses – the landscapes of Estonia are oddly reminiscent of New England – and the older part of Ivangorod. This was only open to local traffic, but I was privileged to be able to walk halfway along it on the Estonian side. It is a square tube, with views over Kreenholm and the river. It was an everyday place for Ivangorod and Narva residents, but to me it was like a secret wormhole from one reality to another. The Narva-2 crossing closed in November 2022, a month after I visited. Roadworks on the Russian side of the main crossing, announced in December 2022, closed the bridge for vehicles, so the main bridge, already quiet, became pedestrian-only.

Wormhole to Russia: Narva-2 border crossing, October 2022.

Having remained an ambiguous space for thirty years, Russia's war forced Narva to choose a side. Particularly in the early months of the war, it was a place where Ukrainians could get from one side of the front lines to the other, via Russia, Estonia, Poland and then back into Ukraine. The Estonian border guards had difficult decisions to make about people with documents from the so-called Donetsk and Luhansk People's Republics, and Ukrainians with Russian documents – while these were illegal, one also had to consider that many people were forced to adopt them. The balance between humanity and security was uncomfortable, and officers felt that it was a major test of their professional skills. As Russia mobilised and war continued, the flow of people slowed down – the Russian authorities were stopping them before they reached Ivangorod. Significantly, a common reaction among the Russian-speakers of Narva to the 2022 Russian invasion of Ukraine was to obtain Estonian citizenship, whether out of loyalty to Europe or to protect their rights in Estonia. Pragmatic considerations, and broader ideas of what constitutes civilised values and which government is best at ensuring them, have determined national identity in the borderlands from Alsace in the 1870s through Silesia in the 1920s to Narva today.

7

The land of amber

(Germany, Russia, Poland)

Fifty million years ago, silent forests of tall trees covered the land by the waters that we now call the Baltic Sea. The trees were of a kind that no human has ever seen, but they were the ancestors of the pines that grow from the sandy soil today. When their bark was damaged, by creatures or by lightning, the trees healed the wound by bleeding. Their resin was tough stuff, resisting biodegradation, gradually hardening over thousands of millennia into a substance that resembled yellow stone. The coasts moved, and some of the fossilised forest was dragged beneath the sea. Some of it would wash up on the shores when stormy weather churned up the shallow seabed, and at some time, over 99 per cent of the way through the history of the resin, a human walked along a damp beach that glistened with golden light and came across a shiny stone that he or she found beautiful. People started to believe in its healing, spiritual power. Thousands of years after that, their descendants found that it was worth trading the stone with the wealthy empire by the Mediterranean, and the Amber Road was charted to take it there via the great crossroads at Carnuntum by the Danube.

The millions-of-years-old resin became the stuff of diplomacy, and rival nationalist claims[2] between entities that meant nothing until the last instant of the amber's existence. Amber came to symbolise the northern shores, and the delicate work of shaping it for ornamental use grew to be a skilled trade in the city of Danzig (Gdańsk). It was a state monopoly, unauthorised harvesting sometimes punishable by death. Polish diplomats and travellers gave amber items as gifts, and in an echo of its Roman journey it played a part in the great cultural exchange between Poland and Renaissance Italy. In 1716 the diplomacy of amber took a new turn, with the gift of the priceless Amber Room from the Prussian king Frederick William I to Peter the Great of Russia. The Amber Room cemented a military alliance between Prussia and Russia against Sweden, an ominous foreshadowing of the brutal consequences of German–Russian friendship for the lands in between. For over two centuries the room was the showpiece of the Catherine Palace, just outside St Petersburg. Amber was scarce, and the craftsmanship involved in shaping it into the richly ornate panels of the room represented extremes of skill and dedication.

In 1941, the leading edge of the German invasion reached the suburbs of Leningrad (as St Petersburg was known at the time) and captured the Catherine Palace. The Nazis had some weird ideas about the aesthetics of amber, linking its northern provenance and golden colour to fields of German corn and the blonde hair of an Aryan maiden.[3] The Germans prised the panels from the walls of the Amber Room, boxed them up and took them to Germany's amber capital, the city of Königsberg in East Prussia. Sometime at the end of the war, the Amber Room vanished. But so did Königsberg itself, as the province of East Prussia disappeared from the map during the bloody destruction of the mid-1940s.

It seems to be written in East Prussia's destiny that it should be an exclave, or perhaps an 'inclusion', a creature trapped in amber. For centuries, the province was of Germany, but not *in* Germany; now a part of it is in Russia, but not *of* Russia. The Kaliningrad oblast – northern East Prussia – viewed from inside the fence is a claustrophobic enclave, a small Baltic republic. It is slightly bigger than Northern Ireland or Connecticut, but unlike those places it is surrounded by a hard border with visa checks and customs controls. From the point of view of Moscow, it might as well be an offshore island – 450km from the nearest bit of Russia proper, about the same distance as Shetland is from Norway. While it is Russian in culture, it has developed a particular variant of that identity, and is more open to neighbouring countries than the rest of Russia. People in the oblast talk about the main part of the country as 'Big Russia' or even as 'Russia', as opposed to their island. It is an echo of its past, as many things are: the Germans who were here a century ago would talk of getting a train 'to the Reich' or 'to Germany' as if they were going abroad.

To get to Kaliningrad from Big Russia, you must fly directly or get your papers in order to do the road or rail transit across Lithuania and either Belarus or Latvia. There are two sorts of passports in Russia, one 'internal' – essentially a sort of ID card – and the other the sort for foreign travel, and Kaliningrad is the one place where even the old people have the second sort of passport because they prefer the train crossing to Big Russia. Many people don't even bother to visit Big Russia – about 40 per cent of the population have never been and many of the younger people prefer to visit the neighbouring foreign countries, particularly Poland. The bounded, finite nature of Kaliningrad gives its people an unusual insight into what it is like to live in a small country. These Russians, for instance, are obliged to care about what Lithuania thinks. The transit links and electric cables cross that country, and there are ethnic Russian citizens of Lithuania who moved to Kaliningrad after the break-up of the Soviet Union but maintain official registration in Lithuania and therefore have Schengen travel rights.

Before Kaliningrad, there was Königsberg. The German province of East Prussia and its capital city were founded by the Teutonic Knights who were fighting a tribal war and religious crusade in 13th-century north-eastern Europe. The native people of the area, the original Prussians, were a Baltic tribe that disappeared from the pages of history in the Northern Crusades – they were, like many people in such episodes, killed, expelled or absorbed, and it is difficult at this distance to establish the balance between these three fates. The marauding Christian knights of the Teutonic Order and the Sword Brothers only stopped reluctantly when they encountered opposition from Poland, whose dynastic union with hitherto pagan Lithuania had Christianised this last holdout. The Poles defeated the Knights at Grunwald (Tannenberg) in 1410 and nibbled away at the Knights' realm for the next century.

East Prussia was never a constituent part of the Holy Roman Empire, which for centuries was the nearest thing available to a political definition of Germany. It was ruled by the Teutonic Knights until 1525, when Albrecht, the Grand Master of the Order, converted East Prussia to a secular duchy with an established Lutheran church, giving Protestantism a firm foundation in Europe. 'Ducal Prussia' was established with the permission of Poland and its rulers gave their allegiance to Poland until 1657; there was already a 'Royal Prussia' under more direct Polish control, which wound around Ducal Prussia like yin and yang. Thanks to dynastic politics of baffling complexity, Ducal Prussia was linked up in 1618 with Brandenburg (around Berlin) under one ruling family, the Hohenzollerns, whose title came from another even smaller disconnected fragment of Germany. The combined realm was part-in and part-out of the Holy Roman Empire, a loophole that was exploited when its ruler (Frederick III) upgraded his title by being crowned 'King in Prussia' in Königsberg in 1701.* So began the rise of Prussia, and eventually the unification of Germany. After the first Partition of Poland in 1772, the Kingdom of Prussia took control of the territory that separated East Prussia from Brandenburg and Pomerania. The latter became 'West Prussia', even though it was in the middle of the kingdom.

City of kings, city of Kant

Having been founded by sword-wielding theologians, East Prussia continued to be a place of both military and intellectual significance. Its towns were founded around fortresses, including the capital city of Königsberg situated on the Pregel river near where it emerges into the lagoon by the Baltic.

While on one level thoroughly German, Königsberg has always had identities for other peoples, something reflected in it having several historical names that are all currently in use. To the Poles, to whose kingdom the city and province had a nominal allegiance in 1525–1657, it is Królewiec (the name has recently replaced Russian Kaliningrad on road signs). To the Lithuanians it is Karaliaučius, which like its German and Polish names refers to its royal status (the king in whose honour it is named, Ottokar of Bohemia, was 'Czech', so it is arguably Královec first of all). As a fervently Protestant city, Königsberg was open to church services in the languages of the city's minorities, and it was a place of refuge for religious dissenters in Poland and Lithuania. It was also the nearest big city for the rural areas of East Prussia, where there had always been some Polish-speakers, and western Lithuania.

A dense townscape of tall buildings along the banks and wharves grew up and the city spilled across the branches of the river. Königsberg became a city of trade and academic exploration. The flat island of Kneiphof, at the old centre of the city, was the site of a cathedral (dating from 1333) and an illustrious university crammed into a narrow riverbank. In 1736, the mathematician Leonhard Euler, enjoying a stroll through the city, wondered whether it would be possible to take a walk

---

*Frederick the Great assumed the title of 'King *of* Prussia' in 1772.

that crossed each of the seven bridges criss-crossing branches of the Pregel once and once only. The answer was 'No', but working out why involved creating the mathematics of topology. Königsberg thinkers developed ideas whose interconnections resonate through the ages: what can we claim as universal, and what are nations and nationalism?

Kant, the secular saint of intellectual Königsberg, was a revered celebrity in his own lifetime (1724–1804); his self-disciplined walks through the crowded old city attracted sightseers. He rarely left the city – a 140km trip outside as far as the East Prussian town of Goldap is commemorated in a monument that still stands there – and he was intensely loyal to and proud of Königsberg. His philosophy is based on universal principles but it is still inescapably the work of a German intellectual, and in his own life he was a proud cosmopolitan alongside his allegiance to his home city. Kant felt that he did not need to travel to discover the world, because the world came to Königsberg:

A large city such as Königsberg on the river Pregel, which is the centre of a kingdom, in which the provincial councils of the government are located, which has a university (for cultivation of the sciences) and which has also the right location for maritime commerce – a city which, by way of rivers, has the advantage of commerce both with the interior of the country and with neighbouring and distant lands of different languages and customs, can well be taken as an appropriate place for broadening one's knowledge of human beings as well as of the world, where this knowledge can be acquired without even travelling.[4]

It is a reminder that academic life, trade and travel were part of 18th-century urban life as well as the 21st. Kant's life and thought are a very borderland mixture of the universal and cosmopolitan with the local and provincial. There was a retrospectively opportune moment in 1758–62 when the city was briefly part of the Russian Empire and Kant became a Russian subject. In those times, a change of sovereignty often did not matter much and there was no contradiction between Königsberg's German culture and Russian rule. The lands along the Baltic already under the Russian crown had plenty of German merchants and aristocratic landowners, so there was not much discomfort at taking in Königsberg. But when the Russians returned in 1945, they came to destroy rather than accommodate that German culture.

One of the students attracted to Enlightenment Königsberg was Johann Gottfried Herder (1744–1803), who came from the small East Prussian town of Mohrungen. Herder's philosophy tried to do something rather unusual: to create a universal argument for the set of feelings that we call nationalism. Much as Karl Marx would have been appalled at a lot of the people and ideas operating under the name of Marxism in the 20th century, Herder would have been distraught at how nationalist ideas evolved after his death. Herder's argument for nationalism is one of the most attractive statements of the ideology. It has the great merit of being universal, in that it is not tied to the merits of one national group over another, or even – in contrast to specific local nationalisms – to what specific qualities differentiate a nation from its neighbours.

Not many people read Herder nowadays,[5] and very few in English. His writing is digressive even by 18th-century *Tristram Shandy* standards – at one stage, during a discussion of irritability, he invites the reader to 'observe the frog in copulation', for instance.[6] Herder contradicts himself, sometimes within a couple of pages. But it is hard to dislike him. He was proud of his German identity, and conversant with French civilisation, but he seemed to love Slavic cultures above all. By contemporary standards he was progressive, loathing slavery and opposing European colonialism overseas as well as the dynastic empires of the continent. Colonialism – even when it claimed to be done in the best interests of the people colonised – was likely to go wrong because the colonisers could not know better than the colonised what was good for them. 'The roses for the wreath of freedom must be picked by a people's own hands and grow happily out of its own needs, out of its own desire and love.'[7]

Herder felt that each nation was appropriate for its territory and while over the long term nations rose and declined, each had a right to exist and was worthy of equal respect. Herder saw nations as collections of people who, by virtue of their common language, plus received traditions and geographical placement, shared modes of thought, values and interests. Government from within one's own nation was therefore the least likely form of state to become tyrannical and force people to act against their own natures. 'An empire consisting of one nation is a family, a well-ordered household: it reposes on itself, for it is founded on nature, and stands and falls by time alone.'[8]

At the time Herder was writing, the nation and the state did not match up in most of Europe. People thought in terms of German and Italian culture, but in political terms Germany and Italy were just geographical expressions because each was divided into a patchwork of small states. Conversely, the great empires ruled from Vienna, St Petersburg and Constantinople all encompassed many cultures and languages. Territories changed hands all the time, without reference to the people who lived in them. The culture of the ruling elite was radically different from that of the people in general wherever one went, and not just in the ways that we now associate with class, education and wealth. They spoke a different language from the people. Frederick the Great preferred to speak French, regarding the German language as a '*demi-barbare*' collection of regional dialects. The Polish ruling class even persuaded themselves that they were really Sarmatians, a distinct ethnicity and culture. Herder's nationalism was not necessarily what we would now call democratic, but it involved the idea of a national *demos* (people in a political context) and a government that was, by virtue of coming from the same habits of mind and the same soil as the *demos*, in line with the greatest happiness of the people. Nationalism was a challenge to the petty power of the princes. The original meaning of *Deutschland über alles* when von Fallersleben wrote it in 1841 was that allegiance to Germany should rank higher than the fragmented principalities into which German lands were divided. Nationalism was also, of course, a challenge to the great empires.

The problem with liberatory nationalism was that the match between nations and territories wasn't particularly good either, and it was probably getting worse even as nationalism gripped the intellectual imagination in the 19th century. Unless geography was particularly firm about the matter – the English Channel, the Alps and the Pyrenees all functioned as barriers – there were no firm lines between peoples. In the west, there was a fuzzy, moving zone where French and German cultures mingled. In the east, language and culture could vary village by village. One nation did not stop where another started. A Hungarian, a Saxon and a Romanian could all look at the same Transylvanian landscape and feel the same powerful emotions of pride and belonging. But whose patriotic feeling would be reflected in the boundaries of a nation state? Who would decide, and how?

Herder's own life illustrates the problem. The small East Prussian town where Herder was born in 1744 was known then, and for the next couple of centuries, as Mohrungen. Although culturally German, there was a Polish minority in the town. It became the Polish town of Morąg in 1945. Herder went to university in Königsberg, studying under Kant, and then worked in Riga, which was then in the Russian Empire but mainly German speaking and dominated by German aristocrats and merchants. He travelled to France and in 1770–71 he had long conversations with Goethe in the agreeable surroundings of Strasbourg, which had been part of France for a century but retained a mostly Germanic streetscape and dialect. Most of the first 27 years of his life were therefore spent in places that for various reasons could not easily be tied down to a single national status. It is therefore curious that he did not seem to have thought through the basic problem that mixed borderlands and cosmopolitan cities posed to his humane nationalist philosophy.

As the philosopher of nationalism Ernest Gellner (1925–95) observed, Herder's mentor Kant had anticipated the fatal flaw: 'partiality, the tendency to make exception on one's own behalf or one's own case, is *the* central weakness from which all others flow; and that it infects national sentiment as it does all else.'[9] My nationalism is an expression of an elevated culture, entitled to every village where one of my people has laid his head; your nationalism is crude, atavistic and provincial. Conflict between nationalisms becomes irreconcilable and aggressive in the border zones without some overall principle or law to govern it.

There is one point in Herder at which there is a suggestion that there are right and wrong ways to run multinational states. He was opposed to Joseph II's decision in 1784 to make German the official language of state throughout the Austrian Empire. He favoured having different languages and laws in different regions, but he stopped short of arguing that the empire should be broken up into nation states. Perhaps, in Herder's world view, there is room for multinational structures after all if they enable people to live their lives in peace as they choose if nation states would prevent them. His first principles should preclude coercing minorities into a nation state, let alone kicking them out of their homes through ethnic cleansing. Nationalism came to include these things in the century and a half after Herder's death, and the scars are still visible in his homeland.

Götterdammerung

As Germany became more economically and politically united during the 19th century, from the Zollverein customs union in 1834 to its culmination in the proclamation of the German Empire in 1871, East Prussia became part of a powerful German national state. There was therefore only a bit over a century of East Prussia being properly linked to Germany. It was an important century, though, in which the railways were built, industry and education took hold and national identities were forged. The overwhelming majority of East Prussians welcomed being incorporated into Bismarck's Reich, but paradoxically this accelerated relative decline and isolation of the province.

The centre of gravity of Germany was moving steadily westwards, towards the port of Hamburg and the industrial heartlands around the Rhine and Ruhr. Königsberg was a long way east of Berlin (over 500km) let alone Cologne (over 1,000km). Larger ships could not make it far enough up the Pregel river to enter the city and a new deep-water port was constructed at Pillau on the outer shore. Rural East Prussia was the sort of place that exported people in the 19th century as work went from the land to the factories.

There was an intimation of twilight in autumn 1914 when the Russians invaded East Prussia, getting as far as Insterburg (now Chernyakhovsk) and the Masurian lakes. The German defenders initially took fright and considered abandoning Königsberg despite its impressive fortifications, before Paul von Hindenburg came out of retirement to take charge. The two enormous Russian armies blundering around East Prussia were outmanoeuvred and defeated, and the occupation of Insterburg ended with little damage after a couple of weeks. Hindenburg was elevated to national hero, with baleful effect on the politics of post-war Germany.

When Poland was re-founded in 1918, East Prussia would once again have to be a separate bit of Germandom beyond it, a sleepy land of Big Houses and wild forests. East Prussia had its ambiguities, particularly in the Warmia region around Allenstein (Olsztyn) where many people still spoke Polish dialects. The Allies insisted on a plebiscite of the population but the outcome in 1920 was a huge victory for the German cause.* People had assimilated rapidly to Germany in the preceding decades, a process that culminated in the Nazis winning large majorities in

---

* Polish sources do provide evidence that there was bias in the administration of the vote and intimidation of pro-Poland campaigners, but the turnout in the vote was high (officially 87 per cent) and the result was a nearly unanimous 98 per cent for Germany in the Allenstein zone.

democratic elections in Warmia; they made it clear that the Warmians were exempted from their racial policies. Even so, the Nazis stepped up cultural assimilation, creating a commission in 1938 to rename East Prussian settlements that had insufficiently Germanic names and banning the use of the Polish language in 1939.

East Prussia's military and aristocratic traditions were increasingly dusty and out of time. Its hereditary Junker ruling class were having trouble paying their way. It was already becoming a place for nostalgia and rural dreams, such as those of Hermann Goering, who took over a vast hunting estate at Rominten in the east of the province, not far from the present-day obelisk where Russia, Poland and Lithuania converge. The regime put up huge memorials to Hindenburg, and tried to recapture the spirit of the Teutonic Knights, crusading and massacring for their cause in the east.

The end for centuries of German life in East Prussia began in summer 1944. At the end of August, Königsberg was within bombing range for the RAF and it was the target for RAF massive raids as part of the same campaign that destroyed Hamburg in 1943 and Dresden in 1945. Death was closing in rapidly from the east as well. The Soviet advance into East Prussia was horrifying in its violence. It was the first part of Germany proper in which the Red Army set foot, and that army was brutalised by three years of Nazi horrors inflicted on the Soviet Union – and by the inhuman and murderous methods with which the Red Army itself was run. When this vengeful force crashed into the Reich, it encountered a world insulated from the hell on earth that had been instituted just to the east of the neat gardens, aristocratic hunting lodges and tilled fields of East Prussia. Soviet soldiers, even if they had not been primed for hatred and violence, could not understand why the Germans had come to burn down their impoverished villages and murder their relatives when staying home was so comfortable.

The first incursion, in October 1944, was pushed back by the Germans after a few days, but left behind plenty of evidence of vicious atrocities in villages such as Nemmersdorf. The Nazi authorities seized upon the evidence and publicised – and unnecessarily exaggerated – the details: women and children were tortured to death and there was a case where a person was crucified on a barn door. The intention had been to stiffen the resistance of the German forces defending in the east and the German people in general by depicting the Russians as a bestial horde. The actual effect was to terrify the people of East Prussia and then in turn the rest of eastern Germany, and civilians started to run away from areas close to the front line. The panic reached Königsberg city and by the time the Red Army reoccupied eastern East Prussia, there was full-scale flight. People took to the sea, attempting perilous foot crossings of the frozen lagoon, or cramming onto ships bound for the west such as the *Wilhelm Gustloff*, which was torpedoed on 30 January 1945 with the loss of nearly 10,000 lives.

Königsberg was ringed by fortresses, largely paid for by the reparations Germany obtained from France in the peace treaty of 1871. As with most investments in forts then, the defences proved useless in war. The siege and capture of the city took three days and on 9 April 1945 the German commander Otto von Lasch surrendered to the Soviets. The city was already far behind the lines as the Red Army had reached the Oder river, only 90km from Berlin. The surrender of the city was final. Stalin had claimed the north of East Prussia, including Königsberg, for the USSR, with the southern half allocated to Poland. The German citizens and refugees were killed or expelled, with only a handful of exceptions.

City of Kalinin

The USSR wanted Königsberg primarily for its use as a year-round port on the Baltic. Russia's naval power has always been fragmented, with open access to the Pacific but with complicated passages to its ports on the Black Sea, the Arctic and the Baltic. Kronstadt and Leningrad (St Petersburg), at the far end of the Baltic, were further from the strategic heartland of Europe and iced up in winter. Kaliningrad's outer port of Pillau (Baltiysk) did not have this problem and possessing East Prussia made it easier to project Soviet power in Europe – and indeed to defend Leningrad and the Russian heartland from attack from the west. A military outpost in the west would also be a useful menacing reminder for Poland that, while it had been vulnerable to Germany from several sides before 1939, its fraternal Soviet neighbour would be there to the north as well as the east.

Another reason for grabbing Königsberg was more primal; the desire of the biggest lion in the pride to tear a lump from the corpse of a vicious enemy and take it for himself. One talks of the 'violation' of borders by invasion, and the invasion of East Prussia was accompanied by bodily violation – rape and casual murder – on a massive scale.

After the horrors of the invasion and the following months, the situation in the city calmed down. Soviet officers and administrators surveyed the mansions and villas of Amalienau, an attractive and only marginally damaged suburb in the west end, and set up home and shop as they managed the transition – the expulsion of the remaining Germans and the arrival of settlers from the rest of the Soviet Union.

In July 1946 the city was officially given a new Soviet name – Kaliningrad, after the recently deceased president of the USSR, Mikhail Kalinin (1875–1946). Kalinin was far from a nonentity, as is sometimes claimed in the west. He was an important figure in Soviet history and his career is a good illustration of the progress and degeneration of the revolution in Russia. Unlike many of the communist leadership, he was genuinely a worker rather than an intellectual. What was truly remarkable about Kalinin's life was that he died a natural death at the age of 70, having survived the purges that cut down so many of his Old Bolshevik contemporaries. When the Soviet government was looking for replacements for the German place names for all its sector of East Prussia, there were hardly any with Russian alternative names. Stalin could honour his fallen henchman and stamp a Soviet identity on this enemy city at the same time.

Erasing old Königsberg for what it symbolised, and the uncomfortable fact that it lacked any Russian history, was part of the plan for the Soviet designers of the new Kaliningrad, but it was not the whole of the plan. As Soviet architect M.R. Naumov put it in 1949:

> The centre of the city as built by the Germans was unplanned, barbaric – which is characteristic of capitalist cities. There were a lot of narrow streets where trams struggled to pass through. On the sites of buildings there will be avenues, green boulevards and parks.[10]

The plan to redesign a higgledy-piggledy old city at lower density with straighter, wider roads, modern buildings and more green space was not hugely out of line with what was happening in western European cities. Other severely bomb-damaged ports such as Kiel and Plymouth were being radically redesigned in similar style at the same time. The ambitious aspect to the new Kaliningrad was not so much in architecture or

urban planning but in Kaliningrad as a place where a new sort of civilisation would be born, a thoroughly Soviet city written on a *tabula rasa*, a
place where people could also start again as empty slates. There were no
Orthodox churches or congregations and the authorities could boast that
the new Kaliningrad was a completely atheist city.

Kaliningrad was particularly tightly controlled by the Soviet authorities because of its strategic location. It was a 'closed city', meaning
that special permits were required to visit. The border with Poland
was closed. The remnant of the 'Berlinka', the Nazi-era autobahn
intended to link Berlin to Königsberg and only partially built, became
an eerie, empty stretch of concrete in the woods of northern Poland
and the approach to Kaliningrad city. The military formed a substantial part of Kaliningrad's population and economy, infusing the whole
province with the mentality of a command society. The area was
repopulated by a mixture of willing and conscripted citizens from all
over the Soviet Union, making it a microcosm and melting pot of the
diversity that existed within the USSR. There are still communities
whose 'home' area has become independent, particularly Lithuania
and Belarus but also from central Asia and all over Russia. People were
atomised and recombined in the laboratory that was Kaliningrad and
the result was Soviet, rather than Russian. It was a city of the USSR
as superpower, a military hub poking out into the west and the home
of some advanced scientific and technical sectors. Kaliningrad is still
proud of its three cosmonauts.

The mostly ruined hulk of the castle of Königsberg still loomed over
the city centre in the 1960s and the question of what to do with it
sparked what by Soviet standards was a vigorous public debate. Fifty
intellectuals – writers, architects, journalists – wrote to the Central
Committee arguing that the structure should be preserved as a historic
monument. The authorities refused the plea, urging: 'Root out the nest
of German imperialism!' Demolition charges started to shake what
remained of the building in April 1968 and it was razed to the ground.

The building that rose in its place was just as emblematic of the Soviet
Union as Königsberg castle was of imperial Germany. It is a large concrete
block of uncompromisingly brutalist design, an asymmetrical arrangement of two slab-shaped towers linked by high-level walkways. The
building, nicknamed 'The Monster', has been regularly rated as the ugliest building in the world. The authorities were aware that it gave their

city a gaunt, sinister image and so it has received a makeover, with blue cladding covering its stained concrete structure, and it projects a certain grandeur from its solitary, depopulated ridge overlooking what used to be the old town. Its proper name is Dom Sovietov (House of Soviets) and it was intended to be a fittingly dominant headquarters for the regional level of the Communist Party organisation.

Dom Sovietov, Kaliningrad, January 2019.

The standard story is that it was abandoned before it could be occupied because it was structurally unsound. The cellars of the castle are still there, several levels deep and mostly flooded, and the weight of the concrete bulk of Dom Sovietov pressing down on these brick catacombs made it too risky and unstable for the party to move in. The deliberately and carelessly forgotten German legacy, therefore, undermines the bombastic Soviet attempt to erase it. It reminds me of the cathedral in Mexico City, which is cracking up because it was built on the unstable ruins of the main Aztec temple. It's a good historical story, a Freudian allegory about repressed material that undermines the conscious mind's attempt to present a smooth face.

The metaphorical story might not be entirely true, though. The building is still there and seems, at least superficially, to be viable. Its extraordinary ugliness was as much to do with its blind, unfinished appearance as its design. I was told another version of the creation story. This goes that the civil engineers and architects realised early in the project that the weight would be a risk, and the designs were amended to reduce its height and bulk. It was on the verge of being occupied in 1991, with wallpaper and working lifts installed in the building, when the Soviet Union broke up and Kaliningrad suffered its economic collapse. By this telling, the structural problems were not with the building at all, but with the Soviet system and its successors.

For the Soviets and Russians, there was additional repressed material associated with the ghostly castle under Dom Sovietov. It was the location where the last authenticated sighting of the Amber Room took place. The disappearance of the Amber Room became part of Cold War politics.[11] For the Soviets, it was deployed as a textbook example of the Nazis' rapacity, an easy way of rousing German feelings of guilt and distracting attention from their own prodigious art theft. The empty walls in the Catherine Palace were a standing reproach, a pre-emption of any German complaints about the annexation of the broken city of Königsberg. The idea that the room was still somewhere in Germany, or perhaps hidden, undiscovered, somewhere under the occult hillsides of Lower Silesia, kept a wound open, served a useful purpose. An alternate theory, that it went down on the *Wilhelm Gustloff*, was less appealing. The whole saga was almost certainly a propaganda narrative. The first Soviet inquiries in 1945–46 found that the room had probably never left Königsberg and it was likely to have been destroyed when Soviet troops burned down the castle, or possibly during the RAF raids the previous summer. It is just about possible that the panels are in one of the poorly mapped tunnels under Dom Sovietov. However, there are still enough parts of the puzzle that don't quite fit – such as when a section, pilfered by German soldiers, turned up in Bremen in 1997 – for there to be room for doubt.

The Soviet government decided in 1979 that it would replace the room with a new one, but progress was slow for the first decade and halted entirely in the early 1990s. However, the Amber Room was tailor-made for a gesture of reconciliation and the German energy company Ruhrgas stepped forward in 1999 and funded the reconstruction, renewing Frederick William's gift to Russia's rulers. The supply of amber was at its peak, as Russian companies strip-mined the substance from pits on the Baltic shore, and the science of how to work with amber had advanced massively from the days when it was a notoriously brittle and difficult substance. The new Amber Room was ready for unveiling by Vladimir Putin and Gerhard Schröder in St Petersburg in 2003, when world leaders were visiting for the tercentenary of the city's construction on territory recently conquered from Sweden. The room was portrayed as a symbol of peace and reconciliation but even then there were troubling overtones – particularly if you were Poland or Lithuania, the amber countries between Germany and Russia.

Kantgrad

Kaliningrad did not cope at all well with the end of the Soviet Union. Though in the Russian Federation, the exclave's identity was based around being Soviet, rather than Russian, a reference point that vanished abruptly. Once Lithuania and Belarus had become independent, it was geographically cut off from the rest of Russia, a revival of its historic status under Prussia and Germany. As a militarised region, Kaliningrad suffered from the run-down of Soviet military forces in the 1990s, losing money and population, which were not replaced by new legitimate sources of growth. What happened instead was a social collapse. Nineteen-nineties' visitors such as the journalists Anne Applebaum and Catherine Scott-Clark describe a crashed-out nightmare city – a degraded environment where nothing made sense and many of the people were lost souls. The enclave's western location and its status as a geographical anomaly made it attractive to organised crime, and by the mid-1990s smuggling of all kinds – mostly cars and drugs – was the boom industry. Despair, rootlessness and economic misery blighted the city.

Kaliningrad's people's knowledge of its history was sketchy. Applebaum found that the only publicly acknowledged reminder of its pre-Soviet past was the bunker from where von Lasch surrendered. The city lacked a proper name, an expression of its rootlessness and artificiality. As in some other repopulated borderlands, local, family, national and official histories were all out of alignment with each other and added to the feeling of living in a dystopian, alienated place. While Leningrad could have a public debate and vote about whether to be St Petersburg once more, there was nothing to fall back on in Kaliningrad. Some alternatives were suggested in the 1990s – going back to its 1945–46 name of Kenigsberg (Кёнигсберг) or renaming it after a less contentious local celebrity by becoming Kantgrad (Kant remained a respectable figure in the Soviet time, to some extent because the debt that Marx owed to Kant made him ideologically acceptable). In the depths of the collapse in the early 1990s there were even rumours – never confirmed – that the province might be sold back to Germany; its post-1945 status had never been confirmed in a comprehensive peace treaty. What would happen to its inhabitants in this eventuality was never made clear, although presumably they would have the choice of becoming German citizens or moving to Big Russia.

Turning up in 2019, I was 20 years too late to experience the Diamond Dogs years of Kaliningrad. Take the cathedral, for instance: when Anne Applebaum visited, she and her companions 'were standing on an island surrounded by polluted canals; behind us stood the roofless, floorless, windowless ruin of the cathedral, picked clean like the ribs of a great beast'.[12] The cathedral was the first big building of German Königsberg to be restored. In 1981, during the late Soviet period, attitudes to manifestations of history and religion started to soften and works started in order to stabilise the remnants with a view to restoring it in the future. After the end of the USSR, Germans, including surviving displaced Königsbergers, started to visit the city and were heartbroken to see what had happened. Deep pockets were opened to fund the rescue of the shattered cathedral, and it was reconstructed between 1994 and 2005. It is technically a concert hall and historic monument. There is an exhibition detailing the destruction of 1944–45 and its rebirth, with a few fragments from the destroyed roof that include a stone bear whose head may be stroked for good luck. The pride and joy of the cathedral is its organ,[13] a magnificent beast with 90 registers and 6,301 pipes, whose unveiling in 2008 marked the return of Königsberg's tradition of church organ music after the destruction of its predecessor in 1944. There are daily concerts, at which the organ is put through its paces, from surprisingly subtle and delicate passages to exhilarating, thumping power. My favourite moment in this grievously damaged but restored place was hearing Boëllmann's Toccata from *Suite gothique*, whose sinister melody when played on the

Kaliningrad organ sounded as if it could summon up ancient Lovecraftian gods.

A strange architectural style has been emerging in Kaliningrad, and one can see examples on the Polish side of the border as well. One could call it neo-Prussian; it is a simplified version of the red-brick Gothic and Hanseatic buildings that are to be found all along the southern shores of the Baltic. The first experiments were along ulitsa Lenina in the late 1980s, but it is the style of choice in heritage areas of the city such as the Fishermen's Village along the branch of the Pregolya river opposite the east end of the cathedral.

The village is a thin ribbon along the riverside, with a large and unwelcoming road behind it and then a vista across a flat island towards the new football stadium. It is pleasant as far as it goes, but there is not much of it. It feels incomplete, and it is hard to avoid thinking of it as a scrap of a larger design that hasn't been built. Architecture as metaphor, again – a one-block-deep attempt to give Russia a western aspect. One interesting restoration landmark near the village is the synagogue, which was inaugurated but unfinished in 2019. It is built from the plans of the original Königsberg synagogue, which was built in 1896 and was the first of the city's grand buildings to succumb to barbarism when the local Nazis burned it down on Kristallnacht in November 1938.

German things are considered desirable in Königsberg/Kaliningrad; having a German house in an old neighbourhood like Amalienau or Verkhneye is a sign of wealth and taste. A local chain of mini-markets is called 'Kant' (not even 'Кант'). Thanks to a wrinkle in the customs and taxation rules, people tend to drive second-hand western cars – often German – rather than Russian models. Unfortunately, though, the tram network inherited from the Germans has shrunk to one rattly line from the western suburbs to the city centre and the heritage area.

There are countless little ways in which Kaliningrad is reclaiming its Prussian heritage, or perhaps a Prussian identity is gradually reclaiming the city. The diet is one example. Kaliningrad Russians eat Königsberger Klopse, the hearty meatballs beloved of the Germans of East Prussia. There has been a revival of Königsberg marzipan. It was an example of Kantian cosmopolitan-provincialism, an industry founded by Italian immigrants that became a local tradition until Kant's city was destroyed in 1945, and now revived. There is a small museum in the red-brick Prussian Brandenburg Gate, with a model of the restored cathedral made from marzipan. Traces of the German past lay neglected for decades but after 1991 a brave minority of contrary Russian eccentrics and antiquarians cherished all the remnants they could find; for instance, there is a museum of German-era East Prussian bricks in Mamonovo.

The Russian Königsbergers drink buckthorn tea, a gloopy acidic concoction of bright orange berries, which, like acquired tastes the world over, is reputed to have health benefits. The sea buckthorn is a tough, gnarly plant that grows along sandy shorelines and whose roots stabilise sand dunes. Encouraging them was part of the Prussians' project to conserve the wild landscape along the Curonian spit, and the hardy people of rural East Prussia looked for sustenance in the berries the buckthorn produced. Now the Russians do the same, and it is not the only piece of local knowledge – urban or rural – that has been rediscovered or reinvented from the 'German time'.[14]

The window for changing the city's official name has closed for the foreseeable future. An official change to the city's name would be a bureaucratic and expensive procedure; the cost and hassle of getting new official stamps and for all the citizens to be re-registered at various offices is not to be underestimated in Russia. Moscow would also look askance at any perceived distancing of the city from its Russian identity. Russia having been re-centralised by Putin's regime, there are no effective local ways of deciding it. The only remaining possibility of a reconciling name is at the airport; there may yet be an Immanuel Kant International Airport, with 'the starry heavens above me' as part of its branding. But the official view now is closer to the nationalist know-nothings who complain about this 'traitor' Kant who wrote 'strange books' and vandalise the memorial sites that exist.[15]

Regardless of official decisions, the informal name of the city is increasingly fuzzy around the edges. If the people of St Petersburg have an informal name ('Piter') for their city, it is unsurprising that people in Kaliningrad want one for their city and their identity. Nor should one be surprised that they find it in the area's authentic local history and therefore it involves variations on Кёниг and a nod to the traditions of East Prussia. The regional bus company is Kenig-Auto, the leading car dealer is Konigsberg, and so on. Talk of Königsberg and people will know what you mean and fewer of them take offence than if you were to keep referring to 'Bromberg' or 'Posen' while in Poland. You can buy, without embarrassment, Königsberg memorabilia that would get you treated with suspicion in Germany as a nationalist. People need to pretend sometimes for official purposes that it is a normal Russian city, but when the state obliges them, for instance by asking a tour guide to emphasise the 'Russian history' for official visitors, the response is mockery.

The economic fortunes of the city have ebbed and flowed with the greater tides of European–Russian relations. There was a lot of optimism in the early 2000s, and it seemed that it might become a western-facing window of a new Russia. As Vladimir Putin put it in 1999, it would be 'the pilot region within the framework of Euro-Russian co-operation'.[16] A radical tax-free status, as a Special Economic Zone, was decreed in 1996 because it was otherwise impossible to attract inward investment to this isolated, militarised and rather frightening corner of eastern Europe. As early as 1998, some industries had started to appear in the area, including auto production by BMW and Kia. The tax advantages were reduced in 2006 and since then the local economy has veered more towards *rentier* and extraction industries like land, gambling, and amber.

Russia's attack on Ukraine in 2022 ended most of the benevolent 'window on the west' possibilities for Kaliningrad; the region's eternal balance between trade and ideas on the one hand and military might on the other tipped towards the latter. It is a base for the navy, and probably for some of Russia's nuclear weapons. What the permanent Kaliningraders, with their European identity and their access to western media, think is hard to know. For now, Kaliningrad represents a primitive, bloodthirsty imperial horsefly trapped in the sticky amber of the European Union. But it is hard for me to give up the hope of an autonomous place with several names, Russo-German-Polish-Lithuanian but above all European, emerging in the future.

8

From Stettin on the Baltic

(Germany, Poland)

From Stettin on the Baltic to Trieste on the Adriatic, an Iron Curtain has descended across the Continent.' [17]

(Winston Churchill, 5 March 1946)

Stettin is not really on the Baltic. It is 60km inland on the banks of the Oder river, south of a large lagoon insulated from the sea by islands.* To get to the Baltic, one needs to navigate one of the channels between the lagoon and the sea proper. The German–Polish border, an unfamiliar and highly contentious line at the time Churchill was speaking, reached the sea at a small port and seaside resort that had just been renamed from Swinemünde to Świnoujście. But Churchill knew what worked when he spoke in public, and the name 'Stettin' sounded good when he said it; this section of the famous speech at Fulton, Missouri would have lost some of its impact if it had started with Winston attempting to growl 'Swinemünde'. It is thanks to Churchill that Szczecin's German name is still widely recognised in the English-speaking world, while Breslau and Danzig are fading from memory.

Churchill deplored the Iron Curtain as a whole, but he had particular objections to the new border between Germany and Poland. Churchill's Fulton speech continued:

---

* The other pedantic point to make about Churchill's speech is that the Iron Curtain as we came to know it before 1989 met the Baltic at Travemünde, the deep-water port of Lübeck nearly 300km further west. At the time Churchill spoke, Germany was divided only into occupation zones by the four powers and not yet into two countries with opposing allegiance; to have conceded an Iron Curtain at Lübeck rather than Stettin would have been diplomatically unwise in 1946.

Winston Churchill peeks through the Iron Curtain, as
visualised by the Daily Mail *cartoonist Illingworth.*

The Russian-dominated Polish Government has been encouraged to
make enormous and wrongful inroads upon Germany, and mass
expulsions of millions of Germans on a scale grievous and undreamed-
of are now taking place.[18]

Poland had suffered grievously during the Second World War. Hitler
had unleashed his war machine on Poland in September 1939, invading
from East Prussia in the north and Silesia in the south. He and Stalin
divided Poland between them. During their occupation, the Nazis
attempted to integrate the west of the country into Germany through
ethnic cleansing, while the residual 'Generalgouvernement' was run as
a slave colony. The Nazis murdered 3 million of Poland's 3.3 million
Jews. When the country re-emerged after 1945, the new boundaries
made it smaller and moved it radically to the west. Poland had gone
from being one of the most multicultural societies in Europe to a

near-monoculture, and border changes and ethnic cleansing removed nearly all its Ukrainian, German and Belarusian populations. The Nazi empire had been defeated but the USSR retained most of its proceeds from the 1939 Molotov–Ribbentrop pact. Poland was compensated with German territory from the west.

The Treaty of Versailles had done a good job in respecting historical boundaries and separating majority German and majority Polish areas, but there were no such niceties at the Potsdam meeting in 1945. In 1945, the Polish–German border moved into what had been indubitably German territory for 200 years or more in sovereignty and longer in culture. Poland's losses to the Soviet Union in the east were compensated by the seizure of a geographically smaller but much more developed region from Germany – everything east of the line of the Oder and Lusatian Neisse rivers, plus an area around Szczecin to the west of the Oder, plus the southern half of East Prussia. The broad, seldom-bridged Oder is a major European river. Its fellow German–Polish border river, the Neisse, is not: it flows into the Oder between Guben and Frankfurt and before its sudden change in status was not much of a dividing line. It is a small river, with several pre-1945 towns having areas on both banks, and there were no significant linguistic or cultural differences between the two sides. At one point, in Bad Muskau, the gardens of a stately home still straddle the Neisse. The idea that this might be suitable as an international border was entirely Stalin's.

The German population of the lands east of Oder–Neisse was expelled in stages after 1945, uprooting around 8 million people, most of whom ended up in West Germany; it was radical ethnic cleansing that would only have been countenanced in the brutal circumstances of the 1940s. Churchill lost the 1945 election part way through, and said afterwards that he would not have approved it. The western powers thought that the expulsion of so many Germans was unconscionable and probably logistically impossible. 'It would be a great pity to stuff the Polish goose so full of German food that it died of indigestion,' mused Churchill at Yalta, articulating a British policy of resistance to pushing Poland too far west as Lloyd George had at Versailles.

The 'recovered' areas were settled by Poles, some of whom had themselves been expelled from the now-Soviet east; communities were moved wholesale and the former Polish identities of some eastern towns have an afterlife in the newly Polish towns of the west; Lwów (L'viv) to Wrocław

(Breslau) is the biggest example. The eastern exiles were joined by people from central Poland, many of whom had seen their previous lives destroyed during the war.

The Oder–Neisse Line was born in blood. Although some of the scar tissue has not healed, it has become a peaceful, agreed frontier where two states co-operate and people may cross freely. Germany came to accept its losses, and put those in the context of the evil that Nazism had wrought on Poland and the rest of eastern Europe. A more confident Poland has started to acknowledge the German history of much of its land. While I approach the line conscious of what it used to represent, it has a different meaning for many younger people who have cycled along the Oder–Neisse Radweg (cycle route), from the romantic crags in the south around Zittau to the encounter with the Baltic at Szczecin or Świnoujście. Many younger Germans do not know or care that this was ever deep inside Germany, assuming that those shaded areas to the east of the country's modern borders had something to do with the short-lived Nazi empire.

There are still buried traumas along the line, half-forgotten remnants of the past that echo with horror and violence, and the sense of a threat

German–Polish border boardwalk at Ahlbeck / Świnoujście, September 2018.

from the great power to the east. You will hear voices reflecting the resentment of the centre that always grows at the edges of the national territory; the people along the line have no great love of the authorities in Berlin or in distant Warsaw. But there is also cause for optimism, that the past can be transcended, ghosts laid to rest and barbed wire torn down.

A line in the sand: Świnoujście/Swinemünde, Pomerania

If you've ever looked at a map of Europe with curiosity, you may have come across the anomaly that is the town of Świnoujście. It is in Poland, but before a tunnel opened in 2023 it was not connected to anywhere else in Poland. It forms an enclave at the end of the nearly entirely German island of Usedom (Uznam). For most of its life the town was known by its German name, Swinemünde; the Polish name Świnoujście has the same meaning: 'mouth of the Świna river'.

Świnoujście does not have much of a pre-1945 history as a borderland, although its national affiliation has been more fluid than one might expect. Sweden was only evicted from its last holdings in Pomerania in 1815, but the river mouth went to Prussia in 1720 and the town was founded in 1748. The little town commanded one of the major outlets of the Oder to the Baltic and had a fine natural harbour, which was augmented by the industrious Prussians with a large canal and two huge breakwaters extending into the Baltic. Swinemünde was also an important military town, with several sturdy red-brick fortresses guarding the mouth of the Swine river from each side. In 1945, German Swinemünde came to an end after nearly 200 years, its people expelled westwards in the direction of Kiel.

The barbed-wire Cold War years continued at Świnoujście (and neighbouring German Ahlbeck) after 1990, as an external border of the EU now ran through the end of Usedom island until Poland joined in 2004. It took another three years but, when Poland's accession to Schengen came into effect in December 2007, border controls were abandoned and there was at last free movement of people between the two parts of the island.

Ahlbeck is now one of the most cheerful border crossings in Europe, if not the world. The German–Polish border meets the Baltic Sea on a wide, sandy beach that looks clean and beautiful on a sunny day. The precise line between the countries is lost as one nears the seashore, but people, often accompanied by dogs enjoying the wind in their hair, stroll back and forward across the line without noticing it. Self-consciously, I marked this softest of soft borders in the sand with my shoe and my finger so that I could take a picture, but I knew that the tide would soon come in and erase the line.

While the border is invisible on the beach (except when a passing Englishman has marked it out), just behind the dunes there is a little monument celebrating not so much the border itself as the possibility of a peaceful, open border between Germany and Poland after centuries of conflict that culminated in the multiple horrors of the 20th. The border monument is a symmetrical steel structure that evokes a bridge rather than a barrier, and is a minor tourist attraction. People walking or cycling among the pines along the 'Europa-Promenade' stop briefly to take pictures, enjoy that border-zone pleasure of hopping back and forward between countries, or use the somewhat malodorous rainwater and solar power eco-toilet by the site, located a couple of metres into Germany. Looking north from the monument – as one tends to – there is a wooden boardwalk that runs literally along the border line between the northernmost of the pairs of small striped obelisks that mark out the boundary between Germany and Poland; an open border of a co-operative future. Looking south, there is a reminder of what the border was like in the past – a bald and inhospitable strip of land that cuts through a forest, and the remnants of the fences that used to pen people in on each side.

Świnoujście is one of the most German-friendly border towns in Poland; there seems to be little awkwardness for the hordes of mostly elderly German visitors who come east for the cheap and tasty smoked-fish shacks and other seaside pleasures. There is a little train that connects only to Germany. There are panels in the town centre showing the streetscape in the German time and giving the German names for streets, and a restaurant – 'Prochownia A.D. 1853' – in a former gunpowder works by the western fort that serves Polish and Prussian staples under the sign of the Pickelhaube. Following Poland's accession to the EU, restrictions on the purchase of property in western Poland by Germans were dropped, and the majority of the cars parked by some of the new blocks of flats near the coast have German registration plates.

Stettin on the border

Stettin was the principal port for Berlin, its infrastructure all pointing south and west. One of the earliest large canals in Europe, the Finow, was dug in 1605 to link the Havel river (and thence Berlin) to the broader Oder. As early as 1800 the visiting future US President John Quincy Adams admired the Oder–Spree and Oder–Vistula canals, but lamented the trade barriers that obstructed progress:

> Their benefit in facilitating the intercourse between the several parts of Germany, and, above all, with Poland, would be still greater than it is, if it were not counteracted by that mutual jealousy which bars the passages between the dominions of neighbouring and rival sovereigns.[19]

As Europe industrialised, and the German states drew together and abolished trade barriers, the Berlin-Stettin corridor became more and more important. The deep Oder–Havel canal was dug in 1908 with a large lift at Niederfinow to raise and lower ships between the Oder valley and the high ground to the west. One of the first long stretches of autobahn to open was the road to Stettin, in 1936.

Stettin, from its origins as a castle town from which Pomerania was governed, developed into a workaday dockland and industrial town; my 1897 Baedeker notes that 'the town contains little to interest the traveller'. When the grievously damaged city was conquered in 1945, it seemed for a while that Stettin would remain in Germany – a German communist administration was installed in the city hall in summer 1945 – or perhaps be a Soviet exclave, as Königsberg was becoming. But it was to be transformed into the north-west Polish city of Szczecin.

The new city was at the far edge of Poland. Its Polish status felt provisional and shaky for a few years after the war; taking no chances, the authorities gave rebuilding it a low priority and building materials that could be salvaged from the rubble were often taken east to contribute to the reconstruction of Warsaw's old town. Later, Szczecin became Poland's naval port, but it was out on a limb in the commercial and industrial map, across a border from East Germany but across the very broad lower Oder valley from the rest of Poland.

What is left of old German Stettin now is not unattractive; the remnants of the historic city by the river are slowly being restored, and the 19th-century new town remains an elegant arrangement of wide avenues fanning out from what was Kaiser-Wilhelm-Platz and is now Plac Grunwaldzki. This contrast between a damaged, sparse old port area and the city centre that relocated after the war was one of several reminders of my own home town, Southampton, which occurred to me when I was in Szczecin.

Szczecin has an urban energy to it, something severely lacking in the flat plains of northern Brandenburg and German Pomerania to its west – the Polish side being livelier and more attractive is a common feature along the lower Oder. As in the period after 1800, the lowering of trade barriers is reviving Szczecin's importance. The canals linking it to Berlin have been rebuilt, with a new boatlift at Niederfinow, and the railway line is undergoing some overdue modernisation. It is a viable long day trip from Berlin even today, and the harsh line between Poland and Germany is blurring. Its German-era brewing tradition has been revived by enterprising Poles. Szczecin's commuter belt extends across the border into Germany, reviving some once bleak and declining villages as middle-class Poles fix up old houses in places such as Tantow. Some border villages are now 20 per cent Polish, a strange reminder of when the Piast kingdom reached slightly to the west of the present border, nearly a thousand years ago.

Much of the rest of the German hinterland of Stettin, though, feels like a neglected corner of Europe. Towns like Schwedt – where the Russian pipelines were plugged in and 90 per cent of Berlin's oil was refined – feel frozen in their East German form. Touring around, one will see the ruins of stately homes that were built by Brandenburg's aristocrats, or by people with new money created in Berlin's 19th-century boom. The red-brick skeleton of Hohenlandin palace, built in 1861 and destroyed in 1945, is witness to the changes wrought by war and communism but now stands in its abandoned estate. Sheep and goats graze in paddocks around its warehouses and outbuildings, the stone eagles over the palace's main door eroding gently. The landscape of post-Prussia starts here and stretches eastwards almost to Suwałki.

Polenmarkt!

I made the journey north-east from Berlin in September 2020, in the company of Jon Worth, a Berliner of British origins. We came to Hohenwutzen village on the back roads, tracing and crossing the canals and river branches heading towards Stettin to the north, Germany in turn narrowing as we were funnelled towards the bridge to Poland over the Oder. But as one crosses the bridge, there is a change from this semi-populated pastoral landscape – suddenly, the road widens, neon signs and petrol stations are everywhere, and a ruined paper factory looms up to the left of the road, the first building in Poland. But the brick ruins are not empty, as the massive sign 'Oder Center Berlin' suggests; in the restored halls, and among the shattered spaces, there is one of the largest marketplaces in Europe – the Polenmarkt (Polish market).

Hohenlandin palace, October 2021.

The market is a miniature modern history of the region. The paper factory was built in what was then the hamlet of Niederwutzen in the late 1930s, its tall chimney and huge square factory halls towering over the Oder and lighting up the villages opposite by night. It brought 400 jobs to the area, but its history was short: the factory was damaged in fighting between the Red Army and the SS in spring 1945 and after the end of the war the machines were carried off to the Soviet Union. The post-war boundary changes awarded the right bank of the Oder to Poland, and the factory was at the westernmost point of the country. The bridges to what was now Germany were not reopened, nobody except border patrols went near the old factory and the place rotted away, forgotten.

In 1990 the area on the German side was rapidly absorbed into the Federal Republic, and therefore the European Union, while Poland went through abrupt economic 'shock therapy' to convert to a market economy. The combination of spending power on the German side and cheap production on the Polish side created places where Polish producers could sell to German consumers, and market stalls appeared at the old paper factory in the early 1990s. Over time, as price levels diverged – particularly for items that were heavily taxed in Germany, such as cigarettes – and demand grew for petrol as more East Germans acquired cars, the Polenmarkt took over more and more of the site. The range of items grew, with wholesale groceries and white goods marketed to German consumers at cheaper Polish prices, although wealthier Berliners regarded it as inferior 'polnische Wirtschaft' merchandise. The poorer inhabitants of the sprawling suburbs of East Berlin, though, looked to the Polenmarkt as a lifeline. There are still three return shuttle buses each day between Marzahn, a huge and notorious concrete residential area built in the 1970s as part of East Berlin, and the market at Hohenwutzen.

Hohenwutzen exists in a peculiar bubble, legally in Poland but substantially an offshore bit of Germany. Its website has the German .de domain name, the language of the market is in German and the currency of nearly all transactions taking place is the euro rather than the zloty. The street names are German, with the main drag named KuDamm after the principal shopping area of West Berlin. The border defines the place, but once you are there it is made as easy as possible to forget that you have left Germany – except that the prices are lower and they sell things that are not legally on the shelves back in Germany proper.

'Lebensmittel – Zigaretten' boasted the signs, and there were certainly a lot of cigarettes, sausages and alcohol – and garden gnomes, for some reason. Cigarettes are dirt cheap in Poland – about half what they cost in Germany – and smokers find it worth the detour to stock up at Hohenwutzen. The maximum amount that German customs officers think is reasonable for personal use is 800 cigarettes and they occasionally enforce these limits across the bridge from the market. As at many cross-border outlets, there are labour-intensive services as well – hairdressers, solariums and nail bars cluster around the market buildings.

There were also fireworks, which are sold only at restricted times in Germany; this part of the market exploded spectacularly in November 2012 when there was a serious fire. But visually, energy drinks were dominant in 2020. Many of the shops were walled in by tall, colourful bluffs and mesas built from cans of high-caffeine fizzy drinks. The reason for this is that Germany has regulated energy drinks. The maximum caffeine content there is 320mg per litre, about the strength of the most familiar brands such as Red Bull. To get anything stronger, the clubbers, fitness freaks and night workers of Berlin have to go to Hohenwutzen, where the rules don't apply. Those fortresses of cans are built of strong

Hohenwutzen Polenmarkt, September 2020.

stuff, marketed with names that are close to but not identical with better-known brands – Pit Bull, Amper, Highlander – with caffeine content perhaps five times the German maximum.

When Jon and I visited on a weekday afternoon, Hohenwutzen was subdued, looking even more like a post-apocalyptic shopping mall than it usually does. The coronavirus had taken its toll here as everywhere. Most of the shops and stalls were quiet. During the first acute phase of the coronavirus crisis, from March to June 2020, the market was closed because its raison d'être, the border, was shut. As at several border towns, there were demonstrations at Hohenwutzen during the lockdown in favour of reopening the bridge. The closures did not just interfere with Berliners' cigarettes and energy drinks, but made life difficult for people in an interdependent border zone where work, shopping and family life can involve crossing the border multiple times.

The border market's functions keep mutating. The European single market, and Poland's rapid economic growth, have narrowed the gap between prices and living standards on each side and taken away some of the market's advantages. We are past the peak of the Polenmarkt as such, with cross-border regulatory and tax differences rather than general price levels fuelling most of the demand. While in its early years Poland was tapping into the windfall earnings of German reunification, it does not make sense to look at it in national terms anymore. The market is now creating jobs and income in a relatively poor area of Germany and a relatively rich area of Poland, mostly at the expense of Berlin.

Not many German visitors to the market go any further into Poland. If they did, they would see a hilltop monument to Polish historical narratives. The Battle of Cedynia took place in the year 972, as the expansionist aims of the Saxon margrave Odo I clashed with the project of Duke Mieszko I to consolidate and expand his Polish state. The battle ended in a Polish victory, but in the context of centuries of wars and skirmishes between Slavic and Germanic polities it was an unimportant engagement. It might not even have happened at this particular bend in the Oder. But historians in the post-1945 People's Republic were under orders to find and celebrate whatever Polish history they could in the western 'Recovered Territories' and Cedynia fitted the bill. The site was dedicated as a memorial in 1959 and in 1972 the millennium was marked with a festival and the erection of a 15-metre concrete Polish eagle glaring westwards from the top of the hill. The interpretive panels are masterpieces of elision, the 700-year period in which Cedynia (Zehden) was under German or Bohemian political control passing unremarked.

The Ghost of Küstrin

(Above) The main street in old Küstrin, looking north to the Berlin gate, before the destruction of the town in 1945. (Below) Photograph taken in October 2018 in the same location.

I came to the border town of Küstrin in search of a place that didn't exist anymore, except as the ruins sometimes called 'Pompeii on the Oder'. While Pompeii was wiped off the map by natural disaster, Küstrin's destruction was the product of human decisions. Before 1945, it was neither a particularly well known nor important town in Germany. It was a railway junction about an hour out of Berlin on the train line eastward to Danzig and Königsberg, a place where the traveller would mark his or her progress as the line crossed the Oder river and a fortified river island on a long viaduct, and the red-brick fortress town on the low-lying peninsula near the confluence of the Oder and Warthe rivers came into view as the train slowed. Seventeen thousand people lived there in the 1890s, a number that reflected the military presence in the town, and rather more in the decades that followed. Küstrin's picturesque Altstadt attracted a few tourists, keen to see a preserved fortress town when so many in Germany had torn down their city walls. But in early 1945 it was the scene of one of the final battles of the Second World War in Europe as the Red Army approached Berlin, and Küstrin was literally wiped off the face of the earth.

Küstrin's history is notorious for an act of extreme cruelty that took place in the fortress in 1730. It was a grim place of exile and imprisonment for the Crown Prince of Prussia, who was later to become Frederick the Great, after his plan to escape his brutal father, King Frederick William, was foiled. The king had long bullied and tormented his son, hoping to beat his foppish intellectual and aesthetic ways out of him and cure him of his attraction to clever, handsome young men. Frederick's favourite companion was the young lieutenant Hans Hermann von Katte. Frederick had taken von Katte into his confidence about the plan to flee to England, and although the lieutenant advised against it, he was unswervingly loyal. The king had them both arrested and confined, and when Frederick was woken on the morning of 6 November he was expecting to be executed. Instead, he was literally forced to witness his lover being beheaded – his desperate pleas that he would give up his right to the throne if von Katte were spared were to no avail. After the execution, according to his sister Wilhelmine's memoirs, Frederick suffered the classic symptoms of what is now known as PTSD, followed by being deeply depressed. He feigned compliance to his father's orders, even to the point of getting married, but he was biding his time. Once in power he was determined to eclipse his father in history, and to live once more as a philosophe surrounded by beautiful things and beautiful men.

When in power after 1740, Frederick's zeal for modernisation and reform turned to the draining of the marshes and the disciplining of the wayward Oder river, which linked his new territories in Silesia to the heartland of Brandenburg. The Oder lands were fairly close to the Polish frontier in those times, although not really a borderland in that sense; it was, however, a frontier territory in the sense of a state shaping the land into its desired image. Starting in 1747, the landscape west of Küstrin was transformed from a boggy wetland into prime agricultural land, to which the Prussian government attracted settlers. In the otherwise sandy, damp hinterlands of Berlin, it became the vegetable garden. To Frederick, it was the 'conquest of a province in peace time' and in terms of the area reclaimed and the eventual success of the settlement, he was not wrong.[20] Another of his enthusiasms, the potato, took root here and has an honoured role in Brandenburg's cuisine to this day.

Despite the remaking of the Oderland into a tame agrarian province, there is a persistent darkness in its history, an evil spirit of pointless destruction that seems to linger in its soil. Massacre's first appointment here was in summer 1758, during the Seven Years' War, when Prussia's army confronted the invading Russians in the fields north and east of the fortress. By the standards of the 18th century, the Battle of Zorndorf was exceptionally brutal – a day of fighting left 31,000 dead or wounded, with both Prussians and Russians waging war with unusual ferocity. The Prussians had been fired up by what marauding Russians had done in the area: 'We were all smouldering with anger over the destruction of Küstrin and the sufferings of the poor country people. The enemy had wasted and destroyed everything, and even broken into churches and robbed them.'[21]

Küstrin suffered only lightly when it fell to the first French units to arrive in 1806. Under the Treaty of Tilsit in 1807, the French, and Polish allies, occupied the fortress as a kind of security deposit from Prussia. When Prussia resumed war against France in 1813, Küstrin was one of several isolated French garrisons east of the Oder and the fortress was besieged for a year, during which the suburbs were destroyed. France was losing the war heavily on other fronts, but there was still room for one more futile act of destruction when French troops pulled out in March 1814 and the fortress was burned down. The siege was not particularly lethal, but of the 4,000 French and Polish defenders only 1,000 were still fit to fight at the end, with the rest in hospital, dead or deserted.

There were centenary peace commemorations in spring 1914, and a stone was erected in memory of Wilhelm von Falkenhayn, an officer who was killed in the brief 1806 battle. Peace in Küstrin survived 1914–18 even as, coincidentally, another von Falkenhayn (Erich) was chief of the General Staff for most of the first two years of the war. The fortress was merely a way station between Berlin and the points to the east where the German army was fighting. The frontier came relatively close again in 1919 with the restoration of independent Poland, whose westernmost town of Międzychód (formerly Birnbaum) was just under 100km away from Küstrin. But as long as Germany did not face any threat from the east, Küstrin remained a sleepy railway and garrison town.

The greatest bloodletting in Küstrin's history started when the Red Army reached the banks of the Oder in the second half of 1944. The Neustadt suburb on the right bank of the Warthe was taken and old Küstrin was nearly surrounded. The fortress town endured another siege, pounded to rubble by the Russian guns. In all logic its 10,000 defenders should have surrendered, but the beleaguered town had been designated a 'Festung' – a fortress city obliged to hold out to the last man, in Hitler's desperate last-ditch defence policy. Eventually, the hopelessness of the position got the better of the last German commander of Küstrin, Heinz Reinefarth, and he led a breakout of the remaining defenders, carrying whatever they could in the direction of the main German lines at the end of March 1945. Around a thousand made it.

The Oder–Neisse partition line between Germany and Poland established in 1945 runs through the middle of the ruined Küstrin fortress complex. The former town centre and suburbs to the east were in Poland, and the river island and a small suburb to the west remained in Germany. Instead of a town, there is a small nebula of settlements around old Küstrin, suburbs without a centre. The largest section is in Poland, east of the Warta river, which bears the name of Kostrzyn nad Odrą and before 1945 was the Küstriner Neustadt suburb of the German town. It was severely damaged and there are a handful of pre-1945 buildings in the town centre, but it is essentially a new town. It is still a railway junction, with a scissor-shaped station that is of interest to enthusiasts for railway architecture. Its population has gradually recovered, although it is much smaller than Küstrin was before 1939 – there are around 18,000 in Polish Kostrzyn and another few hundred in German Küstrin-Kietz. Old Küstrin is now a museum and memorial, a ghostly, overgrown relic. The street pattern is intact, but the streets are empty and pointless; there is no town hall at plac Ratuszowy and the main street (Berlińska) has no buildings on it.

The remnant of German Küstrin is essentially a small village. Border zones were sensitive, secure places and the population of the area was thinned out even further; some houses that had survived 1945 were demolished. The East German authorities decided that any reference to Küstrin was a dangerous ideological deviation that suggested revanchist ambitions against Polish territory. It became 'Kietz', which can mean simply 'neighbourhood'. This non-specific name made it more painfully obvious that it was a part of something that did not exist anymore and could not be named.

In June 1991, not long after German reunification, the border with Poland was opened for local traffic, the first time that this had been possible for decades, and the German section had a vote about the most suitable name for the village. Its people came to the sensible decision that it should be known as 'Küstrin-Kietz'. There were no objections from their Polish neighbours across the rivers in Kostrzyn – mayor Władysław Mysona delivered a warm speech at the official renaming ceremony for his neighbours on 3 October 1991, welcoming the possibilities for co-operation and drawing attention to the problems of neglect that both sides of the Oder had suffered from the authorities in East Berlin and Warsaw.[22]

The rail line was reconnected, at first just for a special service in 1991 but later on a permanent basis. The little station at Küstrin-Kietz is as far as you can go now within Germany on the once-mighty Ostbahn. However, the regional trains out of Berlin go beyond Küstrin-Kietz and serve Polish Kostrzyn. This being a border, the train is sometimes called the Zigaretten-Express because of the amount of smuggling that happens.

Słubfurt: Which came first?

Which came first? Slubfurt, October 2018.

While Kostrzyn exists as a Polish town and a German village separated from each other by the ruined fort, I wanted to see a proper urban area that straddled this historically new border, so I went to the conjoined towns of Frankfurt an der Oder and Słubice. In introducing the German city of Frankfurt an der Oder, one is off to an unpromising start as it invites comparison with Frankfurt am Main. Whatever one's view of the western German financial metropolis, the eastern Frankfurt tends to come off the worse from the comparison. It's the Frankfurt with only one office block tower rather than 'Mainhattan'; it's the Frankfurt with under 60,000 residents and falling rather than over 600,000 and rising; it's the Frankfurt that doesn't have an airport. Since 1945, it has been the Frankfurt that sits on an international boundary. The eastern Dammvorstadt suburb became the Polish town of Słubice when the Oder–Neisse frontier was imposed. The name was a revival of an ancient name for a Slavic settlement in the area, Zliwitz, but Frankfurt's town charter dates from 1253, in the first years of German rule. As with many towns in this area, it is possible to have a pointless argument about which came first, German or Pole.

Under German rule, Frankfurt became a commercial and university city. The city's university was the first in Germany to admit Jews and the medical faculty had trained Jewish doctors since 1678, not that the university met much favour from John Quincy Adams when he came through in 1800: 'The number of students is less than two hundred; of whom one hundred and fifty are students of law, ten or fifteen of divinity; and not more than two or three of medicine. The library, the museum, and the botanical garden, the professors tell me, are all so miserable, that they are ashamed of them.'[23] This seems to be an unusually jaundiced opinion.

Frankfurt university was shut down in 1811 – closing universities was a habit of autocratic rulers then as now – but in modern Europe it lives again. The European University Viadrina opened in 1991, created deliberately as a cross-border institution that was a bridge between Germany and Poland, and indeed between 'eastern Europe' and 'the west' given that East Germany had become part of a united country within the EU. Studying at Viadrina is inescapably, deliberately an international experience. 'This is where Europe begins,' the university announces on the introductory page of its website. It goes out of its way to attract international students and daily life at the university involves crossing back and forward between Frankfurt and Słubice.

The university has created a small youthful quarter in the old town section of Frankfurt and added to the mildly cosmopolitan feel of downtown Słubice, which had been regarded as among Poland's dreariest towns but is now probably the liveliest neighbourhood of Słubfurt for bars and restaurants. The old part of Słubice is a pleasing curve of early 20th-century (and good reproduction) houses, and the city has used some of its European funds to create pleasant parks. But even here, the problematic history and identity of the place cannot be entirely put to the back of the mind – 'NO PAST' reads a creative arrangement of letters on the disused Kino Piast one passes on the way from the Frankfurt bridge further into Słubice.

Disused 'Kino Piast' cinema in Słubice, October 2021.

Frankfurt, if not Słubice, is an uneasy mixture of new German (and Polish, and European) youth and academia and an older population for whom the end of the DDR has been a painful process. When the Oder–Neisse border was imposed in 1945, it did not make Frankfurt an international city; it was a separation line between two communist states that colluded in entrenching the new boundary as the 'peace frontier'. Frankfurt, like the other towns along the Oder and Neisse in East Germany, had been a place for favoured proletarian industries of the DDR, in this case semiconductors, but has faded badly since German unification. The population has been in steep decline, losing nearly 30,000 people, a third of its residents, since 1990.

In trying to create something positive from a borderland location, Viadrina and the cross-border ethos have forced cosmopolitanism on a profoundly provincial city. This may be a working economic and social survival strategy. Current policies seem to be leading to a smaller but possibly happier city that is making the best of its borderland situation.

There are compensations to living in a shrinking city, particularly one that is part of Germany and which has a lively Polish twin just across the sluggish Oder river. The unusual situation of being a university town in steep decline has created some strange phenomena. Housing is nearly free if one knows how to work the system and is prepared to live somewhere moderately inconvenient. The public transport network is excellent for a place of its size; it has a cultural and intellectual life of its own; and sooner or later it will be 'discovered'. Only an hour from Berlin, two hours from bustling, energetic Poznań, Frankfurt will not be on the edge all the time. Trade routes do change, as they did when Frederick conquered Silesia in 1741 and Stalin conquered central Europe in 1945. But the adjustment is melancholy and painful, and if nationalism and the urge to throw up barriers should prevail it will never be complete.

The model East German Frankfurt neighbourhood of Neuberesinchen looks, on a bright autumn day, like a drawing by Le Corbusier. Clean-edged concrete blocks of flats with balconies are scattered, sparingly, through a large park where the leaves on the trees are turning to brilliant reds and golds. Trams trundle around the edge of the park, giving the residents an excellent service to the town centre.

It is only on closer inspection that the reality starts to become apparent. Weeds are starting to grow through the roads that loop through the estate, and the blocks show no signs of being occupied. There are steel barriers to keep drug-users out of the vacant flats while they await the bulldozers. A walk around the park also turns up evidence that this was once densely populated – streets that have their signs but go nowhere and have no buildings on them, and concrete foundations where blocks of flats once stood. Neuberesinchen is dying, so that Frankfurt may survive smaller and perhaps happier. This planned socialist utopia is beautiful in this season, at this stage of the transition from residential area to park, but profoundly sad, an updated version of the ghost town of Küstrin. The chill in the air on an October afternoon seems like a wind blowing all the way in from Siberia.

Neisseblick

Berlin's position far out to the east of 'western Europe', distant from the factories of the Ruhr or the liberal capitalism of Frankfurt, has meant that there has always been something anomalous, something of the fragile glittering border city, about Berlin, a city of immigrants from across Germany and abroad rather than one that relates to its hinterland in Brandenburg. The literal border between Germany and Poland, at Frankfurt and Hohenwutzen, arrived an hour's drive from the city in 1945.

The years when the city was divided and capitalist West Berlin was an island surrounded by communist East Germany were when Berlin was at its most isolated, but it still feels out on a limb. It is a left-liberal internationalist urban enclave set amid conservative nationalist countryside and relations between the two are strained. When I told a Berlin friend that I was going to be travelling in rural Brandenburg and Saxony, he advised me to take care while I was in the AfD-voting Badlands: 'Just don't be black or gay, keep your head down, and you'll be fine,' he told me. So I headed for the town with the Nazi rock festival.

The little town of Ostritz has its share of borderland oddness. The railway line between Görlitz and Zittau weaves back and forward across the Neisse, and at Ostritz the town is on the left bank and the station on the right bank – which was unremarkable before 1945, but since then has put the town in Germany and the station in Poland. Since the relaxation of border controls when Poland joined Schengen in 2007, the little Polish railway station of Krzewina Zgorzelecka has been served exclusively by German trains and nearly all the passengers at the station come and go via the footbridge over the Neisse back into German Ostritz.

At this bridge, we encounter the darker side of this borderland. Signs welcome you to Germany and Saxony. The first building one sees on crossing back into Germany is the (now defunct) Neisseblick hotel. This is unfortunate, not so much because of its aesthetic limitations (it is an unimaginative but inoffensive concrete cuboid) as because it was notorious for its welcoming attitude towards the extreme right. In 2018 it hosted the 'Schild und Schwert' (Shield and Sword) festival on 20–22 April – i.e. an event branded 'SS' starting on Adolf Hitler's birthday, and repeated it in 2019; thanks to COVID, 2020's SS-fest was cancelled. The Neisseblick was to some extent chosen out of necessity because few venues in Germany are willing to accept such unsavoury bookings, but it no doubt added to the appeal that the attendees could look eastwards into Poland and dream of conquest and murder. What defies belief, though, is that the border location was convenient for another demographic attending the festival, namely Polish fascist skinheads.

While Ostritz is part of the most supportive region in all of Germany for the far-right AfD party, there is very little outright backing for the sort of overt celebration of the Third Reich that went on at the SS-Festival. Only 11 people in the town voted for the fascist NPD party in the 2017 elections, while a great deal more – 28.8 per cent – voted for the nationalist right in the form of the AfD. All along the eastern border, the German settlements are hotbeds of AfD support, but on the Polish side liberal forces are stronger in the borderland than in most of Poland. There were two predominant responses to the Ostritz festival by the locals – one was the view that the Nazis were ridiculous and should be ignored while they listened to their stupid music and got their ugly tattoos, while the other was disgust, embarrassment and the determination to resist.

Ostritz had the good fortune to be home to an institution that was capable of being the focus for that resistance. Just south of the main town there is the baroque complex of the convent of St Marienthal, nestling in a riverside hamlet below the main road from Ostritz to Zittau. The convent used to span the Neisse but the lands on the Polish side were lost in 1945; there are currently ten sisters in the community, who live a life detached from secular concerns, be they communist dictatorship or the presence of loutish Nazis in the streets. Much of the complex had fallen into disuse and disrepair during the DDR time, but since the 1990s the sisters have leased a large area to the International Meeting Centre (*Internationales Begegnungszentrum*, IBZ). The IBZ itself is a distinctively German enterprise – cheerful but earnest and painstakingly socially and environmentally concerned. When we visited there were two much larger parties, one of young adults and one of school students; it is a secular institution with moral purpose, suffused with Christian ethics. As the name suggests, it is about dialogue and interchange between people from different places – anti-violence, anti-extremism. Education against racism is part of its mission; the IBZ has produced undercover documentaries about the violent nature of the extreme right music scene ('Blut muss Fliessen') for schools.

We came to see Dr Michael Schlitt, the director of the IBZ, and stayed for a couple of nights at the foundation, feeling as if we were staying in Oxford college accommodation but with a German breakfast buffet that was better than anything I encountered in my student days. He is an engaging, cheerful man, a positive spirit in a region with a lot of ambient negativity. He is an adopted Lusatian, having come from the west in the 1990s as part of the effort to clean up the local environment and stayed ever since. One of his current enthusiasms is for restoring the fruit-growing heritage of Lusatia, and his efforts have taken him to the UK to find seeds to replant traditional apple tree varieties in eastern Germany. After talking for a bit about the environment, the IBZ and the border, Michael Schlitt leaned back and smiled, as if we had been beating about the bush. 'You want to talk about the Nazis?' In conversation, Dr Schlitt always uses the term 'Nazis'. There is no mealy-mouthed talk of 'racial nationalists' or 'the far right'; the focus is on the similarities between this manifestation and the Nazi movement in the years before its explosive growth in the early 1930s. The philosophy of the Ostritz protests is expressed in a banner on a building opposite the Neisseblick hotel, and by Michael Schlitt in conversation. In contrast to the time before 1933:

> One must not wait until the struggle for freedom is called treason. You have to crush the snowball as it rolls: nobody can stop the avalanche.[24]

The dangerous thing about the SS-Festival, to Schlitt, was that it connected aspects of the Nazi subculture – music, tattoos, gangs, politicians and supporters of Nazi ideology in Czechia and Poland. There is a risk of a synthesis, of the whole being more dangerous than the sum of its parts. In his analysis, events like SS are the breeding grounds for violence of the sort that has recently troubled German society, particularly – when we talked in October 2019 – the recent attack on a synagogue in Halle and the June 2019 assassination of Walter Lübcke, the CDU regional head of government in Kassel (northern Hessen) and a strong supporter of Angela Merkel's refugee policies. Permitting a Nazi event unhindered would only encourage more, and allowing the Nazis control of the streets is dangerous. First time round, in 2018, there were two counter-demonstrations, one an explicitly political one organised by anti-fascist organisations such as Rock Gegen Rechts, and one civil society organised by the town authorities, the IBZ and the local churches and civil society groups.[25] There were some delicate issues about co-ordination between the two – some Ostritzers were not happy about the idea of an influx of Antifa activists and even blamed them rather than the fascists for the threat of violence, but peace prevailed.[26] The town

Friedensfest (peace festival) was deliberately wholesome, fun and educational, and political only in the loosest sense of celebrating peace and friendship. It attracted twice the number who attended the Nazi event.

The summer 2019 protests used a new form of resistance. The police enforced laws and confiscated alcohol supplies from people heading to the Nazi gathering, and protesters bought out the town's supply of beer to keep the fascists sober. It was a jolly, clever idea that captures the imagination but it was also risky for the activists involved, who had to face down a large fascist rabble outside the beer shop and experienced violence – the Nazis smashed the windscreen of the IBZ vehicle as it escaped from town with its cargo.[27] The IBZ, being a serious and mostly sober institution, still has a cellar full of anti-fascist alcohol. The numbers of people going to the Nazi festival had nearly halved since 2018, something that can be chalked up as a success in smothering the Nazi network before it has gained strength. There are plans for an alternative festival every time there is a fascist event in Ostritz. The protests helped change, or at least modify, the narrative about Ostritz. Instead of the first reaction and the first search engine results being about 'Ostritz, the town where the Nazis have their festival', it is more likely to be 'Ostritz, the town where they bought all the beer to ruin the Nazis' fun'.

Ostritz may be unusual for being a focus of anti-Nazi protest, but in other ways it is typical of the region of Lusatia (Lausitz) in which it is located. Lusatia is a hard concept to pin down. It is a fuzzy region on the borders of Saxony, Bohemia, Brandenburg and Silesia. When I asked Michael Schlitt what the distinctive features of the region might be, he was initially nonplussed but then told me about the relationship between the landscape and the economic base of the region. Deposits of lignite (brown coal) near the surface were increasingly exploited for fuel, stepping up in the 20th century when electricity generation began in earnest. The brown coal was scraped out of the earth and moved on conveyors to be burned in power stations built not far from the coal deposits. The industry destroyed villages and woods in the path of the open-cast mines. Near Weisswasser, the main road takes an enormous bend around the pit, the old course of the road having been obliterated. Just where the old road disappears, there is a viewing tower over the science-fiction landscape: giant machines crawl over deep quarries that stretch almost as far as the eye can see, the cooling towers of the Boxberg power station visible in the distance.

Power generation had other predictable consequences for the local environment. Under the DDR and into the 1990s, the snow was black on the fields and hills of Lusatia and the air was sulphurous. The corner between East Germany, Poland and Czechoslovakia became known as 'das schwarze Dreieck' (the black triangle) because of this environmental disaster, made all the worse because the national borders running through it diluted the sense of responsibility for what was happening.

German reunification brought a new approach. While politics in eastern Germany is poisoned by a sense of being neglected and scorned, the objective reality is that Germany as a whole has made huge efforts to redeem the disastrous state in which this border region was left. Infrastructure in the east is often new and good – there has been a huge road-improvement programme, which is still going on; the communist legacy in public services was not bad and has been modernised and developed – for instance, Ostritz boasts a magnificent new sports hall. Networks like water and broadband are among the best in Germany. In the can-do spirit of the 1990s, the black triangle was intended to become a clean energy area, with Ostritz being an ecological model town.[28]

To a surprising degree, the project succeeded. Much of the region now looks clean and green and nature and wildlife are protected. Many of the open-cast pits have been filled with water and Lusatia is now a land of lakes and forests – and wind turbines and solar panels. Windsurfing and yachting attract visitors, as do some pieces of industrial heritage like the monstrous F60 conveyor – over 500 metres long, bigger than the Eiffel Tower tipped on its side – at Lichterfeld. But open-cast mining has not entirely disappeared. The Weisswasser pit was reopened, having been closed in 1999, but with various environmental conditions and a clean-up of emissions from the Boxberg power plant, and the Bogatynia mine on the Polish side is still going full steam.

The problem with success has been that the mining and power station jobs that used to exist, and those in traditional local industries like leather and textiles, have mostly disappeared. The tourism and green energy jobs have not been sufficient to replace them. Unemployment during the transition rose to 40 per cent in Ostritz. Like much of East Germany outside the three big cities (Berlin, Leipzig, Dresden), the population has fallen steeply since 1990 in a new *Ostflucht*. Ostritz is down from over 6,000 to around 2,200. Unemployment has fallen too, below 10 per cent, but there is a mismatch between the skilled job vacancies that exist and the labour supply, mostly older and unskilled, that is available locally; the psychological transition between the old industries and the new economy has been harder than the well-meaning reformers expected. Freedom has also brought a rise in border-related crime, such as metal theft and drug trafficking, and a feeling of insecurity and lack of protection from the authorities. The insecurity and alienation that come from depopulation are expressed through suspicion of being taken for a ride by unsympathetic governments, or having immigrants 'dumped' on them, and a sense of post-industrial life being a disappointment after the promise of 1989.

Ostritz is not quite in the corner where Germany meets Poland and Czechia. There is a geographical anomaly at the end of the Oder–Neisse Line, caused by the literal following of the Lusatian Neisse right to the Czech border. There is a small dangling bit of Poland around Bogatynia, a protrusion between the German town of Zittau and the hilly Czech region around Frydlant (Friedland, where the enigmatic Thirty Years' War commander Wallenstein had his principal castle but seemed dissatisfied with its lowly status in the complex hierarchy of the Habsburg and

Ruined monastery at Oybin, February 2011.

Holy Roman empires). The far south-eastern corner of Saxony, just south of Zittau, is a startlingly attractive landscape. When I went there it was during an extremely cold snap in February; the craggy hills and the crystalline white of the branches of the trees took my breath away. There are steam trains out of Zittau to Oybin and Jonsdorf, chugging through what quickly becomes a Romantic landscape of snowy hills, deep dark forests and even a ruined monastery perched on top of a strange sugar-loaf hill at Oybin.

It feels fitting to find a Caspar David Friedrich landscape at the upriver end of the Oder–Neisse Line, a place that fired his imagination more than homely, practical, rational Greifswald back downriver. This part of Europe is strange and beautiful. West of the Zittauer Gebirge there is the Elbe valley and 'Saxon Switzerland' south of Dresden; east of it are the dark hills and mysterious legends of Silesia.

Caspar David Friedrich, 'Klosterfriedhof im Schnee' (1819).

9

The occult romance of Lower Silesia

(Poland, Germany)

Border zones are uncanny. A straight border, separating radically differ-ent places either side of an artificial line, is a strange mirror with a brutal past. A fuzzy border can be destabilising in a more subtle way; one can be unsure about where one belongs as the borderland throws up middle options to what one lazily considers a binary distinction. Areas where borders have changed have another layer of mystery about them. People live among ever-present residues of the lost tribe who occupied the buildings and the land before them, constantly coming across their ghostly legacy. The people who have been displaced, and their children, live with an idea of home that no longer exists. The reality of border life blurs into the literature of horror, the imagining of the Other on the far side of the line.

This German–Polish borderland of Lower Silesia contains a mountain stained by blood since ancient times, the town of Frankenstein, where there is a legend of occult mass murder dating from two centuries before its fictional namesake built his monster, and the divided town of Guben/Gubin where modern scientists splice and plastinate corpses. A 17th-century priest called Arnold Engel wrote that Silesia was a place where 'the art of witchcraft and evil' flourished. The Nazis added their disturbing mixture of modern technology and primitive racial myths to the Silesian landscape. To those attuned to its strangeness, the lower Silesian border is a mythic Romantic landscape lit by the lights of perverted science.

Lower Silesia is now the south-west corner of Poland. Its main city is Wrocław (its name was Breslau in the German years). Its destiny in Poland was one of the most contentious issues between the Allied powers in 1943–45, but it was settled on the Soviets' terms. The fate of Lower Silesia was a by-product of the pressure on Poland from the east – if the Soviet Union were to hold on to its gains from the 1939 Molotov–Ribbentrop pact, then Poland would have to be compensated and the bill would be paid by defeated Germany. This principle was common ground between the Allies, but quite how far it would go was not. There was no dispute over Germany losing East Prussia and Upper Silesia, and that the border between Germany and Poland would be straightened in the north with more of Pomerania going into Poland.

Allied discussions centred around how to divide Silesia. There was a convenient river called the Glatzer Neisse that ran from the hills on the Silesian–Bohemian border down to the Oder, west of the town of Oppeln (now Opole). The whole of the mixed industrial province of Upper Silesia would have gone to Poland; most of it had voted in a referendum to remain in Germany in 1921 despite its majority-Polish population, a sign that national allegiances are much more complicated than nationalists will often concede. The western Allies would let Germany retain the majority of Lower Silesia, and there was little demand from Polish exile politicians to go further. It seemed at the time of the Tehran Conference in December 1943 that this, or something like it, would be the eventual boundary.

As Stalin's confidence grew and the project of imposing a pro-Moscow government on post-war Poland became more realistic, the prospect of pushing the border further west came into view. Stalin's insistence on moving the border had nothing to do with any love of Poland. He hated the country, going back at least to 1920 when Poland defeated the Red Army and drove the Soviets back deep into what is now Belarus and Ukraine. He had overseen the Katyn massacre of thousands of Polish army officers held prisoner in 1940. The reason for Stalin's apparent benevolence towards Poland in the west – which Vladimir Putin recalled menacingly in July 2023 – was that the post-1945 borders gave Russia its most geopolitically secure frontiers in history. Stalin succeeded in extending effective Russian control much further westwards than Tsar Alexander had managed in 1815. It was an astonishing geopolitical achievement.

Instead of the Glatzer Neisse, the Lusatian Neisse (Nysa Łużycka) became the southern end of the Oder–Neisse Line – a demand that the USSR started making overtly on behalf of Poland only at the end of 1944. It made the Polish frontier pretty much a straight line and therefore defensible, and gaining Lower Silesia would mean the transfer of some valuable industrial, mining and agricultural territory that would compensate Poland somewhat for the increasingly certain eastern losses. But the disadvantages of the western border were also obvious. The scale of the ethnic cleansing required was huge, and it would leave Poland dependent on Soviet Russia for its territorial security against German resentment and western reluctance. Lower Silesia was the sugar coating of the bitter pill of accepting Poland's subordination to Stalin's Russia.

Another argument that was used, particularly during state-building in post-war communist Poland, was that these territories were historically Polish and the German presence had been the result of colonisation and settlement and was therefore illegitimate. It is true that Poland now is largely where there was a Polish polity a thousand years ago, although the ideas of what constitutes a nation and a state are so different as to be barely comparable. Over the next few centuries, most of these fragments had been absorbed by neighbouring German or Bohemian states. Silesia and Pomerania became predominantly German, as did some places such as Danzig and Royal Prussia that were still linked to the Polish crown. It is wrong to interpret these population movements and changes in state borders in modern nationalist terms.

The Great Powers were cynical about the 'historically Polish' line of argument when it was deployed at the Yalta Conference in February 1945: Roosevelt joked that if they accepted it then how did Churchill feel about having Britain's 13 colonies back?[29] England had ruled Bordeaux more recently than a Polish state had ruled Hirschberg (Jelenia Góra) but – perhaps fortunately – de Gaulle was not at Yalta to be teased by Churchill.

Recognition was still conditional after Potsdam. The area was 'placed under Polish civil administration' rather than being definitively assigned to Polish sovereignty; the final decision was to be left to an overall peace settlement that would be agreed in future. The Treaty of Paris in 1947 settled the smaller countries' borders but the big question of Germany was left frozen – the four-power occupation continued and two sovereign states emerged in 1949. Their attitude to the Oder–Neisse Line was starkly different. One of the first things that the German Democratic Republic did was to ratify the 'peace frontier' with Poland at the Treaty of Zgorzelec in 1950.

By contrast, the Federal Republic refused to recognise it and regarded the legal boundaries of Germany as those that existed in 1937. For years, West German television would show weather forecast maps that covered lost cities like Breslau and Königsberg. Willy Brandt's Ostpolitik treaties with the USSR in August 1970 and Poland in December 1970 recognised the realities of Germany's eastern borders and West Germany abandoned the pretence that the lost territories were recoverable. Brandt's diplomacy unexpectedly undermined the basis of Soviet strategic dominance in Poland. With the agreement and then working relations established between the two German states in the 1972 Basic Treaty, the idea of German aggression against Poland became implausible and therefore the need for Soviet power to guarantee Poland's frontiers fell away. The last vestiges of a possibility of the Germans reclaiming it somehow by consent were dropped in the treaties that reunified East and West Germany, and in 2007 it became an open Schengen internal border.

There is still an unhealed quality about parts of the Oder–Neisse Line – concrete rubble in the river where there was once a bridge, roads that seem like they are going somewhere but peter out in a forest or on a riverbank, even lost villages and suburbs whose remnants lie deep in the woods. The border has cut and rearranged the ties that bind localities together; often places have been left as inaccessible dead ends rather than linked up properly again with their new trade routes.

On a ruined bridge by the border, Forst 2010.

You will see many of these features in the area around the German border town of Forst in Lausitz. Forst is not a cross-border town, but this is because the eastern suburb of Berge was destroyed rather than being repopulated by Poles. It was a housing development just the other side of the Neisse bridge from Forst's old centre, 1920s German Gothic apartment buildings radiating from the roundabout at the foot of the bridge. The structures were dismantled, except for the base of a memorial and two tall concrete lamp posts by the ruins of the bridge. What was once a crossing point is now a dead end, a corner where few people go unless they are in search of isolation – often, judging by the contents of the open hatchways by the bridge ruin, the sort of isolation that works best accompanied by a bag of beer cans.

Heading away from Zasieki, the rather technical name for scattered houses and empty spaces on the Polish side of Forst, things become even more uncanny. The roads deteriorate sharply unless one follows the main highway from the 'European Union Bridge' just north of Forst. The next tiny village upriver, Brożek, is the start of a maze of narrow minor roads and paved forest tracks into which we blundered, in a large rented Mercedes car, one autumnal afternoon in October. The satnav system became very confused, suggesting random turns and odd detours through the forest. But these were not just any sinister woodland roads. We were getting increasingly lost in a bizarre overgrown Nazi landscape. From 1938 until 1945, this area (then known as Scheuno) housed a munitions complex, the scale of which boggles the mind. Forst-Scheuno extended for miles, over- and underground. There were 394 bunkers scattered across the landscape, linked by 72km of concrete roads. Thousands of workers, initially German but later in the war usually slave labourers – about 25,000 worked at the Scheuno factory for at least a time – produced explosives for the war effort. Despite the Soviet Union carting off most of the working machinery as reparations in 1945, the concrete bunkers and buildings are still scattered throughout the forest, gradually rotting.

Bits of the complex are used for paintball games, but there are stories that some of the wilder areas are still dangerous from leftover explosives. Deep in the forest, as darkness started to fall, Brożek is still a very creepy location. Rather than try to press through, we turned the lumbering car round and beat a retreat to the comforting light of new EU-funded infrastructure.

Travelling south and east from Forst takes one on a long highway –
the rebuilt successor to one of the original German Autobahnen of the
1930s – through an expanse of dark, sterile pine and spruce woodlands.
At a point a little past the site of the famous Great Escape from Stalag
Luft III, one crosses the border between the Polish voivodeships (regions)
of Lubusz (East Brandenburg) and Lower Silesia. There is nothing much
between the German border and Legnica, 120km away – towns are small
and far apart and there is little agriculture. Even before 1945, this was
sparsely settled and sleepy. John Quincy Adams travelled this way in
1800, and felt that the sandy, barren pinelands were 'the abomination of
desolation'.[30] Even homesick German exiles in 1950 were backhanded in
their celebration of the heathlands of East Brandenburg:

> Neumark and Lower Lusatia, Brandenburg country of which has been
> sung: 'meadows, water, sand, that is the Mark land, and the green
> heath, that is its joy.' That which is lost may always be more brilliant in
> memory than it was in reality, and those who have lost their homes
> believe that they have been driven out of paradise.[31]

After becoming part of Poland, these lands were border territory and,
except the ribbon of settlements along the Neisse, the territory remained
nearly empty following the expulsion of the few Germans who had
scratched a living from the sandy soil. It became even more of a forgotten void. But continue south and east, until one is now well into Poland
at Legnica, and the landscape changes again. Fields rather than forests
line the highway; the flat landscape is fertile farmland rather than heath.
In the hazy distance there is a line of mountains running from north-
west to south-east, marking out a definite border to the region – much
sharper than the Neisse and a much older dividing line between different
nations.

The hill country has always had a brooding, mysterious atmosphere. The
Giant Mountains were, to John Quincy Adams in 1800, a place of
'sublime gloom'. There are spiky castles like Książ (Fürstenstein) set on
misty crags, surreally calm spa towns on the lower hills, and smoggy
working-class mill and mining towns like Wałbrzych in the valleys.
    The border with Czechia south-west of Jelenia Góra is set amid wild
forests and steep mountains, another sort of sinister landscape in which

to get lost and confused however powerful and modern one's car might be. The border road twists and turns, a couple of signs formally indicating the point of crossing, but the general area is marked by the standard clutter of truck stops and cigarette shops and a disused pre-Schengen apron for border controls.[32] Lower Silesia is a central-European-style *Twin Peaks* landscape waiting for its David Lynch. As we meandered through the hills, I daydreamed a novel in which an officer Fassbinder from the Berlin *Hauptkriminalamt* was sent in about 1910 to Deer Mountain (Hirschberg, Jelenia Góra) to investigate a strange murder. Our clean-cut agent, however, gets caught up in the life of the town, mundane and supernatural, and perhaps acquires a taste for the damn fine *Kaffee und Kuchen* that had seeped across the border from the Habsburg side of the mountains. It is the sort of place where a fellow could disappear, caught between two worlds.

These woods and mountains are full of mythical creatures. The Riesengebirge were named for a local shape-shifting spirit called Rübezahl (or Rübenzahl), whose natural form was a crouched humanoid with a tail and antlers but who would often appear to travellers as a guide, whose instructions might be good or who might capriciously decide to lead you into a swamp or a wilderness. His slightly disparaging name ('turnip-counter') was not to be spoken, and the mountain people called him instead the 'Giant Lord' or the 'Great Mountain God'. He had not been seen, locals told Adams in 1800, for over a century because a chapel had been placed on top of his home, but the folk names for innumerable natural features attributed ownership to him. Adams was intrigued by Rübezahl, and would ask his guides about the entity. One claimed that he was merely a Bohemian superstition that the Silesians had never believed in, but Adams supposed – almost certainly correctly – that 'a Bohemian guide would have assured me that it was merely a Silesian superstition, which his countrymen had always derided'.[33] Germans, Czechs and Poles all call the range the Giant Mountains, after the great trickster. Rübezahl survived the departure of the German Lower Silesians. He acquired a Polish name, Liczyrzepa, and his legend is part of the shared culture of the Poles, Czechs and Germans of this land.

The most famous mountain in Silesia is Ślęża, a dark obtuse-angled granite peak standing apart from its fellows. Some of the most ancient artefacts in Poland, such as carved stone monuments, have been found around Ślęża, indicating that it was a place of religious significance for the Celtic civilisation that lived in the region perhaps 2,500 years ago. There was something about this hill that struck the wandering tribe as being special and powerful, a natural deity of some sort. The deity associated with this mountain was unlikely to have been wholly benign. We do not know the form that the worship took at Ślęża, but we do know that ancient Celtic beliefs tended towards the bloodthirsty – their warriors were feared for their love of decapitation* and human sacrifice was part of their rituals.

Gory superstition and blood sacrifice have repeatedly haunted the Silesian mountains. There is a story dating from 1582 of a man who bore the name of Johannes Cuntius, and whose reputation was unsavoury in life and terrifying in death. He was reputed, following the intervention of a black cat on his deathbed, to rise from his grave and prey on the living, but the villagers dug up his corpse, hacked it to bits and burned it to put an end to the vampire's midnight ramblings. A century later, witch-finder Arnold Engel wrote that 'many dead men, who didn't die in good faith but had connections with the devil, are getting up from their graves' in the Silesian hills.[34]

The smaller towns in the region were cauldrons of witch-burning during the first decades of the 17th century. It was reported that in Neisse (Nysa), the executioner built a 'huge oven, in which, over a period of nine years, he roasted over a thousand witches, some as young as two years old'.[35] In 1606, the Silesian town of Frankenstein was the scene of a scandalous trial in which it was alleged that a ring of eight gravediggers had poisoned other townsfolk with a concoction they manufactured using corpses, and had also engaged in other disgusting activities such as necrophilia and cutting open pregnant women in order to eat the unborn foetuses. The death toll was supposed to be 1,500 people.[36] The story seems too lurid and implausible to belong to the world of facts. But perhaps there was a small grain of truth, in that corpse remedies were part of folk medicine; the best were derived from healthy bodies, so the executioner was the person to do a deal with, but the gravediggers made do with plague victims. The evidence that the diggers robbed the dead was pretty good; so why not blame them for spreading the plague as

---

*The German name was latterly Schneekoppe, which started as an informal name for what was officially known as Riesenkoppe, 'the Giant's Head'.

well? Garbled versions of the story of the evil gravediggers of Frankenstein seem to have circulated for decades afterwards thanks to the popular media of broadsheets and songs; the story was being told in Denmark in 1673, for instance.[37]

The name of Frankenstein gained another set of associations when Mary Shelley used it for her fictional scientist Victor Frankenstein in 1818. The people of Ząbkowice Śląskie (the Polish name for Frankenstein) are adamant that their town contributed its own grisly history to Shelley's modern Prometheus, scorning rival claimants such as Frankenstein castle near Darmstadt in western Germany.* The oldest building standing in the town, a German merchant's house, is a museum with an entertaining but cheesy chamber of horrors in the basement, and a more literary and historical treatment of the Frankenstein story upstairs. Ząbkowice is an exception to the general tendency for German place names to be erased; there is a Frankenstein ice cream parlour, for instance, trading under the gentle gaze of the monster as brought to the screen by Boris Karloff.†

Frankenstein's legend belongs in a German- and Jewish-influenced cultural tradition, in which a scientist creates something monstrous through the application of science and learning, and is doomed by his failure to understand the force of the irrational. Givers of life, from parents to God, inevitably face ingratitude and rebellion from those that receive the gift. Frankenstein's predecessor, Rabbi Loew of Prague, created his Golem through his scholarship and piety, but found that his creation, too, was beyond his control. Gottfried Herder also created a monster, the ideology of nationalism, out of good intentions, only for it to go on a barbarous destructive rampage.

I was a little startled when I looked at an old map of the region and saw that there was a town called Monsterberg a little to the east of Frankenstein. It lived up to its name as well. In the last decades of German rule, a serial killer called Karl Denke lived in an isolated house on the

---

*The inspirations for Frankenstein are a hotly debated area of literary studies; Shelley drew on and synthesised a rich mixture of myths, imagery and history with her insight about the growing dominion of human science over nature and life itself.
†In a story about changes of name, one might note that Karloff was an Englishman called William Henry Pratt. He chose the name Boris Karloff before his iconic role as the monster in 1931. Bela Lugosi, on the other hand, was a genuine central European borderlander – a Hungarian from the town of Lugoj, which is now in Romania.

edge of town, waylaying perhaps 30 lone travellers as they arrived at the railway station and taking them home to butcher for meat. He ate some himself, and is reputed to have sold some cuts at Breslau's market hall – a building that itself gives one the feeling of being inside the belly of a large whale.

Frankenstein and Münsterberg (as Monsterberg was spelled in more modern times), like the rest of Lower Silesia, passed from Germany to Poland in 1945. There were several years of work for Polish historians and linguists in producing Polish names for the settlements in the 'Recovered Territories'. Some of them, such as Breslau/Wrocław, had reasonably well-known modern Polish names already (the Polish language, just like English, does tend to have its own versions of town names across the world, from Londyn to Nowy Jork). Others bore Germanised versions of original Slavic names. But there were a few, like Frankenstein, where there was not much of a guide for the Polish linguists; the town name derived from it having been settled by people from Franconia in northern Bavaria who brought with them a stone reputed to bring good luck ('it didn't work', as a modern Frankensteiner mordantly told me). German Frankenstein became Polish Ząbkowice Śląskie – the root of the new name 'ząb' meaning tooth, probably from a legend of a hero and his single-toothed baby son. But it feels like a reference to the fang of the Slavic vampire replacing the Germanic mad scientist.

Buried treasure and Nazi tunnels

The 20th century, rather than replacing superstition with rationality, created a new layer to the occult landscape of Lower Silesia. On a hill near Waldenburg (Wałbrzych), the Nazi authorities built a square memorial to German Silesians killed in the First World War and the 1920s Silesian conflict, plus some SA thugs who had died in brawls. The mausoleum, the Totenberg, had a large eternal flame lit by gas from the mines, casting an eerie glow over the town. The flame is out but the Totenberg stands there, growing more creepy year by year – a place with an unheimlich energy about it, a place where people go to commit suicide.

The Nazi legacy extends below ground. The communist Polish authorities securing the 'Recovered Territories' encountered more recent evidence of the uncanny and the bloodthirsty. They discovered concrete bunkers scattered throughout the Giant Mountains near Wałbrzych and Świdnica, and iron shutters behind which huge tunnels, some easily big enough for trucks and trains, led into the darkness under the hills. This labyrinth of tunnels had been dug, mostly by prisoner labour from the local concentration camp of Gross-Rosen, in 1943–44, but the Nazi engineers and soldiers who had commanded the operation had fled and the documents explaining the project and its purpose had been destroyed. The tunnel system is vast and eerie, but it is probably a small fragment of what had been intended. There is another part of it below Książ castle, which had been intended to be a command bunker for the foreign ministry and the Führer. Prisoners, housed in a small satellite camp amid the woods of the aristocratic estate, were still digging here as the Red Army crossed the Oder.

The lack of definite information about the secret underground Nazi project in the Riesengebirge has made it a place with its own modern mythology: 'secret underground Nazi project' is a very mythogenic location for our times, in Poland as well as England. The local history shelves of bookshops are full of lurid covers and promises of horror and buried treasure. It is said that the prisoners who built the tunnels were killed either at the time or when the area had to be abandoned in the face of the Soviet advance in 1945, but no such graves have been found. Nor has about half of the concrete Albert Speer – Hitler's chief architect and minister for armaments and war production – said was used in building it, which would have been a substantial proportion of Germany's entire output. The most likely explanation is that the stories were exaggerated, that someone was defrauding the dying Reich by billing it for goods that were never delivered. But it is also possible that there are further secrets to be discovered and gaps through which they might have vanished: industrial or scientific material left would have been transported to the Soviet Union after 1945, and the remaining site was a military area under communist Poland. Small parts of it are now open to visit.[38] The tunnels have still not been fully mapped.

The soil of Lower Silesia has other secrets. When the Germans were expelled, they were not allowed to take more than a suitcase with them, and no valuables. Many people decided to bury money, jewellery, their best crockery and anything else that was portable and valuable. In 1945 they had hopes of being allowed to return following a final peace treaty; it hardly seemed possible that Lower Silesia was forever lost to Germany.

So throughout the region, the new Polish inhabitants kept on finding buried treasure, and secrets hidden behind hastily built walls and floors in their unfamiliar new homes. There are still almost certainly some caches of gold and jewels hidden in chimneys and buried in the woods. In Wrocław I was told a story about buried treasure in the forests of Lower Silesia. In recent years an old German man, with several younger friends with short haircuts, crossed the border and went to dig in an obscure location. They returned a couple of hours later, but Wrocław organised crime keeps an eye out for this sort of mission and the German car was held up by a gang on the way back to the border. The Germans were relieved of two crates, which the Polish gang were disappointed to find did not contain gold but instead an archive of SS documents that had been hidden by their owner. Deaf to the muse of history, the gang ended up selling the documents to a private collector in Switzerland.

There was enough truth, therefore, in the myth of buried treasure for it to exert a strong hold on the imagination of the people of Polish Lower Silesia, particularly as many of them originated from much less developed villages further east to whom the ordered Silesian-German farms, houses and roads were signs of unimaginable wealth. This naturally encouraged people to imagine larger truths behind the domestic secrets they sometimes uncovered.

There are periodic bursts of speculation that gold and art looted by the Nazis, perhaps even the legendary Amber Room, are hidden somewhere in the dark maze under the Silesian mountains. For decades, enthusiasts have ranged the hills armed with new technology, lately ground-penetrating radar, looking for evidence of missing treasure. So far nothing has been definitively proved and some of the most exciting speculations have been disproved. But still, there is a lot of missing treasure and a limited number of mysterious locations where it might be. In 2015 another cycle of investigation started, centred around the possibility that an entire Nazi train full of gold was hidden somewhere in the tunnel system under Książ castle. Nobody found it, but perhaps the Silesians found gold in a different way. There was a flood of journalists and writers and treasure-hunters, all pumping money into the local economy, and the episode raised the profile of this corner of central Europe and added to its mysterious reputation.

No rest in peace

In the real world, the dead do not rise from the grave to trouble the living, but rather the living do not allow the dead to rest in peace. Being dead has not excused people from being conscripted into war in 20th-century central and eastern Europe; graveyards are still military and cultural battlefields, and the living still fear the presence of the dead. The gravediggers still have their secrets. The region is full of neglected, deliberately forgotten graveyards.

Throughout Poland, Ukraine and Belarus there are villages with no Jews, but with a Jewish cemetery on the edge of town known to older people if they care to admit it. When I walked from the eastern Polish village of Krasiczyn into the hills in search of the fortifications of the Molotov Line, I came across the remnants of one such cemetery that was marked out by new wooden fences and in which the couple of gravestones still standing had little stones of remembrance placed on the top according to Jewish tradition. A recent monument states 'Cemetery of the Jewish Community of Krasiczyn Until the Year 1941. Remember OUR OLDER BROTHERS IN FAITH, REST IN PEACE.' It was put up by the Catholic parish of Krasiczyn village in a relatively unusual act of respect and remembrance. Elsewhere across the blood-soaked landscape of the eastern borders, there are places where locals and people scattered across the world come to find old Jewish tombstones used as paving slabs and foundations and restore them to their appropriate dignity.

At the other end of Poland, in Brożek near Forst, there is another cemetery, but nobody has made a gesture of respect here. I only discovered it when I was looking for something else, namely a Nazi weapons factory. But what I found was the resting place of some people who had died before Nazism was a term that anyone knew; people whose home was a village that had existed for centuries as Scheuno without feeling themselves part of any racial struggle. Their mossy, anonymous graves lay in the forest, their tombstones having been smashed in vengeful fury in the 1940s. The Germans were long dead, but they were still a threat to the Polish nationalist claim to Brożek. Their individuality, their memories and their relationship with the land had to be destroyed. Unfortunately, nobody has come back to repair the cemetery and restore the presence of the people below the rectangular stone boundaries. I could make out the site of the old church and the gates from the German time, but the footprint of this site of remembrance was fading and maybe in another twenty years there will be nothing left.

Abandoned German cemetery, Brożek (Forst-Scheuno), October 2019.

Since the 1990s there have been projects to restore neglected places associated with the German past. Where the young Poles who joined the restoration could find the original markers or even fragments of stone and porcelain, these were put back in place. In some places, priests with an interest in history and reconciliation, like the one in Krasiczyn, have encouraged restoration. Many of the surviving bits of German signage in smaller communities are connected with religion, such as tombstones and wayside shrines, perhaps adding to the air of the supernatural that is associated with the German past. There are even some examples, unthinkable before 1989 and probably for some time after that, of Germans who had been expelled in 1945 coming home in death. In 1992 Günter Grass wrote *The Call of the Toad* (*Unkenrufe*), which envisaged and satirised the desire of the children of pre-1945 to return to Danzig or

Wilno to rest in peace where their stories began. But most Germans whose home this was before the 20th century lie unacknowledged, forgotten.

I still wonder, whenever I go to western Poland or to eastern Europe, about the lives of the people whose pasts are now lost, the people who are dead twice over – with nobody to remember them or tend their graves. There were people in those Jewish cemeteries in places like Krasiczyn whose grandchildren paid their respects in 1935, thankful that life had evolved and improved since the Europe of pogroms and ghettoes. There were guiltless Germans lying beneath the moss in Brożek, who had tended the fields or taught in schools decades before any Nazi planner had decided to put a weapons factory there. The places where borders have changed are sinister, but beyond that they are charged with melancholy feelings of loss and absence that people struggle with for generations.

Central Europe

Hungary in its modern borders

Austria/Hungary pre-1918 and the modern states
A Hungary's current border
B Slovakia
C Croatia-Slavonia
D Banat & South Transylvania

Hungary's temporary territorial gains 1938–41 from
1 Czechoslovakia
2 Romania
3 Yugoslavia

Austrian half of the Empire before 1918

PART THREE
Centre

10

Heart of Europe

I can't define central Europe, but I know it when I see it. I have often found myself sitting at a table outside a bar in a harmonious town square, looking across at a hotel or a town hall as the evening sun lights its façade, painted in the warm imperial Habsburg yellow shade called Schönbrunner Gelb. I raise a glass of invariably excellent beer to this vague region where I feel unaccountably at home, despite linguistic incapacity and my deeply English roots. I might walk back past baroque churches and floridly ornate theatres, the shadows of the merchant houses lengthening as the sun goes down.

My vagueness about where central Europe begins and ends is widely shared; there are probably as many definitions of central Europe as there are people who have thought about the subject. The father of the concept, the German liberal politician Friedrich Naumann (1860–1919), had no definite borders in mind but thought of Germany and Austria-Hungary as its core. Others regard central Europe as being the countries between Germany and Russia that share certain general similarities – mostly Slavic, non-Orthodox in religion, and with non-autocratic traditions like the rule of law and civic self-government. For me, its limits are similar but not identical to the boundaries of the empire of Austria-Hungary as it existed in around 1900. Central Europe, to most people who feel attracted to the concept, carries connotations of pluralism, high culture and intellectual endeavour – a place averse to simplistic solutions. Naumann was sentimental about the diversity of his *Mitteleuropa*, imagining in a flight of fancy that:

The whole is alive like a mighty forest with tall trees and undergrowth, with evergreens and fir-copses and a thousand small bushes and flowers. It is like a sea in which all sorts of fish disport themselves. And nowhere are limits or divisions sharply fixed. All is in flux, pushing and pressing in confusion, whispering and shouting, pleading and scolding, praying and calculating.[1]

That vision, organic and pluralistic, is now acutely nostalgic. Central Europe was profoundly changed by the traumas of the 20th century. National boundaries appeared in new places across it in 1918–21, fixing those 'limits and divisions' in place through military facts on the ground, the deliberations of the Paris peace conferences and sometimes local popular votes. The new national states were much less tolerant than the old empire, and they were also divided by boundary disputes. The Nazis destroyed one of the foundations of central Europe, its Jewish population,* in the Holocaust. The reckoning in 1945 meant the expulsion of most of the Germans who had lived in scattered communities across the region for centuries. Two of the binding forces of central Europe were gone. The nostalgic central European identity must acknowledge that the absences – the Germans and the Jews – are still to be felt and worried at, like missing teeth whose empty space is more palpable than the healthy teeth that remain.

The 1940s undid the pluralism of central Europe, as its states were remade by violence and ethnic cleansing as close to national monocultures as possible. Having briefly been a German imperium, most of central Europe now fell under the political control of Moscow. It became 'eastern Europe'. The authorities insisted that Russian replaced German as the regional common language. The western image of it changed from chaotic pluralism to drab, grey uniformity. Cold War Europe was divided into East and West. For many people in the west there had always been a border in the imagination, a place – usually a bit to the east of where one came from – where the orient began and civilisational standards dropped. The Iron Curtain made the boundary – literally – concrete.

Milan Kundera, in exile in France, wrote a powerful statement in 1984 reasserting the lost central European identity. His essay *The Tragedy of Central Europe*[2] argued that the region was essentially part of the cultural and political west. Soviet domination of the region after 1945 had forced

---

* To the Czech novelist Milan Kundera (1929–2023), the Jews of central Europe 'were its intellectual cement, a condensed version of its spirit, creators of its spiritual unity'.

the region to look east, artificially severing the connections to the west that had fuelled central European civilisation for centuries. It drew a sharp distinction between Russia and the heart of Europe. Russian absolutism was an alien imperialist imposition. 'Nothing could be more foreign to Central Europe and its passion for variety than Russia: uniform, standardizing, centralizing, determined to transform every nation of its empire . . . into a single Russian people.' Prague, Budapest and Warsaw had been kidnapped from their true home.

The problems of central Europe in the 20th century were the problems of Europe in concentrated form. How was it possible to reconcile the demands of nationalism, for sovereign states bounded by firm borders, with the reality that people with different identities live intermingled with each other and won't stay in place? How could one gain the benefits of free trade and economies of scale in a world of small nation states? Must there be borders, and if there are, how can their tendency to divide us and make people poorer be mitigated?

The tragedy, Kundera argues, was that the Habsburg empire did not evolve into a federal state of equal peoples before it was shattered into fragments by total war in 1914–18. According to the Jewish writer Joseph Roth,

'The most powerful experience of my life was the war and the end of my fatherland, the only one I have ever had: the Dual Monarchy of Austria-Hungary.'[3]

The Dual Monarchy ruled not only over modern Austria and Hungary, but also Slovakia, Slovenia, Croatia, Bosnia-Herzegovina, nearly all of the Czech Republic, big parts of Romania, Poland, Ukraine and Serbia and smaller parts of Italy and Montenegro. A third of the 27 countries in the EU have roots in the old empire. Roth's nostalgic loyalty for the fatherland that vanished in 1918 suggests that this curious country (or was it two countries, or 20?) had merits despite its complexity and occasional absurdity. As a Jew, he instinctively felt safer under a regime that recognised difference and let minorities live, and feared the consequences of trying to implement the idea of the nation state in central Europe.

My fondness for central Europe has a lot to do with the Habsburgs' legacy. Its large cities – Vienna, Budapest, Prague, L'viv – are among the most attractive in Europe, and the flowering of culture and architecture in the 1870–1914 period is a major part of their charm. The empire also scattered opera houses and theatres across its length and breadth, to smaller towns all the way from Eger (Cheb) in the west to Czernowitz (Chernivtsi) in the east. I have visited a lot of local museums during the travel for this book, and the broad story of nearly every town in the Habsburg empire is the same. While the empire did not standardise language or religion, it did foster a certain neo-baroque, pastel-washed urban form. As Nada, who showed me around the eastern Croatian city of Vukovar, explained, 'every town in the empire looks a bit the same'. The universal story is not a bad one: baroque early 18th-century churches, fortified walls knocked down, new schools, paved streets, wise men with bushy beards, emancipated Jews, a grand railway station, electric light, trams, Art Nouveau style, baroque local democratic politics. Life got hugely, rapidly better for a lot of people.

The Dual Monarchy was not quite like other things that called themselves empires by the time Roth was born in Brody, a small town at its eastern edge in what is now Ukraine, in 1894. It was out of its time, a pre-nationalist creation holding back the tide, but perhaps also an antidote to the bloody simplicities that took hold once it was gone. The empire's politics increasingly revolved around managing the complex mix of nationalities living within its borders.

But what were the alternatives to Austria-Hungary? The answers that people produced during its twilight, and the way things turned out after 1918, are full of lessons about borderlands and interdependency, how to distribute power between region, nation and supranational government, and what language one should be expected to speak and where.

The radical solution of breaking up the empire was not popular. Everyone grumbled about how Austria-Hungary worked, but it was the sphere in which one did politics, even nationalistic politics aimed at getting hold of power and resources for a people within the empire. The internal politics of the EU are not dissimilar. The symbols that bound the Habsburg empire together were highly conservative; the army, the bureaucracy, and above all the figure of the emperor Franz Joseph (reigned 1848–1916), devoted to duty and correct form, stern and whiskery. There were surprising wellsprings of loyalty to the emperor among all nationalities and classes. None of the crown lands (except a few all-German areas forming the core of Austria) represented one single nationality, so using pre-existing borders would only create several multinational states where previously there was just one. Nor was it possible to redraw the boundaries to correspond with nationality. The decline of the Ottoman Empire was a frightening portent of what might happen when nation states emerged and fought for territory. As the Ottomans retreated, violence and terror was visited upon Muslims and minorities and the mixed borderlands were unmixed into rival nation states through ethnic cleansing.

It makes no sense in central and eastern Europe to think of the 'First World War' as something that ended cleanly on 11 November 1918. These battles were a new phase of the war, between rival nationalisms and the forces of reaction, liberalism and communism. Successor governments had control in their capitals but their borders had not been established and there were many areas that were disputed between the new states and neighbouring powers – Italy, Serbia and Romania.

The empire had created a huge space in central Europe where the rule of law, civic equality, freedom of movement and open trade prevailed. At the end of 1918 it was clear that borders would go up across the region, but not where they would be or how restrictive they would be for people and trade, or how minorities would be treated if they found themselves on the wrong side of a new border. The decisions taken in those few months, at central European military checkpoints and in the back rooms of the Paris Peace Conference, shaped the map of Europe that we have today, and have influenced the course of history for over a century.

The successor state

(Czechia, Slovakia, Germany, Austria)

I'm very fond of the Czech Republic, its people and their sense of humour. A Czech joke is often not 'funny' in a direct sense, but an espresso shot of despair at the state of the world that invites a wry smile in return. Take, for instance, a conversation I had with An Eminent Czech (AEC hereafter). He had married an optimistic, smiley American and was introducing her to his homeland and his home village. They went to a pub in the village and she tried to engage the locals in conversation. She asked a man at the bar what he did, and he replied, 'I work,' looked away and took another gulp of beer. Undaunted, she asked what he liked doing: 'Drinking.' She tried again and asked what he did when he was at leisure and not drinking: 'I go and pick mushrooms in the forest.' 'That sounds lovely!' 'It's not. It's horrible. I hate mushrooms and I hate the forest.' 'Why do you go then?' 'Because it's the only place I can go where that sour, evil old witch I married won't come with me.'

Czechoslovakia was the only place with a significant proletariat that installed a communist government on its own initiative, and Czech literary culture from Kafka ('an old-style Czech intellectual – a Jew who wrote in German', according to AEC) onwards is accustomed to the idea of making the best of living under an absurd regime. When I got to know the country a little, I was pleased to find fellow believers in the opinion that Kafka's *The Trial* is really a comedy.

Old maps of Europe, even if they are attempting fidelity to the geographical facts, will sometimes indulge in a flight of fancy when they depict the lands now known as Czechia, the Czech Republic.* The

---

* The fact that the name of the country is itself a bit fuzzy should tell us something. In 2016 the foreign ministry announced that the previously unusual form 'Czechia' was the preferred English version, while 'the Czech Republic' had previously become standard since 1993. It was an anomaly, in that, if this logic were consistently

region is garlanded with a linden wreath, or shown as a grove at the centre of the continent. Linden trees have symbolic associations with healing, protection and fertility in many European folk traditions; their heart-shaped leaves convey another association, that of Prague and its region being the 'heart of Europe' – both geographically and spiritually. The life of this grove is bound up in its mysterious central city of Prague, but also amid the leaves that define its borders. Bohemia has often been an ambiguous place, at the western edge of the Slavic lands and subject to the influence of Germany and Austria along its borders.

Czechia may be a new state but its physical borders are some of the oldest and most stable in Europe, though they have tended to mark out vaguer entities than modern nation states. Other than for the odd few years here and there (most recently 1938–45), the horseshoe of low mountains around the west of the country has been a border on every political map of Europe since the seventh century CE. The other boundary of the Czech lands, in the east, is nearly as clear. It runs along the tail (Moravian) end of the Beskid mountains and then the Morava river – whose German name 'March' evokes a frontier. This one is centuries old as well and before 1918 it was the border between the Hungarian and Austrian sections of the Habsburg empire.

Czechoslovakia inherited the empire's existential dilemmas about nationality and borders in 1918 and its eventual fate, as it divided into its component parts in 1993. Its 20th-century history, of ethnic cleansing and domination from dictatorships imposed from Berlin and Moscow, was incomparably more brutal than the quarrelsome final decades of the old empire. The 1940s, central Europe's bloodiest decade, created a monoculture in the Czech lands. Tomáš Masaryk (1850–1937) founded Czechoslovakia with the enlightened but impossible dream of nationalism with a human face, of being a democratic nation state while home to several nations. Two generations later, in 1968, Alexander Dubček tried Soviet bloc 'socialism with a human face' only for his country to be occupied by the Warsaw Pact – the only military alliance in history to

---

followed, we would have referred to 'the Slovak Republic' and even 'the French Republic' as well. Further, the term Česke can be translated depending on context to the Czech nation or, particularly in place names, to the geographical area of Bohemia. Bohemia is the western side of Czechia centred on Prague; Moravia is the eastern section centred on Brno. The country also contains a little bit of Silesia.

have solely invaded its own member states. The history of the lands at the heart of Europe demonstrates that nationalism and communism have more in common than the proponents of either ideology are willing to admit.

The Czechs were clearly a people, but creating a Czech nation state was going to be difficult. Most reforming Czechs in 1914 had believed in a confederal version of the Habsburg empire rather than the nation state, and there were good reasons for that. The essential problem was that there were a lot more Germans and Russians than there were of anyone else, and in a competition of nation states they would be too strong in comparison with everyone else in central Europe, including the Czechs. Without an economic, political and military alliance, the nation states would be vulnerable to being picked off one by one by Germany and Russia. The economics of competing nation states did not work for the Czech lands; industry had developed with an empire-sized market of 52 million people and without free trade it would wither in a state of 12 million.*

The next problem was that it would be impossible to draw clean national boundaries around a Czech state or anyone else's – populations were hopelessly mixed. Bohemia-Moravia was at the same time the only available Czech national home but also a land shared with a German population who had been there for centuries. Most of the Bohemian Germans lived in the crescent along the borders with Germany and what became Austria, and this is where a lot of the mining and manufacturing that created the region's wealth was located. Without it, a Czech state would be poor and virtually impossible to defend. With it, it would have a large enough German minority as to put in question its claim to be a nation state. While the borderland was mostly German-inhabited, there was no sensible way of separating out the two populations. Whatever line one chose, there would be a lot of people on the 'wrong' side of it – Czechs in industrial Brüx (Most) and Germans in Brno (Brünn) to take just two glaring examples.

Czech nationalists at the end of the 19th century looked towards the neighbouring territory across the border in the Hungarian half of the empire, where Slovaks formed a local majority in 'Upper Hungary' – the

---

* Czechoslovak politicians tried to set up a central European common market in 1936 but were not successful.

southern slopes of the Carpathians. The national project became 'Czechoslovak' based on shared linguistic and cultural features between Czechs and Slovaks. Masaryk, as a son of a Czech–Slovak marriage, was inclined to see the common features between the two sides although he identified as Czech. Both nations were Slavic subjects of the Habsburg empire and felt second-class compared to German-Austrians and Hungarians in that political system. It was sensible, in 1918, for both sides to join forces to form a stronger country that would be more capable of independent action than either could achieve alone. But they were not, as people sometimes claimed in 1918, 'one people divided by a thousand years of history'. Czechoslovakism never replaced either previous identity, although people – particularly Slovaks – even now feel a sense of a cultural space based on the former state.

As a new state and a new national project, Czechoslovakia's boundaries were a matter of doubt and debate between the development of the idea and the final determination of its borders in 1920. The Allies undoubtedly showed favouritism towards the Czechoslovaks. The new Slovak border cut across several old-established Hungarian counties. The Czechs were also allowed a few nibbles across the other side of the historic border, mostly to take control over railway lines. There is a 'border mansion' in the vast estate at Valtice (Feldsberg), formerly the property of the Liechtenstein family, with a ballroom that straddles the frontier between the historic provinces of Moravia and Upper Austria. It stopped being on the border in 1920 when the Czechs were awarded a tiny piece of Upper Austria. In the north, Czechoslovakia acquired a little area from Germany at Hlučin (Hultschin), a peculiar place where the people spoke a Czech dialect but identified as Prussians and voted for the German nationalists.

Even counting Czechs and Slovaks together, just over a third* of the citizens of the new country were from various minorities – Germans principally, but also Magyars, Rusyn-Ukrainians, Poles, Roma and Jews, although some Jews identified as Czechs by nationality. Most of Czechoslovakia's neighbours felt aggrieved by where the Paris treaties

---

*According to the 1930 census; note that censuses were used as a political/ethnographic tool in mixed central and eastern European states and empires and the scale will be tilted to maximise the number recorded as Czech (51 per cent) or Slovak (16 per cent).

had drawn the border lines and aspired to redraw the map to the new state's disadvantage. To remain intact and develop as a country, Czechoslovakia needed collective security and the support of the British and French – the Russians were in no position to prop it up in the inter-war period – to preserve its territorial integrity. There was an ominous signal in 1925 when the Locarno agreement between Germany and the western powers guaranteed Germany's frontiers in the west but remained silent about the eastern side. Even the most democratic German polit-icians under Weimar hoped for boundary revisions and felt a need to look out for Germans who were citizens of other countries. Poland and Hungary also cast covetous glances at Czechoslovak territory. When the disastrous era of boundary revisionism began in the 1930s, Czechoslovakia faced danger from all directions.

Sudeten elegy

The 'Sudetenland' did not exist before about 1930. That was a blink of an eye, in historical time, before it was at the centre of the Munich crisis of 1938. It was a grievance exploited by Nazi Germany to expand its territory and shatter the rival state of Czechoslovakia.

'Sudetenland' was a circular definition in that it was used to group those places where the Germans of Bohemia-Moravia lived – there was no 'Sudetenland' on the map of 1937 comparable to Alsace-Lorraine or West Prussia. There is no trace, for instance in my 1896 Baedeker's *Austria*, of the Sudetenland as a distinct pre-existing region. The Sudeten locality was near the mountains of that name, which are in the north-east of the Czech lands around the town of Liberec (Reichenberg), and a Sudetenlander was someone who came from there. 'Sudeten', rather like 'Czechoslovak', was a modern construction to channel people into a nation-state model that did not really fit.

Throughout borderland regions – Alsace, Silesia, the Sudetenland – crude definitions of nationality crash against the subtle realities of people and lived experience. For centuries, Czech or German was not a rigid distinction in Bohemia-Moravia. Families could contain both, not only as a result of German-Czech marriage but also through situ-ations like an educated child being German-speaking in the city and Czech-speaking with their parents. Masaryk, the founding father of the Czechoslovak state, had a Czech mother who had a German education and was more fluent in that language than in Czech. Konrad Henlein, who led the Sudeten German party that pushed Nazi demands in the 1930s, had a Czech grandfather and a mother with the very Czech surname Dvořáček.

The difference between Czechs and Germans, as it is in many borderland and disputed regions, was about class and the contrast between town and country as well as nationality as such.

The Depression of the early 1930s had a disastrous effect because it shattered the industrial economy of north Bohemia. To make it worse, the bogus Nazi economic miracle across the border exercised a magnetic attraction after 1933, and Nazi propaganda flooded into the German areas of Czechoslovakia with little hindrance. Domestic Nazi and far-right German parties were banned in Czechoslovakia in 1933, but quickly replaced by the Sudetendeutsche Partei (SdP) led by Konrad Henlein – of whom history books record that he was a gymnastics teacher. I imagine everyone who writes a book, and a fair proportion of readers, can recall something from their childhood that makes the idea of a PE teacher leading a fascist movement seem appropriate.

The international situation darkened dramatically in March 1938 when Hitler's Germany absorbed Austria. The Czech lands were surrounded on three sides by Greater Germany, their head in the lion's mouth, and the Sudeten leadership and their sponsors in Berlin ramped up the tension. The idea of redrawing the border, rather than trying to decentralise Czechoslovakia while maintaining its integrity, took hold with disastrous consequences. British prime minister Neville Chamberlain sent the pliable former Liberal politician Lord Runciman (1870–1949),[4] who had smoothed over other disputes in the interests of the British state, to Czechoslovakia to find facts and mediate.[5]

Runciman's sympathies were with the Germans and his son was active on business with Germany and knew several Nazi leaders. Runciman's mission involved social and hunting trips to the chateaus of Bohemia, mixing business and pleasure in the sort of milieu that was familiar to the British elite. When I visited north Bohemia, drawn by its borderland history, I discovered that I was sleeping in the room just below the study where Runciman had contemplated coloured maps in the company of the local aristocracy in an effort to find out where exactly the Sudetenland was, and how it should be governed.

Zámek Červený Hrádek, Jirkov June 2019.

I was staying in the west wing of the Hohenlohe-Langenburg castle on a hill outside the town of Jirkov (Görkau). The chateau – under its Czech name of Zámek Červený Hrádek (it has always been the Red House, even though its colour scheme no longer fits the name) – is now a hotel. One of the pleasures of borderland travel in central Europe is that there are many castles and manor houses that have been turned into affordable, comfortable hotels and the Red House looked to me, as it did to Runciman had I but known, like a pleasant perch from which to contemplate the Sudetenland. The house looks out on its beautiful but run-down parks and a lake where fish will sometimes jump and flop back into the water so fatly and loudly that the noise is audible from my room. I sat by the lake one morning reading Joseph Roth's *The Radetzky March*, thinking that the Hohenlohe-Langenburgs could easily have just escaped from the novel's pages. Most of the masters of the Red House had been prolific hunters, the corridors bristling with the antlers of slain beasts just like the homes of their equivalents in the sparse lands of East Prussia or the Scottish Highlands. One can make out the alignment of the exotic trees, suggesting the layout of the formal park during the aristocratic German time. There are overgrown grottoes and fountains long since run dry, where privileged children once played and where stiffly attired gentlemen like Lord Runciman walked and talked business.

Runciman accepted all the Sudeten demands for autonomy, and the Czechoslovak government moved a long way to concede them, but the international situation prevented a last-gasp solution. *The Times*, strongly under Chamberlain's appeasing influence, endorsed border revision – transferring the Sudetenland to Germany. Hitler stepped up his demands at the Nazis' annual rally in Nuremberg on 12 September and Henlein fell in behind him; rioting broke out in the Sudetenland and the government imposed martial law. Chamberlain went on his two flying visits to Berchtesgaden and Bad Godesberg, conceding more each time, and delivered his famous, scandalous, ignorant verdict that the Sudeten dispute was 'a quarrel in a faraway country between people of whom we know nothing'. Runciman's mission was converted into being a fig-leaf for surrender, and he put his name to a report that discarded all the options he had been exploring and endorsed transfer to Germany. Runciman, who 'felt quite broken and pathetic',[6] got his reward by returning to the Cabinet in October 1938. He was celebrated in song by Sudeten Nazis:

> *Wir brauchen keinen Weihnachtsmann,*
> *Wir haben unser Runciman!* ★

The Munich diktat to the Czechoslovaks was signed by Britain, France, Germany and Italy on 30 September 1938. The annexation of the Sudetenland was shockingly rapid. The next day, 1 October, Eger was occupied by German Freikorps units. Over the next week German troops moved into four zones of the Sudetenland, while an international panel scrambled to delineate a fifth zone, which would define the new German frontier. In November, the Sudetenland was formally absorbed into Nazi Germany.

The details of the agreement were if anything even more squalid. The Czechoslovak army was instructed to leave all its materiel in place. The border hills bristle with the bunkers the Czechoslovaks had built in

---

★ Idiomatically, 'who needs Father Christmas when you have Runciman?'

the 1930s, but they fell to the Nazis without a shot. The Nazis had their lists of opponents to round up, as the Sudetenland had played an unheralded role as the sole surviving centre of anti-Nazi German politics. German trade unionists, social democrats and communists who did not escape were persecuted and 20,000 vanished into concentration camps. The Runciman report had recommended that the Czech government should ban anti-German 'agitation' on its territory; thousands of dissidents were expelled from Prague across the new border.

Jews faced discrimination and mob violence straight away. Nazis burned down the two synagogues in Eger a week before the Munich agreement, adding to the reputation the town already had as a hotbed of extreme anti-Semitic German nationalism.[7] The Nazis attempted to expel the Sudeten Jews across the new border into Czecho-Slovakia (as the state became after Munich) but the government would not accept them; they were shunted around and ended up in camps on the Hungarian–Slovak border. As displaced people, without a state to call home, they were the easiest for Hitler's allies Slovakia and Hungary to deport to Auschwitz in 1942–44.

The boundary between Sudetenland and the rest of Bohemia-Moravia remained in place after March 1939 when what remained of the Czecho-Slovak state collapsed under Nazi pressure and a protectorate was established in the Czech lands as a kind of colony, in that it was overseen by German appointees and obliged to conform to German policies but not technically part of the Reich. The protectorate, and the supervised independence of Slovakia, were intended at the time to be examples of how some sort of national life could survive under German tutelage.[8]

Within three years, the Sudeten Germans found that their new citizenship involved sending their young men to die in the snows of Russia.[9] Once the honeymoon was over, the cultural differences with Germany proper that were always there started to rankle. Just as the people of Luxembourg and Alsace were regarded with condescension in the Nazi Reich, so too were the Sudeten Germans. The only member of the SdP trusted with a serious role in the Reich was the extremist anti-Czech racist Karl Frank.* The journey from being valued racial brothers to

---

*Frank was executed for his crimes by the restored Czechoslovak government in 1946. Henlein had a succession of more minor roles. He was captured by the Americans and committed suicide in custody in Plzeň in May 1945.

being backward provincials with funny accents fit to serve as cannon fodder was a very short one.

Czech exiles were embittered by the experience of the war and, once the German empire was retreating, ideas about how the country should be reshaped after the war became increasingly crude and radical. Most exiled politicians favoured doubling down on the Czechoslovak national idea at the expense of the national minorities, particularly the Germans, who were increasingly seen as a hostile element that needed to be expelled.

By the time Czechoslovakia was liberated, politics in this complex modern society had been crudely simplified into Czech/German, patriot/collaborator, worker/exploiter binary divisions. Nazi barbarism, and the nationalist reaction that it evoked, ended six centuries of pluralism in Bohemia – a place that gave its name to an idea of cultural liberalism. There are few better examples of the harm that nationalism, fascism and communism did to European civilisation in the 20th century than the scarred Sudetenland.

The end of German Bohemia

'The final solution to the German question'
President Edvard Beneš, 28 October 1945

Czechoslovakia resumed its existence when the government-in-exile returned in May 1945 and the agreements of Munich and Vienna became void. The Sudeten Germans were held collectively accountable for the crimes of the Nazi regime and became enemies rather than citizens of the restored state. The worst incident in the first weeks after the war took place after an explosion in Ústí nad Labem (Aussig) on 31 July 1945. Panicked Czechs assumed it was the work of a stay-behind Nazi terror organisation, the much-feared network of the 'Werewolf' group. In truth, Werewolf barely existed, but even its name was a frightening evocation of secret, inhuman terror. Germans were lynched and thrown into the river. This murky incident encouraged the Czechoslovak government, already intending to expel a large proportion of the Sudeten German population, to move towards a complete cleansing, a 'final solution' as Beneš infelicitously dubbed the process. There was an obvious element of repaying Nazi crimes in kind in the persecution – the

Germans were forced to wear armbands bearing the letter 'N' (for Nemečky, the Czech word for German) and camps were established whose gates were adorned with the Czech translation of 'Arbeit Macht Frei'.

The Ústí massacre was part of the initial phase of 'wild' expulsions, in which the worst elements of society led the violence. Criminals would descend on German houses, looting the contents and killing the occupants if they failed to flee in time. The terror encouraged many Germans to run away. By the end of 1945, expulsions were not exactly the 'orderly and humane' method specified by the Allies at Potsdam, but less arbitrary and lethal – and more efficient. Most were expelled across the border to the Soviet-occupied zone that was to become East Germany, while others went to Bavaria and Austria. The expulsion of 3.5 million people, nearly a quarter of the state's population, was largely complete by the end of 1946.[10]

Ethnic expropriation is a sadly effective way of building nationalist loyalties. Nazi Germany pioneered this, by seizing Jewish property and making Germans complicit by distributing the benefits. But communist-nationalist governments in Poland and Czechoslovakia excelled at the technique. People could rely on them to protect their new property from Germans who wanted to come back. Exploitation of hatred, using the methods of national socialism, was part of the reason why genuine hopes of creating a good nationalist and socialist society were so quickly disappointed.

Far from suppressing nationalism, communism exploited it. The dissident generation of the 1970s and 1980s were anti-nationalist. President Václav Havel, at the cost of some popularity, said in March 1993 that the expulsion had been 'morally wrong'. The dissidents thought seriously and compassionately about their legacy, particularly as the scale of social and environmental disaster in the borderlands became clear. The dissident philosopher Petr Příhoda (1939–2014) thought that the new settlers had no 'relationship to work, nature, the landscape, not to mention the local monuments of the past' and that the loss of the Sudeten Germans deprive the area of 'tradition, attachment to the Heimat, informal human relationships and accumulated moral and cultural values'.[11] The land was therefore unloved and there for its economic use value rather than anything deeper; the abuse of the borderlands was part of the general moral crisis of communism.

The dissidents still do not carry the majority of public opinion with them. Borderlanders themselves still have anxieties about losing the only home they have, and people in the interior are also unsympathetic to the vanished Germans, no matter how positively they view being part of Europe now. As recently as 2013, the borderland played a part in the presidential election between the nominally left of centre populist Miloš Zeman and the centre-right Karel Schwarzenberg. Schwarzenberg (1937–2023) was from the Bohemian aristocracy, and particularly from the oldest, most Habsburgian part of it, which was bilingual and bicultural between Austrian-German and Czech. He had lived in exile in Austria from 1948 to 1990, and the idea that he was basically a German was used against him in Zeman's successful campaign. Schwarzenberg himself thought that the expulsions were against human rights law and was accused of 'speaking like a Sudeten German' for his thoughts. There is still a legal amnesty in place for Czechs who committed crimes against Germans during 1945–46.[12]

The language of blame for the tragic outcome is inappropriate. It was a consequence of using nationalism as the main organising principle of states. As soon as one starts talking about the nation state as some sort of ideal form of government, one is condemning the mixed, the ambiguous, the borderland identities as defective. The 'solution' to the 'problem' is always going to be assimilate, expel or kill.

The orchard in the forest

You can still spot the border of the former Sudetenland, although it is not marked on maps and signs. The Sudeten landscape is sparse, underpopulated. A walk in the countryside can involve strange discoveries of abandoned villages and farms that have stood vacant for decades and reverted to woodlands and scrub. One might be walking through the birch and pine and suddenly find a ragged square patch of apple trees, the gnarly remnant of a German-Bohemian farmer's lost orchard.[13]

There were simply not enough dispossessed Czechoslovaks to repopulate the border regions once the Germans had gone – only a few tens of thousands. There was nothing similar to the wave of millions of displaced Poles who needed places to live and were housed in ex-German territory in the west. The population of the rural border area has remained well below 1938 levels. While there had been significant minority Czech populations in the industrial towns, the rural areas had been nearly completely German and it was here that the rupture with the past was total.

The stretch along the south-west and west that bordered Austria and West Germany was largely rural, including the dense, dark Šumava forest. This section was part of the Iron Curtain, and during the 1950s this became a highly secure, militarised region. The immediate vicinity of the border line was a forbidden zone, the population completely cleared and replaced by fortifications. At first the zone was strewn with land mines, but in the early 1960s this was replaced with electric fencing and barbed wire. There was a controlled region within the actual border, varying between 3 and 30km in depth, from which 'inimical' people were evicted in 1949 and 1950. Only some of the pre-1938 Czech residents could stay. The population of this outer zone were subject to strict controls but also given incentives to co-operate with the border guards and report people they suspected of trying to make an illegal border crossing.

Border security involved cunning as well as brute force. There was an elaborate operation in the years around 1950 that involved setting up a fake border strip. The idea was that escapees would find their way across the zone and then meet a friendly 'American' officer on the other side who would greet them with whisky and ask them about their contacts and friends back in Czechoslovakia. But the escapees were still on Czechoslovak territory and the 'American' was working for the intelligence service; the escapees would be handed over to the prison system and their friends would be arrested or watched.[14]

The Czechoslovak authorities cultivated a glamorous reputation around the border guard. They borrowed from history and myth, taking up the iconography of a medieval order that existed to defend the borders of the Czech lands against German marauders. The border guards became heroes of television, cartoons and pulp fiction in communist Czechoslovakia, as they combated criminals and American agents who were undermining the socialist republic. The 1959 film *Král Šumavy* (*King of the Sumava*, limited English release as *Smugglers of Death*) centres around the hunt for the boss of a network that was helping people escape to Austria. The film was vastly successful at the time, with 4 million people seeing it at the cinema.

Many Czechs were open to the heroic image of the border guard, more so than in most of the Soviet bloc states along the Iron Curtain. History and geography gave resonance to the idea of the defence of the Slavic Czech lands against the encircling Germans. Support was highest in the border region itself, where many of the guards and their families settled and where the communist regime was associated with defending Czech ownership of the property from which the Sudeten Germans had been expelled. The guard defended against the perceived threat of the expellee Germans coming back for their property or the West Germans demanding border changes. These were not entirely fanciful concerns either, as the exile lobby was a strong force in West German politics in the 1950s and 1960s. There is nothing quite like the revulsion that Germans feel about the *Grenztruppen* of East Germany. The psychological shadow of the Iron Curtain darkened the urban hinterland rather than the border regions themselves. It produced a sense of claustrophobia and isolation that marked Czech intellectual and everyday life. Although most people never saw the border, there were common fables, for instance of a father and child seeing the barbed wire and watchtowers. The child asks, 'Who lives behind all that?' The father replies, 'Us.'

The twist to the *King of the Sumava* story is that it was based on real life, and that one villain of the piece lived long enough to see his country decide that he was a hero after all. Josef Hasil – like Paul Grüninger, a border officer with a perspective of conscience – became disillusioned with what he had to do as a border guard after the communist coup of 1948 and decided to help people get to the west. Hasil was arrested and imprisoned, working as a forced labourer in the mines of northern Bohemia, before he escaped in May 1949 and crossed to the west – where he promptly linked up with the US Counter Intelligence Corps and continued to 'walk' agents and escapees out of Czechoslovakia through the south Bohemian forests. As the physical barrier along the border became more formidable, this approach stopped working and the US authorities lost interest in Hasil. He emigrated to Chicago and lived a largely anonymous life as a working-class immigrant American. He was recognised at last in 2001, when he received the Czech Medal of Honour from President Havel, and died in November 2019.

Bohemian Hammer

I was staying on the German (Saxon) side of the Krušnohoří (Erzgebirge) hill in an attractive little town called Annaberg-Buchholz. I decided, fairly randomly, to get the train across the border as far as Měděnec (formerly Kupferberg), a small Czech town in the mountains between Annaberg and the industrial town of Chomutov. I wanted to experience that frisson of crossing the border, particularly a border as vexed as this one, and see for myself the deserted landscapes of the former Sudetenland. The sleepy railway line crosses the border over a valley between the German village of Bärenstein and the small Czech mill town of Vejprty (formerly Weipert; Bärenstein has always been Bärenstein). The landscape is very hilly; the train takes a slow, curving route through the forests. As I sat looking out of the window, I was sometimes showered with leaves clipped by the train, falling from trackside trees into the carriage. 'Leaves on the line' – the bane of autumn rail travellers in Britain – and even 'leaves in the train' are familiar to the German and Czech railway companies. The line was once useful as a mining railway, but it now runs only at the weekends and the locals are outnumbered by hikers and cyclists. Most of my fellow travellers were lean, Lycra-clad Germans with their bikes.

In Czechia, as in Britain and many other countries, closing a railway station is a difficult legal process and therefore they tend to remain open. The line through the Krušnohoří region has lots of little stations, many of them standing on their own or serving only a couple of cottages. Some of the small villages in the hills even have two stations, dating back from when these hills were a densely populated rural-industrial region. Měděnec's first station was busy even decades after the expulsion of the Germans, because a large iron ore mining complex, the last new mine in the Erzgebirge, was sunk here in 1968 and remained operating until 1997. As the square-faced Czech diesel train trundled off into the distance, I felt the silence and remoteness of being somewhere that was at the same time deeply rural and post-industrial, deliberately emptied.

The forests cover what used to be villages and farms before the expulsions. The newer mine complex stands empty and grown over. I was

Měděnec: abandoned countryside with abandoned mine, June 2019.

tempted to explore but I was too fat to get through the gap in the gate, a bit too old, and a long way short of being capable of talking my way out of any trouble in Czech. I started up the road to Měděnec village and came to the hillock that gave the place its German name of Kupferberg – a protrusion on the landscape riddled with tunnels excavated over centuries of copper mining. The view from the top gives another insight into the region. Měděnec village has a sparse, pruned look about it. It was never a metropolis, but its population – stable at around 1,000 to 1,200 from 1880 until 1940 – dropped by 80 per cent by 1950 after the expulsion of the Germans. Since the end of mining it has halved again, and it is home to only 159 people. Former German houses were demolished, particularly when the main road through the village was widened and straightened in 1970 after the opening of the new mine. Wandering around Měděnec is eerie. It is a village of empty spaces, odd grassed-over or overgrown lots abutting on inhabited houses, industrial remnants and silence.

There's nothing particularly special about Měděnec, except that it had the last functioning mine in the region, and that one end of it commands a fine view from a peculiar rock formation known as the Sphinx. From there, one can gaze out over the Ohře valley like a character from a Caspar David Friedrich painting. The next station after Měděnec is Rusová (Reichsdorf), a village that has entirely vanished.

(Above) Reichsdorf, 1960s and (below) Rusová 2002.

Walking north back towards the German border takes you through tiny hamlets like Horní Halže (Oberhals), where the small German-era church has been restored. As the traumas of the 1940s, for both sides, become historical rather than living memory, the number of such places has grown and the senses of defensiveness and bitterness have diminished. German descendants of the people who lived in Oberhals can come in the summer and work to restore the church to what it looks like in the framed postcards on the wall of their house in, say, Augsburg, and nobody takes it as a territorial claim. The last couple of decades have seen some of the linguistic iconoclasm of the 1940s, in which German signage was methodically destroyed, softened by compassion. Horní Halže has a memorial to its sons – mostly but not entirely men with German surnames – who died in the Great War under Austro-Hungarian colours. Měděnec has a bilingual memorial to the dead of both wars, with the non-specific, non-nationalistic sense of loss one finds in war memorials across the borderlands of Europe.

The border between the Czech hill country of Krušnohoří and the German hill country of the Erzgebirge is the Polava/Pöhlbach, a gentle stream that flows through a few villages. I crossed over this soft, internal Schengen border at České Hamry (German name Böhmisch Hammer, i.e. Bohemian Hammer). It was a hot day and I had a beer at the Habsburg Inn, one of the last buildings on the Czech side, before walking across an undramatic little bridge to the polysyllabic German village of Hammerunterwiesenthal. A steam train took me back to Cranzahl with nary a checkpoint or shred of barbed wire to be seen, and then a regular train deposited me, footsore and weary, at the bottom of the hill in Annaberg-Buchholz.

The urban borderland

'How bad can it be?' my father asked me. It was December 2014 and we were planning a journey from the delightful small town of Litoměřice back towards home, with places booked on a night train from Ústí nad Labem to Oberhausen in western Germany. The choice was about how much time to allow in Ústí between the local train and the night train. I was aware of Ústí's reputation and counselled that we should minimise our stopover. My dad has a cautious approach to time that I have not inherited; I deferred and so it was that we visited Ústí. We devised the plan of walking with our luggage from the Ústí west station where the Litoměřice train arrived, through the city centre to see what it was like and to get some dinner, and then to the main station where the night train would pick us up.

It did not turn out to be a brilliant plan. Ústí seemed to be closed; there was an empty area by the first station, a straggly street leading into town, and the town square was a sad concrete wilderness. Going to the main square in most towns in Czechia (and Poland, and Germany) is usually joyous and colourful, particularly in December – one should find mulled wine, sausages, trdelník (a sort of spiral doughnut that is marketed as a Czech speciality) and music. But it was dark and cold and quiet in Ústí. Although I did not have high hopes, they were disappointed. It's usually possible wherever you are in Czechia to find a cosy, traditional style pivnica (pub) where one can kill time while enjoying some stodgy food and excellent beer. We did find one in Ústí, but there were people queuing out of the door. Maybe there was a special event, or maybe it was the only decent pivnica in central Ústí and everyone who liked a pub with a non-threatening atmosphere huddled together for comfort. We ate in a brightly lit fast food restaurant near the main station and I got some supplies for the journey from a Vietnamese* shop – crisps, cans of beer, bottles of water. We then sat, for a long time, on a lonely bench at the station waiting for the train. I opened up a can and started drinking to anaesthetise myself. It had only been two or three hours, but Ústí had already got to me.

For most Czechs and Germans, the images conjured up when thinking about the Sudetenland are unpleasant. The Czech television drama *Pustina* (*Wasteland*), about political chicanery in a dying town in the coalfield, was another manifestation of its sinister reputation in popular culture. The borderlands of northern Bohemia embody some of the worst features of being on the edge of a country – ethnic cleansing, poverty, ugliness, crime, environmental degradation and a pervasive sense of decline and alienation. In elections, turnout is lower and voting

---

*The communist era meant cultural exchange between Czechoslovakia and Vietnam, fellow members of the Soviet bloc. Czech brewers helped out with Vietnamese beer production, for instance. Many of the small shops and 'Chinese' restaurants in Czechia are run by Vietnamese families.

for extreme or protest parties (including the far right and the Communists) is higher than in the rest of the country. It has a reputation for insularity and racism; in 1999 the authorities in Ústí put up a wall in one of the most depressed areas of the city to separate Roma from Czechs. The physical wall came down but the segregation is still there. Buses go from Teplice to far-right demonstrations in Dresden. In the first decade after the fall of the Iron Curtain, the Czech borderlands gained a new sort of edgy, nasty reputation, for cross-border prostitution and chemical drugs of dubious quality. The police were few and far between, and had a reputation for being corrupt.

To Czech governments of today, the industrial zone in north Bohemia presents a complex of economic, environmental and health problems. Before 1945 it was the most productive, richest region of Bohemia-Moravia but it is now the poorest. Unemployment is particularly high in the belt of territory between Karlovy Vary in the west and Liberec in the east, and is also high in most of the rest of the former Sudetenland. Ambitious and educated young people tend to move to Prague or elsewhere in Europe and not return. It has a particularly bad case of the legacy of mining and heavy industry that one can find in similar regions in other countries, aggravated by its borderland status and the dead weight of its history.

In 1948, the Sudetenland was supposed to become a working-class Utopia, a focal point of the new identity of the country. In contrast to what happened in Poland, where villages were transplanted whole from Belarus or Ukraine to the former German areas in the west, the Sudeten border towns and villages were resettled by people from all over Czechoslovakia. Old identities would be submerged as citizens of a new national and socialist community were created. The problem that had emerged in 1918 of being a big industrial complex within a small country would be solved by mining and manufacturing in north Bohemia serving the entire Soviet bloc, where it would be among the most modern and productive regions.

North Bohemia in the late 1940s was a place of opportunity. It was the Wild West of communist Czechoslovakia. The most debatable places like Cheb (Eger) and Aš (Asch) in the west were reserved for the most reliable cadres. But people who had something that they would rather forget – such as membership in a collaborationist organisation, or debts, or a stale marriage – could reinvent themselves. Czech pioneers could claim property from the banished Germans and settle the new frontier with a clean slate. No matter what one's pre-1948 background might be, one could become a good Czechoslovak proletarian in the new borderlands. Movement was not always voluntary; the former Sudetenland was also a dumping ground for less respected citizens of the new Czechoslovakia such as Hungarians and Roma, setting up ethnic tensions even in this ethnically cleansed territory.

To see the urban borderland at its most bizarre, one needs to travel a few kilometres west of poor, drab Ústí to the city of Most, the subject of a moving work of social and environmental history by historian Eagle Glassheim. The historic town was formerly Brüx to the Germans; both of its names mean 'bridge' but the visitor may be surprised that there is no river and no bridge in Most. This is because the river, bridge, old town and all disappeared in an enormous pit after the authorities decided in the 1960s to exploit the coal reserves under the town.

As bulldozers destroyed its streets and buildings toppled into the abyss, the derelict old town of Most had a strange afterlife. In 1968, during the brief period of liberalisation, the makers of the American Second World War film *The Bridge at Remagen* decided to shoot many of its scenes in Czechoslovakia. The unannounced appearance of American actors in Nazi uniforms caused understandable anxiety in the places they filmed. Old Most played the part of the western German town by the bridge. The filmmakers did not have to change much, other than to paint on a sign or two pointing towards 'Rhein', but the architecture in the background is obviously from well to the east of the Rhine. They could smash places up in the battle scenes if they liked, as it was all being destroyed anyway. There is an iconic scene in the film of an American tank driving down a dilapidated baroque street while the buildings collapse. In the story, this is because of bombardment. But look carefully, and you can see the charges from the controlled demolition that the Czechoslovak authorities had arranged around the filming timetable.

The film crew found that central European political problems were not over. The choreographed scenes of American tanks trundling through the destruction were overtaken by the real thing as Soviet tanks rolled into Czechoslovakia to suppress the Prague Spring. The Americans, and some of the Czech crew while they still could, headed for Austria and abandoned the rest of the shoot. In his haste to escape, Robert Vaughn left his doctoral thesis in his hotel room; it was recovered via the US Embassy in 1970.

The last people left in the decaying city were the Roma, most of whom came from Slovakia in the late 1940s; it tended to be the poorest and most troubled parts of the community who chose to stay in the ruins of old Most. Eventually, when it became physically impossible to stay, they were rehoused in a bleak and isolated estate in Chanov, away from the rest of new Most; Chanov has a terrible reputation as a ghetto and a pool of squalor, even by the standards of urban north Bohemia. One building from the city centre was spared; in 1975 the church of the Assumption of the Virgin Mary (parts dating back to 1517) was trundled 841 metres from its original site to safer ground. A small group of old-style buildings huddles around it, the last isolated remnant of the historic city.

The communist authorities were proud of the engineering achievement of moving the church, and unapologetic about the destruction of the old city. The heritage was German anyway and didn't fit. Moving the city freed up an awful lot of brown coal to burn, certainly enough to pay for building a new, modern town. The new city was carefully planned and the architectural design is boldly modernist. There are straight-edged blocks of flats in a surprisingly green townscape of lawns and avenues.[15] That the town ultimately failed is not the fault of the architecture and planning. It was down to this version of Most being built, like its predecessor, on foundations that would ultimately hollow out and bring the place down. This time it was not the physical foundations that gave way, but the economic and social ones.

The environment was the first thing to fail. The ever-faster extraction of brown lignite coal, and the burning of the coal in smoky power stations and factories, put enormous quantities of pollutants into the atmosphere. Chemical plants puffed out their share of noxious emissions. The north Bohemian towns had been harshly industrial since the late 19th century but by the 1980s the air quality had degenerated so much that going out in the dark foggy streets could give you a headache and streaming eyes. Mortality rates climbed alarmingly. In 1987 Eduard Vacek, an electrical engineer from Teplice, could write that 'they're waging chemical warfare against their own people'.[16] The toxic air led to citizen protests even in this model communist region of one of the more repressive of the Soviet bloc states.

Airborne pollutants acidified the soil of north Bohemia and were carried on the winds across the border to the west, where they fell as dilute sulphuric acid rain. The forests started to wither and die. The west, other than the Sudeten expellees, had largely forgotten about the region since 1945 but it was now a continent-wide public health concern that could no longer be ignored. The reaction to the environmental crisis – from scientists and activists on both sides of the border – was another strand in the knitting together of the new post Cold War Europe. The Bohemian smog bowl, particularly alongside the Chernobyl disaster in 1986, was an inescapable demonstration that it was impossible to confine problems within national borders.

The lost Sudetenland

The expellees in Germany tended to settle in the southern states of West Germany, in Baden-Württemberg and Bavaria, or in Saxony in East Germany where Sudeten identification was heavily discouraged. After the first few years, their feelings about their lost homeland were complicated. There were vague, emotional hopes that perhaps there could be some deal with Czechoslovakia about transferring some of the territory to Germany, to preserve a scrap of the old Heimat. The exiles also held on to the hope of a right to return, or at least some restitution for the seizure of their property, but this was forlorn. The accounts coming out from the old homeland – depopulation, rural dereliction, urban squalor – were deeply painful. Their nationalism made explicit a feature of many nationalisms; it was about a place that did not exist. The pain was not always expressed in suitably diplomatic ways; there was an undertone of 'we civilised Germans built this over centuries and you barbarian Czechs ruined it'. The migration of the 1940s severed the connection between the people of the towns of north Bohemia and the history of the places where they lived. It is only latterly that some of the reconnections have started to be made.

In the late 1990s a number of young Czechs from the region formed a group called Antikomplex to encourage a greater sense of ownership and belonging in the region, which involved engaging with the real history of the places that make up the former Sudetenland. As one of them, Tereza Vávrová, put it to me: 'People in the Czech borderlands still feel they're using property that's not theirs. They feel like guests, not rooted in their landscape, settled in a region that didn't belong to them' and that feeling generates a sense of fear and uncertainty. The environment was treated like a rented flat, not a home. The older generation were defensive, fearing being judged by their successors for what they did in desperate times. Examples of Czech-German reconciliation among the generation who were there in the 1940s are touching but rare. People did not have the vocabulary to talk to each other across the boundary without triggering powerful emotional defences.

There are glimmerings of hope that northern Bohemia might be becoming more 'normal' as new generations put down roots and establish an honest relationship with local history and identity in the knowledge that they are there to stay. Although the hilly geography does not encourage it, cross-border contacts are growing. As well as shopping trips back and forward across the border, there are school and cultural links, but nothing like the dense network of connections between France and Germany across the Rhine at Alsace.

Just on the Czech side of the border with Austria, there is a corner of the woods marked on the map as Zvonková. Once upon a time, whether this was technically Bohemia or Austria made little difference; the dominant power was the Schwarzenberg family, whose nationality defies precise analysis. Zvonková is a Czech version of its German name, Glöckelberg – Bell Hill – and by the woodland path you will find a pretty, spiky little church with bells in its steeple. But there is only one house by the church. The original inhabitants were expelled in 1945 because their family homes were a few metres the wrong side of the line. The church and its graveyard were trashed; not only were they German but they were in a sterilised, secure frontier area. The displaced Glöckelbergers built a small church in Austria, just south of the border post with a view over the forbidden, lost land. But before memories could fade entirely, the border became permeable again. The church was cleaned up and restored in the 1990s. When I visited in 2022, I read the funeral notices of the last few Glöckelbergers; it felt like a victory over the inhumanity of those lines on the map.

For the first time in centuries, the Czech lands are safe in their long-established place on the political map of Europe, as an independent yet interdependent entity, their borders secure but increasingly invisible. It is too happy an ending to be a punchline for a Czech joke.

12

The peaceful battlefield

(Austria/Hungary)

When I first came to Vienna, I arrived from the east. This had been unusual for several decades before 1990, but in Vienna's glory years it had been the usual pattern. In the early years after the fall of the Berlin Wall, the eastern aspect of Vienna came rushing back, like blood into a leg that had gone to sleep after being sat upon for a while. It was a tingling and painful but optimistic moment in central European history. As well as inquisitive backpackers re-crossing the vanquished Iron Curtain, there were people from all over central Europe coming to Vienna to sell antiques and handicrafts and market gardening produce in the former imperial city. It was not just geography – Vienna is well to the east of Prague – that made it an unconvincing part of the west. It was always affiliated to central Europe, even when the binary division of the Cold War seemed to make that description redundant. There had been something borderline about Vienna even at the height of its imperial power, when Metternich sensed the Orient beginning in the city's eastern suburbs.*

Part of the legacy of empire is that the web of cultural connections and identities and economic connections that empire creates does not disappear, and that means people from all over the empire want to be in the metropolis. Habsburg civilisation was powerful and attractive enough to make Vienna a symbol and a magnet for people throughout its cultural space, long after the imperial state had shattered. The eastern Jews came to Austria, but Austria came to the eastern Jews first.

The old border between Austria and Hungary runs south from the Danube through the little town of Bruck an der Leitha: not quite as close

---

*The precise quotation varies; the boundary is sometimes located at the Landstrasse.

in as the Rennweg, but only 40km south-east of Vienna and within easy commuting distance. As its name suggests, there is a bridge in the middle of town over the Leitha, a minor river, like the Lusatian Neisse, which became well known as a result of being designated a border. The two halves of the Habsburg empire were called 'Cisleithania', the country this side of the Leitha, for the collection of lands ruled by the imperial council in Vienna, and sometimes 'Transleithania' for the Hungarian kingdom. Although both sides are now in Austria, one still crosses between the federal states (Länder) of Lower Austria and Burgenland at the bridge. On the east side, there is a bust, with a splendid moustache, of the old emperor, but it is in his capacity as Ferenc József, king of Hungary, and the Hungarian coat of arms decorates the plinth. The late empire bred complexity, with subtle differences between 'k. und k.' – kaiserlich und königlich – for all-empire state business and k.k. for the Austrian side only. Divided polities are prone to raising lexical issues to importance, hence the vexed question of whether the Northern Ireland office of deputy First Minister has a capital 'D' in 'deputy' or not. Critics like the novelist Robert Musil (1880–1942) called the Habsburg state 'Kakania', a name with a deliberate whiff of scatology.

The lands just east of the Leitha had become known as 'German West Hungary' at the turn of the century because although they were in Hungary, they were mostly German-speaking and within the orbit of the German-Austrian cities of Vienna and Graz. Several Burgenland villages have names suggesting patriotism of the particular 'protesting too much' quality one sometimes finds in the borderlands: 'Deutsch Jahrndorf', 'Deutschkreutz' and so on, not to mention 'Kroatisch Minihof' – there were more Croats than Magyars in German West Hungary.

When the empire broke up, Austria and Hungary fell out over the lands beside the Leitha. Both countries were regarded as defeated enemies at the Paris Peace Conference, so there was little for the Allies to choose between them on that count. Hungary claimed the western counties as an integral part of the political and economic unit that made up their old kingdom, but the Austrian claim was based on national self-determination because of the overwhelmingly German population of the area just across the Leitha. The issue festered for a few years, with the region being the location for an attempted comeback by the Habsburg emperor Karl and the foundation of a 'Banat Leitha' republic. The Allies started to worry that it would lead to war, and in 1921 they decided to award most of the land to Austria but hold a plebiscite in the main city of Sopron (or Ödenburg, as the Germans called it). Surprisingly, and perhaps dubiously – there were allegations that the conduct of the vote was biased and influenced by the Hungarian army – the majority in Sopron chose Hungary. The city became a salient of Hungary sticking into Austria's new federal state of Burgenland.

After 1945, the German population remaining in Sopron was mostly expelled or fled into Austria. The post-war boundary was sealed tight. Closed gates on old main roads were replaced by barbed wire. Hungary was under Soviet domination and Burgenland was in the Soviet occupation zone until the Austrian State Treaty of 1955 restored sovereignty.

The Cold War frontier blighted Burgenland, and the western end of Hungary, for decades. It was a bleak, redundant corner of Europe. From the Austrian side, Burgenland was a dead end – a flat, poor region without a significant town, bad transport links and not on the way to anywhere except a stretch of the Iron Curtain. From the Hungarian side, Sopron stuck out as a salient with Austria on three sides, and was therefore also a dead end from the perspective of Budapest. Sopron was suspect from a security point of view because of its border location and people were initially discouraged from settling in such places, although it was not depopulated like the Czech borderlands. Until the 1980s people needed a permit to go to Sopron and security police patrolled the trains looking for people who were trying to defect to the west.[17]

The first attempt to break down the divide was the false dawn of 1956. The revolutionary Hungarian government of Imre Nagy (1896–1958) lifted border restrictions and from 23 October people were free to cross over into Austria. A trickle of people crossing turned into a flood with the increasingly violent situation in Hungary and the looming threat of Soviet tanks. On 4 November the Red Army arrived at the border posts in the west of Hungary and tried to seal the border again. There were desperate scenes as people struggled to cross the small bridge near an Austrian village called Andau. The fields on the Austrian side became a refugee camp. The Red Army blew up the little bridge on 21 November but there were still people escaping before the fences and watchtowers were built up during 1957.

Austrians rushed to provide food and clothes and shelter for the refugees and help them adapt to life in Austria. This generosity could not be sustained, and people started carping and complaining as people do, but it was a moment in which the new independent, neutral Austria took an opportunity to show itself in a positive light. Other western political leaders, having done nothing to help Hungary in 1956, used Andau as an example of the inhuman consequences of communism; US vice president Richard Nixon visited Andau in 1956.

Communist authorities in Czechoslovakia and Hungary were guardians of the locked external gate of the Soviet bloc, and there was almost as extreme a situation as existed at the Berlin Wall. The architecture of the border strip was rural but still ferocious, with armed guards stationed at watchtowers and deep defences of barbed wire and other obstacles to prevent people swimming across rivers or running across the fields. In the 1950s and 60s, there was even a minefield.

Burgenland seemed to be the graveyard of the idea of central Europe. Divided, ethnically cleansed, poor and remote, a hard border gouged through the middle of this once ambiguous land. But the middle refused to stay buried. Burgenland is where the Cold War ended and central Europe was reborn.

A picnic on the border, 1989

'the official program was overturned, but as it turned out later, so was all of Eastern Europe'[18]

There is a field on the border of Hungary and Austria, not far from Sopron, where the decisive battle that ended the Cold War was fought on 19 August 1989. It was fought peacefully and joyfully, by 10–12,000 people having a nice picnic, listening to some speeches by democratic activists, and celebrating their renewed closeness to their Austrian neighbours. The nearest thing to an offensive was when a group of about 150 East Germans broke through the padlocked gate and escaped into Austria. They were unopposed; the Hungarian border guards were technically under orders to shoot the escapees, but they looked at each other, and the peaceful scene before them, and tacitly agreed that they would not raise their guns. It was the beginning of the end for the whole Soviet bloc. As Helmut Kohl said at the time, 'the Hungarians have removed the first stone from the Berlin Wall'.[19]

Hungary had changed a lot even by the start of 1989. It had the reputation of being 'the jolliest barracks' in the grim army camp that made
up the Soviet bloc. Compared to the other satellite states, there were
high living standards, social peace and – as long as one didn't go too far
– a measure of cultural and intellectual freedom. Hungary's still nominally communist government started dismantling the country's border
fortifications on 2 May 1989, converting it into a normal-looking international border. One of the last sections was ceremonially removed on
27 June. The Austrian and Hungarian foreign ministers, Alois Mock and
Gyula Horn, jointly severed a length of barbed wire at Klingenbach, on
the road from Sopron to Vienna; Mock's bolt cutters now repose in
Austria's new museum of contemporary history.

It was at this moment, of a democratic movement pushing at a yielding
door, that a number of activists in Sopron and Debrecen had the idea of
having a 'Pan-European Picnic' on the Austrian border, and the date of 19
August and the location of Sopronpuszta, a field twenty minutes' walk
north of Sopronkőhida prison, were chosen. Opposition printing presses,
recently illicit, churned out invitations to the picnic.

It acquired official recognition when Imre Pozsgay, minister of state in
the Hungarian government, announced his support, and Otto von
Habsburg came, representing the European Parliament and the West
German political establishment. Otto, as the notional occupant of the
Habsburg throne since 1922* and long-standing advocate of European
Union encompassing the east, brought a pleasing sense of restarting a
more benevolent international order. It was certainly a contrast to his
father's desperate, conspiratorial attempts to establish a base in the region
in 1921 in order to reclaim the Hungarian throne. The Sopron field
marking the modern border between Austria and Hungary was an
appropriate place to start the reunification of the continent and the start
of the realisation of the old dream of confederal unity between the
peoples of central Europe. Otto, on once being told that a football match
would be Austria-Hungary, asked 'but who will we be playing?' He was
sending up his own dynastic status, but also looking forward to a future
where borders would soften and vanish.

The slogan of the picnic was *Baue ab und nimm mit* ('Break it down

---

* Otto formally renounced any residual claim to the throne in May 1961, declaring
himself a loyal citizen of the Republic.

and take it with you'); everyone was allowed to cut a piece of barbed wire and take it away as a memento. The organisers started off giving out certifications of authenticity but the forms ran out after an hour. It was a much bigger event than anyone expected, and the unplanned, unofficial decision of the East Germans to take matters into their own hands when the official opening of the gate was delayed gave it even more significance. The first group of 150 were followed by several hundred more. At the end of the day there were a couple of dozen East German Trabant cars left abandoned by their owners as they fled across the border into Austria. There could scarcely have been a more contemptuous way of rejecting the East German regime than to abandon amid picnic litter and detritus the cars that served as a status symbol and for which people spent years on waiting lists.

The Hungarian security authorities initially tried to close the Sopron salient to prevent East Germans from escaping, but they gave up after a few weeks and on 11 September the border was officially thrown open. The East German refugees who had gathered in camps and in the grounds of the West German embassy in Budapest were allowed to leave. The easing of border controls between Hungary and Austria, and the Hungarian decision not to enforce visa requirements, effectively shorted out the entire Iron Curtain. East Germans on holiday in Hungary had the option of following the trail westwards to the Austrian border rather than north and homeward. The western side were making it easy, with Austrian border officers supplying the necessary paperwork for DDR passport holders to acquire West German citizenship. It did not take long for queues of Trabants to form at Hungary's western borders. The Hungarian government seemed unconcerned by these developments, a practical demonstration that the liberal communist regimes had abandoned any sense of having a duty to maintain their fraternal parties in power in the rest of the Soviet bloc.

The founders of the Pan-European Picnic wrote in the distinctive idiom of the democratic movements of 1989: a pure, even naïve, expression of universal progressive ideas couched in didactic, somewhat Marxisant phrases – an inevitable consequence of an eastern bloc higher education:

It is obvious from many centuries of historical development that the only chance for world-wide peace is a better understanding among the peoples of the world and the demolition of barbed wires and cultural barriers raised by political chicanery. By the end of the 20th century Europe has to become a home for all the peoples inhabiting it: a land of pure human relationships, ignoring differences of nationality and ideology. The next century cannot be an age of war and hatred.[20]

The vision of the people who made the 1989 central European revolutions has more in common with the 1968 protest generation in the west than official memory likes to remember now. The Pan-European Picnic's agenda went further than bringing democracy to Hungary – it was about a free, united and anti-nationalist Europe and it is therefore still a bold, countercultural challenge. Social democracy and the Habsburgs had, as in 1910, found some common ground after the rude interruptions of nationalism and communism. In 1998, János Martonyi, foreign minister in Viktor Orbán's first government, linked the picnic to Hungary's accession to the EU, calling it 'the message and symbol of a united Europe'.[21]

The Burgenland border has been reconnected. Hungary joined the EU in 2004. The bridge at Andau was restored by the Austrian army and reopened on 20 September 2006. Since 2007, the Austria-Hungary border has been a Schengen internal border and therefore more open than it was even when the two countries made up the pre-1918 empire. Sopron and the region in general is no longer a dead end but part of the corridor between the two old Habsburg capitals of Vienna and Budapest.

Sopron has an accepting attitude to the area's German cultural heritage, which contrasts with many Polish and Czech border areas. In one of the old town's squares there is a touching memorial to the thousands of German Ödenburger who were expelled in 1946. It is a stone tablet with a jagged crack down the middle; on one side a street scene of Sopron and on the other an empty street with boarded-up buildings. The motto 'Mergitur, non submergitur' comes from Sopron's mayor Cristoph Lackner (1571–1631); a concise statement of the ethos of multiculturalism and the memory of the peaceful co-existence of Hungarian and German in the city. Since the fall of communism, often narrow-minded and nationalist when in power, street signs in central Sopron have been in both Hungarian and German in a restoration of an old bilingual tradition in the city.

Having been a depressed town when the Iron Curtain surrounded it on three sides, its current good fortune has given Sopron the problems of success. Sopron is within commuting distance of Vienna. There are a couple of trains an hour taking about an hour and a quarter to make the journey and a lot of people have decided to take advantage of this and travel to Vienna for work. It has some borderland peculiarities, such as the profusion of dentists who have set up shop in Sopron and whose clients come mostly from over the border in Austria or Germany.

We talk rather glibly, particularly in countries that are far away from the former front line, about 'the fall of the Berlin Wall' as being a key moment of history. There was an epic, symbolic quality to the wall coming down at its Berlin strong point. It had been such a focus of western defiance from John F. Kennedy's declaration* onwards and had seen so many valiant attempts at escape since it went up in 1961. Far fewer

'Mergitur, non submergitur' memorial to the expelled Germans of Sopron. January 2019.

★On 26 June 1963 President Kennedy spoke at a rally in West Berlin, declaring 'Today, in the world of freedom, the proudest boast is "Ich bin ein Berliner!"'

people know anything about the story of the Pan-European Picnic and the East Germans who made a break for it months before the wall came down, or the Hungarian reform communists who blew up the whole rotten structure of Soviet domination.

We can read the fall of the Berlin Wall in nationalist terms, stressing the yearning for Germans to overcome the artificial division of their country, and in triumphalist terms as demonstrating the superiority of the western way. The Pan-European Picnic fits less comfortably in an Anglo-American narrative. It was explicitly about European unity, and embraced all the dimensions of that idea. It was about overcoming the Cold War division of Europe, and the combination of Austria, Hungary and Otto von Habsburg inevitably invoked the idea of a multinational, civilised, co-operative space in central Europe. The Martonyi of 1998 was quite right to link the mission of the picnic to EU accession. What had seemed absurd, impractical idealism in 1989 was achieved in 2007 when Hungary joined Schengen and the border controls finally vanished.

Central European history is not short of ironies. Hungary was first to dismantle the barriers and seek the reconstitution of central Europe within the EU, but also first to twist those ideas into a mutually hostile relationship with western Europe. The Hungarian government of Viktor Orbán has subsequently decided that barbed-wire fences and division are good things after all. The reasons for this reversal are to be found in the contemporary politics of conservative national populism, but also the deeper history of the Hungarian part of central Europe and the legacy of past boundaries.

13

The other side of the gateway

(Slovakia, Austria, Hungary, Czechia)

Slovaks get annoyed when people forget they exist. It happened a lot in the Habsburg empire, when they were under the thumb of the Hungarian kingdom. It happened in Czechoslovakia, and it still happens a bit even now, after thirty years of independence. Central Europeans, according to Kundera:

> cannot be separated from European history; they cannot exist outside it; but they represent the wrong side of this history; they are its victims and outsiders. It's this disabused view of history that is the source of their culture, of their wisdom, of the 'nonserious spirit' that mocks grandeur and glory.[22]

The Slovaks are the quintessential central Europeans in this respect. The existence of their country was denied under Hungarian rule and subsumed twice into Czechoslovakia; 'independence' in 1939–45 meant submission as a satellite of Nazi Germany. Slovakia was invaded three times by Russia: in 1915 to conquer, in 1944 to defeat fascism and in 1968 to squash the democracy that the Slovak Alexander Dubček (1921–92) was trying to introduce to Czechoslovakia. Independence came in 1993 not as part of a triumphant liberation national movement, but almost accidentally as a result of self-interested political manoeuvring.

Slovakia appeared on the map as an independent country in January 1993. Bratislava became capital of a new national state. This was quite a turn-up, as it had started the century called Pressburg, and had previously done a couple of centuries as capital of Hungary. The idea of this Austrian-Hungarian city becoming a Slavic capital would have seemed preposterous at any time before 1918.

I first came to Bratislava on the train from Prague during an Interrail trip in September 1990. When we arrived, it was evident that we had crossed some sort of border from the language on the signs – while Czech bristled with accents, Slovak looked less intimidating, the word for railway station being the nearly familiar *stanica* rather than *nádraži*. We rented rooms from one of the people who were touting at the railway station – I seem to recall that we communicated with the landlady in German. The house was in one of the suburban vineyard-covered hills that form a collar around the north side of Bratislava. It was an attractive location but the bedroom was horribly dusty, and Bratislava was the last time I ever had a full-scale asthma attack.

Bratislava has little of the architectural formality and pomp of a capital city, still less the aspect of a communist capital where spaces need to be cleared for mass mobilisations. It is a medieval-baroque mixture, with an imposing castle overlooking the town and the sweep of the Danube, but with some chaotic post-war intrusions, most unforgivably a late 1960s highway that bulldozed the former Jewish quarter and severed the castle area from the old town and therefore the two most interesting bits from each other.

In 1990, we travelled the short distance between Bratislava and Vienna on an infrequent clanking old-fashioned compartment train with plush seats and the strong smell of cigarette smoke. It stopped for a long time at the border while Czechoslovak border guards perused passports and paperwork. I was slightly nervous about the crossing because the export of Czechoslovak currency was technically illegal and we were still carrying a significant quantity of the stuff, having been unable to spend it all during a lavish last dinner at the grandest hotel post-communist transitional Bratislava could offer. But there was no problem, of course, and my passport was duly stamped out of 'eastern Europe' at the border station of Devínska Nová Ves.

The reconnection of central Europe has remade Bratislava as a boom town in a strategic location, or perhaps restored its pre-1914 relationships. While border areas tend to be poor, capitals tend to be wealthy and the proximity of Vienna makes the far west of Slovakia a particularly privileged border zone. In 1991, VW established a car factory in Devín, not far from where we had crossed to Austria, and has become a huge production plant employing more than 10,000 people on an average salary of over €2,000 a month.[23] Slovakia overtook the UK as a car-producing country in 2020.

There are now at least two trains an hour between Vienna and Bratislava, most of them commuter-type services, because the Vienna metro area broadly defined extends over the border. One of these trains is a real border-buster: this Vienna regional service starts in Bratislava before crossing over into Austria, winding through the Vienna suburbs and back out again, over into Hungary at Sopron and then back out to an Austrian town called Deutschkreutz, where it terminates – probably out of sheer confusion as to which country it is in. Ryanair at one time flew into Bratislava airport advertising it as Vienna, with the Slovak capital's name in parentheses and small font. However careless of Slovak national pride, there can be few more conclusive badges of central European identity than that.

Just opposite the west side of Bratislava city centre, the Slovakia–Austria border takes a swing inland on the right bank of the Danube. Nearly all of Slovakia is on the left bank, but there is a flat patch of Slovak territory on the other side about 22km north–south and 4km east–west where the river bends to flow southwards. This Transdanubian foothold, previously part of the border region of German West Hungary, was established in 1919 to give Czechoslovakia control of a small stretch of the Danube. It was grabbed by Germany after the 1938 Munich agreement and reverted to Czechoslovakia in 1945, when most of the non-Slovak inhabitants were expelled. The brutalist concrete Petržalka suburb was built here in the 1970s. Another small section, comprising the villages of Čunovo, Rusovce and Jarovce, was transferred from Hungary to Czechoslovakia in 1947, largely to facilitate the expansion of the port of Bratislava but also to allow the constricted city a bit more room to grow. These villages, although they are now suburban boroughs of Bratislava, still have some Hungarian and Croat inhabitants.

Past Čunovo, one quickly reaches the Hungarian border. On the modern motorway crossing, there are booths to buy the different national permits to go on toll highways and the sort of HGV-only checks that seem to the non-trucker population like mysterious rituals, which take place at weighbridges even within countries. The border between Hungary and Slovakia runs south-west from Čunovo through the fields, with parallel muddy tracks on each side of the border and the occasional marker stone between them with 'S' on one side and 'M' (for Magyarország) on the other. There was older signage from less benevolent times at this border, when it was strung with barbed wire to keep the people of the fraternal socialist nations of Hungary – with its dangerous liberalism – and austere Czechoslovakia apart. One of these lonely wooden posts, planted in the fertile alluvial soil, had sprouted branches and formed an image straight from the liminal imagination of David Lynch.

'WARNING: border' sign on the frontier of Slovakia and Hungary near Čunovo, December 2018.

I was startled several times as I walked here, when my footsteps triggered the sudden eruption of an enormous hare from the bushes at the border, followed by the creature running in a zigzag line across the undefended border into a Slovak or Hungarian field. Onwards a little further, I came to a little sculpture park at the corner where Slovakia, Austria and Hungary meet, and I added another Dreiländereck to my list.

The destiny of the area around Devín and Bratislava was written in stone and water. If you look at the region as central Europe, it is a junction point. This place is the crossroads between the Danube going west to east and the Neolithic Amber Road from northern Europe to the Mediterranean. If you think in terms of east and west, it is a portal between the two. The Iron Curtain slammed shut right across it during the Cold War, making it the border between the western and eastern Europe of that period. It has been the edge of the Roman Empire, the place where the military city of Carnuntum rose and, in 374 CE, fell to German 'barbarians' as the empire crumbled.* Migrating Hungarian warlords were stopped here by the western powers a few centuries later. The Danube makes a gap in the mountains between the Alps to the west and the Carpathians to the east. Devín's principal landmark is a castle on a crag, ruined by Napoleon's troops in 1809, from where one looks across the Danube to a similar hill at Hainburg in Austria; the twin hills remind one inescapably of a gateway. This stretch of the Danube has

Devín castle, overlooking the confluence of the Danube and Morava rivers at the Austria–Slovakia border, December 2018.

---

*Carnuntum had symbolic significance for the esoteric German far right; the Pan-German occultist Guido von List (1848–1919) wrote his first novel about it.

been known for centuries as the Porta Hungarica. When I visited Devín in 2019, it gripped my imagination much more than the low-key attractions of central Bratislava.

When I crossed at Devínska Nová Ves in 1990 it was the remnant of a sensitive, forcefully guarded Cold War frontier. While I could, as a tourist, feel like I was in a scene by John le Carré as the stern Czechoslovak officers with peaked caps inspected my passport, it had recently been all too real. Less than a year before, the Morava river was the line between dictatorship and freedom and people risked their lives trying to swim across. Below the old castle, the Czechoslovak border authorities had built newer installations, not so much to guard against invaders from upriver but to provide vantage points to arrest or shoot those who were trying to escape. The whole area was considered so sensitive in communist times that when the Slovak artist Jozef Chrena was painting the river, an officer of the border guard came up to him with the surreal instruction that it was forbidden to paint the Austrian side.[24] Not that there is much of interest on the Austrian side anyway – just some woods that look very similar to the sort of woods one can find easily enough in Slovakia.

Borders of the imagination: meat feast at the Pizzeria Bathory

I am among a small category of people who watched Eli Roth's *Hostel* films for geopolitical insight. For the uninitiated, these films were made in the mid-2000s and involve naïve American backpackers being lured to a luxurious hostel in Slovakia. The gormless young men in the first film are spun a tale about Slovakia being full of beautiful women who are desperate for sex. The lads seem to find that the story is true when they check in at the hostel, but it is a trap and the travellers are taken to a scary abandoned factory where wealthy sadists are allowed to torture and kill them, having paid a criminal organisation called Elite Hunting for the privilege.

The *Hostel* films use Slovakia as a generic eastern Europe of the imagination; the presentation has little to do with the real country. Filming took place in readily identifiable locations in Czechia, notably Prague and the delightful riverside town of Český Krumlov in southern

Bohemia. The Czech crew were having a joke at Slovakia's expense – the two countries will always share enough for a bit of humorous needle with each other. While *Hostel* cannot have encouraged tourism in Slovakia, Eli Roth was probably right when he said that the target audience were the sort of people who did not have passports and wouldn't travel in Europe anyway. The rest of the audience would be in on the joke, particularly since *Hostel II*, which involves women travellers entering the hostel environment. There is a call-back to the idiocy of the men in the first film, in which a character laughs and says that there hasn't been a war in Slovakia since 1945. Milan Kňažko, a Slovak actor, former minister of culture and veteran of the dissident Public Against Violence movement, plays the evil big boss of Elite Hunting, a person very much in favour of violence.

The films tap into a deep vein of western thinking about the east. Go through those gates, the Porta Hungarica, and you cross the border into 'here be monsters' territory. Life is cheap and in the words of the Dutch torture freak in *Hostel*, 'you can pay to do anything. An-y-thing.' The police are corrupt, the children are feral, and there are decrepit factories, squalid basements, thuggish men and whorish women, and costumed people doing folk dances everywhere you look. In the era of internet-fuelled urban legends and conspiracy theories, dark concepts like torture tourism or snuff movies end up being attached to locations like eastern Europe or South America, which are the shadow sides of the 'developed' west (or north), and we want to believe that they are real. But, peeling back another layer, the freakish employees of the torture factory are there because they are the servants of an evil whose source is closer to home than we like to believe. This eastern Europe of the imagination is a Jungian construct, the 'shadow aspect' of the west that projects its own unconscious and disavowed evil urges onto people who are other. The customers in the *Hostel* films are from western Europe, the United States and Japan – their jaded plutocratic indulgence leads them to seek the ultimate rush of murder. One of the customers is a wealthy American woman called Mrs Bathory, and here we go deeper into the relationship between borderlands and horror.

The scene in *Hostel II* featuring Mrs Bathory is probably the most disturbing in either film. The nicest and most naïve of the young American travellers is suspended over a small, empty pool.

Mrs Bathory comes in, strips off and starts to slash and stab the victim while she, ever more ecstatically, enjoys the feeling of the warm blood shower on her skin. The original Elisabeth Báthory (Báthory Erzsébet, 1560–1614) was a Hungarian noblewoman who appears in the historical record as a serial killer of monstrous dimensions. The body count usually associated with her is 650 victims, mostly young women who were killed in acts of torture and bloodthirsty sexualised sadism. She was reputed to bathe in the blood of servant girls in the belief that it kept her beautiful and young-looking. She had 36 mansions and castles from Deutschkreutz in modern Austria to Nyírbátor in eastern Hungary, but she is most associated with Čachtice (Cséjthe in Hungarian) in western Slovakia, not far from the Dreiländereck where Czechia, Austria and Slovakia meet. She was arrested in 1610 in her manor house in the town, and she spent the last four years of her life in solitary confinement in a bricked-up room in the gaunt, cold castle on top of the neighbouring hill. Báthory's ancestral coat of arms looked like something from a heavy metal fan's T-shirt: three dragon teeth and a rather smaller dragon coiled around the crest. She was born with Dracula in her bloodline.

Vampires are creatures of the borderlands. They hover in a liminal place between life and death, crossing back and forward and failing to pay due respect to the most important hard border that can exist. They are buried, and rise, at the unhallowed ground of a crossroads at the edge of the village at midnight. Modern vampire legends are also tales of the borderland in a more literal, historical sense.

Báthory's story[25] inspires and shapes western vampire lore. The one image we have of her is a portrait in which she looks young, pensive and somehow slightly wrongly put together – her high forehead, bulging eyes and pale skin all seem uncanny. It is not hard to imagine her having fangs and drinking blood, but that is to get the wrong end of the causal arrow – our idea of vampires looks like Báthory, rather than the other way round. There is a direct connection between Báthory's sexuality and the idea of the lesbian vampire, a staple of the modern imagination from Sheridan Le Fanu's *Carmilla* (1872) to innumerable 1970s exploitation flicks and indeed to *Hostel II*. As an aristocrat, like Lord Ruthven in Polidori's 'The Vampyre' (1816) and Dracula himself, the legend of Báthory is part of the upward social mobility that vampires have achieved over the centuries from their origin as bloated grave-dwelling peasant zombies to the creatures of wealth and taste we know today. The vampire is hard to resist as a symbol for the cruel, exploitative and decadent upper classes draining the life from rural serfs.[*]

Portrait of Elisabeth Báthory aged 25, contemporary copy of a 1585 original.

It was a cold, misty afternoon when I came to the village of Čachtice, but there I stop being Jonathan Harker en route to his appointment with Count Dracula. A cheerful Roma guy at the railway station in the nearest town, Nové Mesto nad Váhom, helped me interpret the bus timetable and showed me over to the taxi rank, where the driver showed no reluctance to take me towards the village of the vampire legend.

---

[*] It was also used in anti-Semitic propaganda – to some extent under the Nazis but probably even more by their predecessors in turn-of-the-century Vienna. This would depict Jews as vampires, fusing the blood-libel with the image of Jews as exploitative financiers.

When I arrived, the innkeeper was pleasant and let me have the room early, and never once muttered anything about 'not holding with strangers round here' or warning me against going up to the castle. I arrived on the first day of spring. The people of Čachtice were celebrating with a ritual in the ruins of the Báthory castle in which an effigy of the dark Slavic goddess of winter and death, Morena, was burned and the arrival of Vesna, the benevolent goddess of spring, was celebrated with a libation of milk. The ritual was followed by a religious procession around town and a meeting in the square, near the Báthory statue, where the mayor and priest spoke while a man dressed as Death stood silently behind them. Slovakia may be Catholic, but it's never as simple as that.

There's often a slightly shamefaced attitude to locations associated with notorious people, welcoming the tourist money but despising the ghouls who have come to look at the lair of the monster. In Braunau am Inn there is a retired man who spends a chunk of each day sitting near Hitler's birthplace telling people who have come to look at it that they should be ashamed of themselves. Čachtice, though, gladly caters to morbid curiosity.* The long, anaemic-looking face of Elisabeth Báthory peers down everywhere, haughty and inscrutable. Since 2015 there has been a prominent wooden statue of her in the main square of the village. I ate twice at the Pizzeria Bathory, and the kebab shop across the road will do you a 'Báthory burger'. There is a more direct connection between the sanguinary local wine and the murderous celebrity who appears on the label; Báthory studied viticulture and founded the local wine industry. The headquarters of the wine co-operative stand on the site of her mansion house and still uses the foundations for storage. Whatever else she was, Báthory was an inquisitive and organised person.

People have ambivalent feelings about Báthory because there is no simple answer to the question 'did she do it?' We do not even have an agreed idea of what 'it' actually was. The evidence for some of the florid claims that attach themselves to her memory is nearly non-existent. The first published account of her crimes was over a century later, and

---

* My Baedeker's *Austria* of 1896 points out the ruin of the castle and the legend that Báthory is 'said to have murdered 300 young girls in ten years in order to restore her youth with their blood' (p344) – another example of how 'dark tourism' is a much older phenomenon than we tend to think.

therefore more distant from her time than 1970s books claiming that Jack the Ripper was a member of the royal family were from the Whitechapel murders of 1888. She almost certainly never bathed in blood. She is unlikely to have thought that blood rituals would keep her young and beautiful. This seems to have been a later invention, to create a reason for her crimes that would fit with the idea that a pathetic pursuit of beauty was the only possible motivation for a woman to do such horrible things. By 1610 she was fifty years old, which was an advanced age at the time. Because the only authenticated portrait we have of her is from when she was twenty, our imagined Báthory is forever that languid young woman, while the real Báthory aged as the years passed by. Nor is there any respectable evidence for a body count of 650. This figure comes from a single person, who allegedly saw it written in Báthory's personal journal, which has never been found or shown to have existed. The allegations made by witnesses at the trial amount to about 80 murders.

There are a few people who claim she was innocent of all charges; that her castle was not an abnormally bad place to work by contemporary standards. In this reading, she was trying to cure people who fell ill, by experimental medicine or indeed by going back to the herbs and potions of folk medicine that was often dismissed as witchcraft. The 2008 film *Bathory: Countess of Blood* starring Anna Friel depicts her as an intelligent, progressive woman who was the victim of misogyny and political plotting. People in Čachtice tend to admit that she was cruel and committed murders, but attribute this to her having been mentally ill. The political overtones, of a predatory Hungarian aristocrat bleeding the life from Slovak peasants – and indeed the interpretation that the Hungarian was the innocent victim of political schemes cooked up with the monarchy in Vienna – are obvious.* It was probably the case that her trial was political, aimed at appropriating her wealth, but that there was some truth to the allegations. For aristocrats like Báthory, servants were property and cruelty had a similar status to tax evasion in modern Russia – everyone did it, but the authorities were only interested if it was politically convenient to inquire.

Báthory's life, despite its apparent aristocratic comfort, was lived on a military frontier in a climate of violence and inhumanity. Hungary was

---

*Though it should be noted that Slovak historians and writers have also advanced the revisionist case about Báthory.

divided into three parts, one of which (Royal Hungary) approximates the area of modern Slovakia. The long frontiers between these Hungarian entities were porous, and there were near-continuous border wars between the Turks and the west. The rival armies inflicted horrific cruelties on each other, and plundered the towns and villages they encountered. There was little law and order, and brigands and local warlords were also threats to life and livelihood in the borderlands.

These were not remote concerns for Elisabeth; travelling from one of her castles to another involved lengthy journeys through sinister, depopulated countryside and the constant paranoia that the Ottoman Empire would resume its advance north and west – she lived in the middle of the period between the two sieges of Vienna in 1529 and 1683. Even Čachtice, in the far west of Slovakia and adjacent to the Austrian and Moravian heartland of central Europe, was one of a string of castles built as a last line of defence against the Ottomans along a ridge overlooking the Váh river and was an active military base during her time. The next town down the valley, Pistyán (Piešt'any) was a famous spa whose mud bath resort was owned by fellow aristocrat Count Erdődy. During Elisabeth's time (1599), Ottoman forces raided the resort; they killed all the male patients and abducted the women.

Nobody knows for sure where Báthory is laid to rest. She was initially buried in Čachtice but then apparently removed after protests. She was supposed to be in the family vault in Nyírbátor in eastern Hungary but was absent when the site was investigated in 1995. Some villagers in Čachtice think she is still in the crypt under their 13th-century church. The Catholic Church and the local priest, however, shudder at the thought of a Báthory tomb, and the people it would attract. They are worried enough about the dark glamour of the area and there are local rumours of Satanic rituals taking place at night in the castle.

Báthory and the borderland history have given Čachtice a creepy atmosphere. The village is honeycombed with tunnels running at cellar level or slightly below, a system that developed when Čachtice was on the military front line. There is a story, which seems implausible to me but who knows, that there was a tunnel running from the village up the hill to the castle perched on its bleak crag. There are similar places across the contested frontiers of medieval and early modern Europe, where the border between different realities could be above and below ground, and between different parts of the mind. Christianity could not entirely displace Vesna and Morena in Slovakia or indeed in Ukraine, where a wartime video in 2022 depicted a vengeful Morena cutting a Russian invader's throat with a scythe. New borders and national identities overwrite rather than erase the old. The smudged old borders of Hungary, and of the frontier between Christendom and Islam, are still there and still have power.

14

The Trianon complex: Hungary and its neighbours

(Slovakia, Romania, Ukraine, Serbia, Croatia)

In 2020, the polling organisation Pew asked the people of several European countries whether there were parts of other countries that 'really belong to us'. The country that was unhappiest with its borders was Hungary: 67 per cent felt there were bits of Hungary governed by other states. Hungary's population was even more certain about having designs on their neighbours than the Russians, who had a 53–33 majority for claiming places outside their borders.[26] Historical borders and empires do not have the same prominence in any other European country – not even, until recently, in Russia.

Given that leaving international borders alone is a cornerstone of the international and European order, and that – other than a few years when it was Hitler's ally – Hungary's borders have been stable for over a century, Hungarian irredentism is extraordinarily strong; the pre-1914 imperial kingdom still lives on in the imagination of modern Hungary. The map of the kingdom, shaped – to my imagination at least – a bit like a beaver with coastal Croatia as its flat tail, or possibly like a brain, is everywhere. When I saw it on an old map on a restaurant wall in Szeged, I chose to view it as a bit of atmospheric nostalgia, like a map of an old county in an English pub. It may have been, possibly. But there is no such excuse for the huge map of the imperial kingdom on the wall of the Hungarian foreign ministry, or on a scarf worn by prime minister Viktor Orbán to a football match in Greece in 2022. The scarf was particularly crass at the time, as it expressed a territorial claim on Ukraine and was therefore in part agreeing with those in Moscow who proposed partitioning Ukraine and 'returning' western sections of the country to Hungary, Poland and Romania. The old maps are not harmless antiquarianism, but a present threat to the integrity of borders elsewhere. As well as the tangle of material interests, Orbán and Putin are united in the view that borders are not sacrosanct and that the diaspora of a dead empire is more valuable than the other citizens of independent foreign countries.

Hungarian governments down to the present one have cultivated a sense of grievance that other countries, including the UK and Germany, have let go.* Austrian and Polish links with their former borderland and imperial possessions tend to take place with painstaking displays of reciprocity and respect that are lacking in Hungary. Hungarian education and public discourse always refer to places within the crown lands of St Stephen by their Hungarian names. Timişoara in Romania is still Temesvar, Košice in Slovakia is still Kassa. This policy contrasts with the inconsistent, embarrassed German way of dealing with their former territories. The Deutsche Bahn website will answer queries about trains to Breslau, but the timetable it produces will always refer to Wrocław. There are no such post-imperial hang-ups in Hungary. Hungary's attitude to boundaries is an example of the national myth of Hungary that it is not Hungary that is marching out of step – it is the rest of us who don't understand how to do western civilisation quite as well as the Hungarians do.

The name of the Paris chateau of Trianon is at the centre of the Hungarian historical complex, for it was there that the treaty was signed in 1920 that reduced Hungary from an imperial kingdom covering a large area of central Europe to the present relatively small nation state. The Paris peace treaties were based on two considerations: 'national self-determination' for the peoples of central Europe and the punishment of the defeated Central Powers. Hungary's semi-independent status under Austria-Hungary gave it the status of a defeated enemy, despite the efforts of the post-1918 revolutionary government to distance itself from its imperial predecessor. Imperial Hungary's rule over many minorities – even on the most accommodating definition, only 55 per cent of its population were Magyars in the 1910 census – made it a prime candidate for radical boundary changes. The kingdom lost land in every direction. Hungary's biggest and most painful losses were Slovakia ('Upper Hungary')

---

*In Germany, 30 per cent felt that there were parts of Germany run by other countries and 62 per cent did not; given how deep the Oder–Neisse Line cut into historic German territory in 1945, how many people are descendants of expellees, and the persistence of the issue into the 1970s, this reflects a strong taboo on nationalism.

to Czechoslovakia and Transylvania to Romania. Croatia-Slavonia, semi-autonomous before 1914, seceded from Hungary and joined Serbia in a new south Slav state. The city of Fiume (Rijeka), Hungary's port on the Adriatic, was contested between Italy, Yugoslavia and a curious Futurist regime established by the Italian poet Gabriele D'Annunzio (1863–1938).* Several areas went from Hungary proper into Yugoslavia,† including the mixed Vojvodina region north of Belgrade. Serbia and Romania quarrelled over Banat, the region that straddles the modern border between the states near Timişoara, and the effort by locals to establish a multi-national republic was squashed by the nationalist powers in 1919.

The Trianon border put a third of the ethnic Hungarian population outside the new Hungary and included a few minority populations within it who accounted for around 10 per cent of the post-1920 state's population. The national boundaries ran through areas that had Magyar majorities on each side that were largely cut off from each other by the imposition of hard borders. It was experienced by Hungarian national sentiment as unfair and punitive. Their advocates argued in vain in Paris for the retention of the whole kingdom as one unit, but they ended up losing most of the small arguments of detail as well as their main case.

The Hungarian geographer and politician Pál Teleki (1879–1941) produced one of history's most famous maps, the Carte Rouge, to bolster Hungary's claims to dominion over a large area of central Europe. Teleki's map is a masterpiece, but it is also manipulative. It attempts to represent population without distorting geographical scale by down-weighting rural areas and leaving gaps where a traditional map would have a wash of colour. The Carte Rouge would be a splendid work of abstract art, from the school of Paul Klee, were it not so thoroughly representational. While the aim of a proper weighting for urban populations is reasonable, Teleki used other tricks of visual persuasion. Hungarian populations are depicted in a glowing bright red (hence the name of the map) while others are in more subtle colours, particularly Romanians – shaded in pink, they are made to seem almost-Hungarian.

Even in the Carte Rouge, though, it is obvious that there are good grounds for cropping the Hungarian kingdom – contiguous areas of

---

* Fiume was briefly a Free City like Danzig but was divided in 1924, most of the city going to Italy and the Sušak neighbourhood to Yugoslavia.
† Formally titled the Kingdom of Serbs, Croats and Slovenes until 1929.

Slavic peoples – Slovaks and Ruthenes – in the north, Croats in the south, Germans in the west and Romanians in the south-east. Though fuzzily, one can see the outline of Trianon Hungary in the Carte Rouge. Teleki himself argued that the 1914 kingdom should be treated as a unit for historical and economic reasons, somewhat against the more limited ethnographic claim that his map implies.

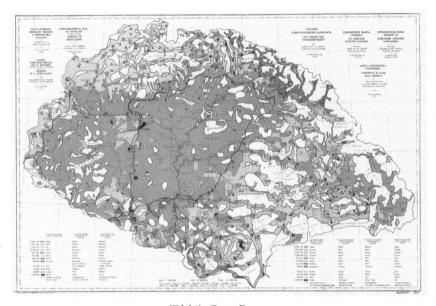

Teleki's Carte Rouge.

It is probably futile to imagine what a 'fair' settlement with Hungary would have involved in 1919–20. It might have avoided the sorest point of the Trianon settlement at the Csallóköz (Grosse Schütt) flatlands between branches of the Danube near Bratislava, or put a city or two such as Subotica (Szabadka) back in Hungary, but it could not possibly meet Hungarian nationalist demands. A new Hungary based on national self-determination would inevitably have been a lot smaller than the kingdom had been in 1914. It would have been impossible to gather all the Hungarians in one country without sweeping in millions of people from national minorities who had no reason to trust a Hungarian-run state to respect their rights. Conversely, the mixture of populations in the borderlands meant that however sympathetically one drew the lines, there would be Hungarian minorities in neighbouring countries. In drawing the new map of Hungary, there was a wide range of possible outcomes that balanced the existence of minorities on both sides, and all the other practical and historical considerations.

Nem! Nem! Soha! (No! No! Never!)

After democratic and communist periods in 1918–19, the pendulum of Hungarian politics swung back to aristocratic conservatism with the counter-revolutionary White Terror. Admiral Horthy ruled as regent in the absence of a royal head to wear the Crown of St Stephen. ('What kind of crazy-ass country is this?' asked President Roosevelt at a briefing. 'A kingdom without a king ruled by an Admiral without a navy?') The state was a peculiarly Hungarian mixture, with a formal parliamentary system disguising an authoritarian reality just as it did before 1918 and has done since 2010.

The dominant ideology was conservative, nationalist and anti-urban rather than fascist in the strict sense. The grievance of Trianon was ever-present, poisoning relations with Hungary's neighbours and serving the same purposes in domestic politics as the German stab in the back legend. Despite signing the diktat, Hungarian governments and public opinion never accepted that Trianon was final: 'Nem! Nem! Soha!' (No! No! Never!).

The language of grievance went to wilder extremes in Hungary than in Germany in the 1920s. Hungary was literally compared to Jesus Christ as having been crucified and awaiting resurrection. On a less exalted plane, Hungary was held to have been 'mutilated' by the Trianon borders, using the metaphor of the country as a physical body.

Restoring the old kingdom was an impossible dream but treaty revision did not appear to be. The Hungarian government conducted extravagant lobbying and propaganda in western Europe.[27] As with much about Hungarian politics, the present is rooted deep in the past; the post-2010 Orbán government has modernised the techniques of the interwar regime to create a foreign clientele for its own version of reactionary conservatism.

Inter-war Hungarian propaganda image of the
'mutilation' inflicted by the Treaty of Trianon.

Hungarian lobbying converted Lord Rothermere (1868–1940), propri-
etor of the *Daily Mail*, to the cause in 1927 and he used the pages of the
newspaper to argue that Trianon should be revised. Rothermere was
dazzled by Hungarian hospitality, never more so than when some
Hungarians – who had no power to make it happen – suggested that he
would make a suitable occupant of the vacant Hungarian throne. Like the
Sudeten German aristocracy with Runciman, the Anglophile Hungarian
elite knew the codes for their British equivalents. Rothermere was
impressed by the 'chivalrous' Hungarian national character, and believed
that their love of sport and their parliamentary system made them the
nearest thing to the British that one was going to find on the continent.

Rothermere's argument was that settling Hungary's border disputes
by negotiation and granting reasonable concessions 'as a measure of
appeasement'[28] would enable the countries of central Europe to put
these squabbles behind them and establish co-operative relationships.

The numbers and geography in Rothermere's proposal were wayward, but that has never greatly troubled an Englishman drawing lines across maps of other people's countries. His proposed borders included about 1.3 million Hungarians rather than the 2 million that he suggests, and the almost equal number of Slovaks, Romanians and Croats transferred into Hungary go unmentioned.

The triumph and disaster of Hungary's revisionism 1938–47

Benito Mussolini was a much more useful convert to the Hungarian cause than a British newspaper baron. Italy, despite getting a good deal from the peace treaties, was unsatisfied because the promises of the London treaty of 1915 were not fulfilled. D'Annunzio, dictator of Fiume, coined the term 'mutilated victory' and fascism took up the cry and looked to the Balkans and Africa for expansion. Well before Nazi Germany, a revisionist axis developed between Rome and Budapest.

It was only when Nazi Germany threatened war over the Sudetenland that the revision of Trianon became possible. The agreement was signed in the Belvedere Palace in Vienna, where 30 years earlier Franz Ferdinand's circle dreamed of a federal central Europe. Calling in the Great Powers was an established way of sorting out boundary disputes widely used in the early 1920s (for instance in Silesia and Teschen with the Conference of Ambassadors), but this time the great powers deciding border issues in eastern Europe were the two leading fascist states. It was an alarming sign, on top of Munich, that a new model of diplomacy was in the ascendant in Europe. Instead of Wilson, Lloyd George and Clemenceau parcelling out territory, it was now Hitler and Mussolini.

Annexation seems to bring a violent surge of primitive triumphalist emotion, as seen in Austria and the Sudetenland. It was the same in the new Hungarian lands. The Czechoslovak border gates were lifted and the Hungarian army and people crossed, fiery torches blazing in the dark as they seized the land. Even some Hungarians wondered what they had unleashed.

Rothermere joined the Hungarian celebrations at Kassa (Košice), newly reclaimed from Czechoslovakia. His description is pure nationalist kitsch:

While the organ rolled out its Te Deum, we passed up the dim nave between two ranks of beautiful Hungarian girls in their folk dress—costumes that had been hidden during the twenty years when the dress was forbidden, dresses that had been handed down from grand-dame to grand-daughter for this day of freedom and rejoicing . . . These people were free again![29]

In Rothermere's lyrical account of cheering crowds, the Slovaks, who made up about half the city's population* in the late 1930s, are completely invisible, except to be described as 'an alien race . . . regarded as inferior in history and culture'. His claims about bans on traditional dress and parents speaking Hungarian to their children were utterly untrue. The Hungarian high school in Kassa/Košice was open throughout the interwar period and was provided with a taxpayer-funded new gym in 1935.

The next and biggest coup for Hungary was the recovery of northern Transylvania from Romania in the Second Vienna Award of August 1940, dictated by Hitler's foreign ministry in Berlin. It was a dark moment in European history, after the fall of France, Romania's traditional ally, and while the Molotov–Ribbentrop pact between Nazi Germany and Stalin's USSR was in force.

Hungary was drawn inexorably into the orbit of Nazi Germany. It signed the Tripartite Pact in November 1940, as did its neighbours Romania, Slovakia and Yugoslavia that winter. But there was a coup in Yugoslavia in April 1941, and the new government in Belgrade defected from the pact rather than comply with Hitler's demands to allow German forces passage on their way to bail out the Italian invasion of Greece. The response was a brutal invasion of Yugoslavia by Germany, Italy and Hungary, despite the signature of a Hungarian–Yugoslav friendship treaty only months earlier. Prime Minister Teleki, belatedly realising where his strategy since 1939 had got him, committed suicide, leaving an excoriating note to Horthy:

We have become word-breakers—out of cowardice—and broke our promise of the eternal friendship agreement . . . The nation senses that we have cast away its honour.

---

*Kassa had been 40 per cent Slovak in the 1880 Hungarian census. The politicised censuses of 1910 (Hungarian) and 1930 (Czechoslovak) put the Magyar proportion at 75 per cent and 18 per cent respectively.

We have sided with the villains because the atrocities they reported are a pack of lies. There were none against Hungarians and none even against Germans! We will be robbing a corpse! We will be the most miserable of nations. I did not hold you back. I am guilty.[30]

Hungary's thirty pieces of silver were paid in territory from former Yugoslavia – half of Vojvodina (Bácska, to be precise), southern Baranya and two smaller pockets further west (Prekmurje and Medjimurje). In less than three years, Hungary had nearly doubled in size and increased its population by more than 50 per cent. The changes brought over 2 million Magyars into Hungary – but they also swept a similar number from minority populations into a hostile nationalist state.* Many of the minorities struggled to provide paperwork when the borders changed, making them vulnerable to the authorities. None suffered as much as the Jews; refugees and those in the newly absorbed areas were among those deported first, before the principal Hungarian Holocaust in 1944.

Hungary's expanded territory lasted only as long as the German empire that had made it possible. The turning of the tide at Stalingrad in the winter of 1942–43 meant that sooner or later Stalin would be drawing the boundaries. The moment came quicker for Hungary because Romania switched sides; the Axis powers were rapidly chased out of temporarily Hungarian Transylvania. On 25 October 1944 the last part was 'liberated' when the Soviet army defeated German and Hungarian forces at the Battle of Carei, a border town dominated by the palace of the Hungarian Károlyi family and still a town with an ethnic Hungarian majority.

Revisionism had brought Hungary nothing but disaster – diplomatic isolation between the wars, the stagnant economy of closed frontiers, the moral degradation of collaborating with Hitler that Teleki decided to pay for with his life, and complicity in the even greater crime of the Holocaust. It ultimately led to military defeat and occupation at the hands of the Romanians – again – and the Soviets, the return to the Trianon borders (minus three villages), communism and the loss of

---

* Among these minorities, however, were a couple of hundred thousand Germans who would probably have preferred to live in Hungary. On the other hand, there were many Jews counted as Hungarians in 1910 who would probably have wanted to live in countries other than the anti-Semitic post-1920 state.

independence that was so cruelly apparent in 1956. In contrast to countries such as Poland and Czechoslovakia, where ethnically cleansed border zones were part of the communist-nationalist formula, Hungarian nationalism was taboo during most of the communist years in power.

The relationship between Hungary and the minorities in neighbouring countries remained uncertain for a long period after the return to democracy. There was a small flurry of discussion around 1990 about trying to reopen the matter of Hungary's borders, particularly given clashes between Romanians and Hungarians in Transylvania. But the issue quickly died down. After the return of Orbán in 2010, there was a new approach. The Hungarian state gave the Hungarians across the border citizenship rights in 2011 and voting rights in 2012 and 1.1 million had taken up the option by 2022. The Orbán government also turned on the taps for funding of organisations, cultural activities and propaganda, and by 2022 this had increased tenfold.

There is nothing wrong with a government engaging in cultural promotion abroad, and there are several other cases where the core state of a people dispersed across borders has been generous with citizenship. Ireland's welcome to people born in Northern Ireland and those with an Irish grandparent is an example, as is Romania's acceptance of the descendants of pre-1940 citizens. But the Orbán government's programme has several sinister features. Cultural output is heavily skewed towards the official interpretation of history and identity, which is exclusive and conservative, verging on propagandist. Hungarian-language information online is dominated by nationalist propaganda. The flow of money is earmarked for organisations that are effectively part of the Fidesz regime, and there is little accounting of how it is spent. At election times postal votes are loosely distributed, and the 2022 elections were marred by allegations – which the Hungarian Electoral Commission could not investigate because its jurisdiction stopped at the border – of misconduct, including alleged destruction of ballot papers near the Transylvanian town of Târgu Mureş.[31] The published election results showed a 94 per cent vote for Orbán's party among the Hungarians across the border. Meanwhile, the Hungarian diaspora elsewhere, including 118,000 in the UK, were largely neglected because they tend to be young and cosmopolitan and not supportive of the regime. The Organization for Security and Co-operation in Europe (OSCE) election observers found a 'pervasive overlap of government information and ruling party messaging' in the 2022 election.[32] Electoral manipulation and the use of official resources for government candidates and propaganda has a very long history in Hungary, dating back to the previous conservative regimes before 1914 and between the wars.

Even if one accepts the Hungarian nationalist objections to Trianon as they were in 1920, the question remains of what purpose can be served by dwelling upon century-old injustices now. Most borders have some element of unfairness, but most countries' political cultures are not poisoned by it. The Orbán regime, like Horthy's before it, feeds on those emotions of resentment and stimulates them at every opportunity.

The regime was not going to miss the centenary of Trianon, which came on 4 June 2020. The new memorial took the form of a gouge in Alkotmány utca, the street facing parliament, which represents the 'mutilation' of Trianon. It consists of a deepening slash, reminiscent of the Vietnam War memorial in Washington, DC, the walls chiselled with the names of every settlement in the pre-1914 kingdom. The places are jumbled together, the still-Hungarian mixed with the Hungarian towns and villages beyond the present borders and with the (Hungarian) names of places that had never had a significant ethnic Hungarian population. At the bottom of the slope there are two gaunt stone columns, and an eternal flame behind them. The columns had the sombre quality of the central memorial of Treblinka, which I had visited not long before, and the eternal flame evoked Yad Vashem. The Trianon memorial in Budapest is an obscene spectacle, appropriating the imagery of the Holocaust for a century-old nationalist grievance about borders.* It is a resentment factory, with no message for the future.

In all but the most intransigent nationalist terms, European integration all round was as close to an answer to the Trianon Question as anyone could ask. The EU means minority rights on both sides of borders; it should enforce a set of rules on, for instance, Romania in how it treats the Transylvanian Hungarian population, even if it needs diplomatic and

---

* There are hardly any German memorials to the lost territories. There is a certain irony to some Polish ones, in that they mourn the loss of the Kresy to the east without acknowledging the Germans expelled from the west.

*Trianon memorial, Budapest, with the parliament
building in the background, January 2022.*

commission pressure to be implemented. It may be imperfect, but it is a huge improvement in terms of the rules, the recourse to law by the population affected, and the commitment of the member states that existed under the League of Nations' guidance between the wars.

But Orbán's Hungary overtly aspires to be an ethno-state rather than a civic one: 'the government that took office in 2010 made it clear that they think in terms of nationality, not borders', according to Péter Szilágyi, the ministerial commissioner for Hungarian communities abroad in 2019.[33] The problem is that borders matter, and the state system we have is based on territorial sovereignty including that of Slovakia and Romania.

The new partium

Hungary's economy has been heavily dependent on inward investment in the west of the country. But to the east it is slipping behind on a historic scale. Debrecen and Oradea are neighbours, a similar distance from each other as Nottingham and Sheffield, and before the First World

War they were both in Hungary. They each had their local peculiarities, Debrecen as the 'Hungarian Geneva' with its Protestant heritage and proud memories of the declaration of independence in the unsuccessful 1849 revolution, and Nagyvárad (as the Hungarians call Oradea) with its Jewish and Romanian minorities. It was one of the more painful cuts of the 1920 Treaty of Trianon when Oradea was allocated to Romania. There is a statue in its theatre square to the wily Queen Marie, whose lobbying efforts at the Paris Peace Conference resulted in Romania's generous 1920 frontiers. Nagyvárad became part of Hungary again in 1940–44 but the old border was reinstated by the Allies and there it has stayed.

Despite their proximity, a railway journey between Debrecen and Oradea involves a change at Püspökladany and a grimy stopping train towards the border across the flat east Hungarian plain. As Romania's land border is not in Schengen, there are passport inspections and stamps on both sides of the border. There is also a time change, as Romanian time is an hour behind Hungary. The journey effectively takes the best part of an afternoon. Borderland travel is often like this, with through trains arranged for the convenience of people travelling between the national capitals rather than the local inhabitants. I wanted to explore this little-known region, and see what the lost Hungarian cities looked like and felt like over a century after Trianon. Were they still missing their motherland, or had they moved on with the times?

I found Oradea, at least, to be an attractive and lively city, with a surprisingly successful economy and a sense of purpose. The centre is a festival of turn-of-the-century architecture – Hungarian Art Nouveau, German-Austrian Jugendstil (the boundary between these is pretty loose) – much of which has been recently restored with generous EU funding. The confected style, and the bright pinks and blues of the newly repainted facades, give the city a cheerful look. While there are no grand Viennese-style cafes, Oradea has several modern hipster coffee establishments where multilingual young people operate sleek, mysterious machines in the constant search for a cleaner, purer brew. Several of Oradea's coffee places were founded by young Romanians coming home after working as baristas for the major chains in London. Modern Oradea seems comfortable with its traditional borderland identity; there is no attempt to deny or expunge its Hungarian history. The Hungarian patriotic and democratic poet Endre Ady (1877–1919), who lived here around 1900, has a street named after him, and he is part of a statue in the main street commemorating the founding of the city's literary society. Ady's lap is worn shiny from people sitting on it. Oradea still has a Hungarian minority of 25 per cent and Hungarian-language educational and cultural facilities. One sees not only official bilingualism but also private enterprise using both Romanian and Hungarian to advertise.

Like many successful borderland cities, Oradea has an official ethos of unity in diversity, regarding its Hungarian and Jewish history as assets and its central European location as an advantage. Part of Oradea's strength has been in building up its university and attracting international students, who contribute to its youthful bustle, and to its diverse image. The drainage covers in the pavements feature the city's emblem and its name in four languages – Romanian (Oradea), Hungarian (Nagyvárad), German (Grosswardein) and . . . English ('City of Oradea'). The English seemed an unnecessary duplication when I first saw it, but now I understand. Being an open place, a borderland in the good sense, involves a relationship with the international English present and future as well as the languages that have made the city what it is now.

Oradea has achieved something remarkable in the last 20 years. The physical renewal of its beautiful Art Nouveau centre is an outward sign of its economic success. Romania has been a poorer country than Hungary for centuries, but it is rapidly catching up and the border region has overtaken the neighbouring parts of eastern Hungary. As on the German–Polish border, the border towns on the traditionally poorer side of the line are some of the fastest-growing and most liberal places in their country while the traditionally richer side is more stagnant and nationalistic.

Oradea and its hinterland are more prosperous than Debrecen across the border, an extraordinary change since the 1990s when Debrecen was an El Dorado for impoverished Romanians in need of consumer goods. There are Hungarians who commute across the border to this welcoming city, a trend accelerated by the decline of the forint and the stability of the leu on international markets despite Romania's dysfunctional politics. Reuters reported (9 January 2023)[34] on one example: 'Zoltan Dio, a theatre set designer who lives near Hungary's second-biggest city Debrecen, has been working across the border for years . . . "If I get an assignment in Hungary, then after much haggling I can charge about two-thirds of what I get in Romania with no questions asked."'

Triplex Confinium

Hungary's feelings about borders have even deeper roots than Trianon 1920, as I found when I visited another of the Trianon boundaries, this one in the far south of the country. It all looked a bit post-apocalyptic as I trudged towards the border post at Kübekháza; the plains are not inviting in mid-January. The road stretching in front of me was empty, and the fields either side were flat and bleak. Freezing fog hung in the air, smudging any light that tried to pierce the gloom. But gradually the lights of a lonely border post came into focus, then the shape of the makeshift buildings, then the fences and barbed wire that started on the right-hand side of the road. I was being watched. The sight of a man walking, alone, 3km from the nearest village, towards the border was an unusual one – at least, walking in the direction I was travelling. I was wary, curious. And so were the guards.

The object of my quest was a few metres on the Serbian side, so I had to pass through the border control. I put on my most law-abiding facial expression as I approached the side door of the Hungarian officers' hut, the door opened and a young man leaned out and asked me, first in Hungarian and then in English, where I was going and how I had got there. I explained that I had walked from the village, and wanted to see the Triplex Confinium, and got out my phone to show him the object of my journey. 'It's a waste of time,' he warned me. I explained I was interested in borders and I'd been to the equivalent point at the other end of the country, in Rajka near Bratislava. I played the English eccentric abroad as hard as I could; it was a role I certainly felt I could inhabit. 'Everyone needs a hobby, I guess,' said the young guard, and after a quick scan he returned my passport. Then I walked about 10 metres to the adjacent hut, where an older Serbian border guard with a moustache reminiscent of his Habsburg predecessors examined my British passport, an exotic item for quiet Kübekháza/Rabe. He said he would keep my passport while I had a quick look at the Triplex Confinium and took photos.

Despite its science fiction name, the Triplex Confinium is a low-tech, triangular stone column. Each side of the obelisk bears a national emblem and a date – 4 June 1920 – when the Treaty of Trianon established it as a

Triplex Confinium and Kübekháza border crossing, January 2020.

boundary point. Before that, all three sides of it had been in Hungary and this point is far from forgotten on the Hungarian side. The monument used to stand at the precise point where the borders of Hungary, Serbia and Romania meet, a junction point between Magyar, Latin and Slav, Schengen, non-Schengen and non-EU, but it was moved a few metres in 2015 when the border was fortified and now stands on Serbian territory.

I then headed back across the border controls, and in a technical sense something extraordinary happened. I turned up at the Serbia–Hungary border without documentation and was waved through. This border is among the hardest in Europe, fortified since the migration crisis of 2015 with barbed wire and watchtowers. To Hungary's leaders, the border fence that starts at Kübekháza is a symbol – and practical demonstration – of their resistance to migrants, particularly if they happen to be darker skinned or Muslim. Orbán's fence crackles with paranoia and defensiveness. It is the spiritual successor to one of the big, historically resonant boundary lines of European history – the Military Frontier between Habsburg Christendom and Ottoman Islam. And I had just strolled across it.

As I went back through the Hungarian control and exchanged fare-wells with the guards, the young man told me to keep my passport easily to hand. I was already conscious that as a man walking alone, underdressed for the freezing conditions in an open leather jacket, backpack on my shoulder and with a non-existent grasp of the Hungarian language, I looked at first glance like the sort of person Orbán wanted to throw out of the country, except that I had light hair and white skin. My trip to the Triplex Confinium had been a success, but it left me uneasy. That I could wander back and forward, to the amusement of the guards, was surely the definition of white European privilege. If I had been a UK passport holder of Middle Eastern or South Asian origin, how would I have fared? I am sure my documents would have been given a more thorough going-over, at the very least. Without wanting to believe any of the officers I spoke to were racist individuals, I knew that the system they worked in was not designed to be fair. I could cross and re-cross, but many other people were help-lessly stuck on the far side of the mirrors. At the fence between the border post and the Hungarian interior there was a sort of scarecrow, a stick figure dressed in women's clothes and carrying a purse, looking in but never crossing over. She seemed to me to represent the nowhere-world of the border for the less privileged, stuck permanently in limbo amid fences and guards.

No immigration patrols stopped me as I returned to the bright lights of Kübekháza village, but I had one unusual encounter. A man – I will not describe him in any more detail than that – greeted me. We had a conversation, or rather he spoke gesture-augmented Hungarian and I expressed my acknowledgement and thanks as best I could; I assumed he was asking me what the hell I was doing. I ventured that I was headed for the 'autóbusz' to Szeged and he pointed me in the right direction and smiled and waved. The reason I am not describing this kind fellow is that I think he assumed I had some sort of irregular status at the border and was trying to help me. Being a good Samaritan to asylum-seekers and immigrants carries legal penal-ties in 'Christian' Hungary and I have no wish to repay his kindness by getting him into trouble.

My Samaritan is probably safe from social ostracism in Kübekháza. It's an oddly liberal and tolerant little place that has kept re-electing its mayor, Robert Molnár, while he has condemned the border fence and most of the works of Orbán in outspoken terms.[35] Maybe it is down to the always ambivalent attitudes of border villages to having barriers slammed down, but maybe it is also that Kübekháza has multiculturalism in its blood. It was founded as a Swabian German village, Kübeckhausen, and despite the loss of most of its Germans in 1945–46 it is determined to hang on to the cultural heritage. You can see representations of dirndl and lederhosen and Alpine cows on posters advertising its shops and facilities. On the Saturday morning when I went from the nearby city of Szeged to Kübekháza, the bus was full of people going to the German market in the village.

The first that the people of Kübekháza knew about Orbán's fence was when the barbed wire was rolled out on Monday 13 July 2015. Molnár was woken up by a phone call from a farmer's wife from the edge of the village: 'Mayor, they are destroying my land!' she shouted through the receiver. Startled, he asked her what was going on. 'The soldiers! They are driving with large trucks over my yard.'[36] It was a classic tale of borderland sensitivities; the trampling on the borderers' rights without even the formality of getting planning permission – in the name of state security, and the unease that border people feel on seeing soldiers and fences and watchtowers. The tradition enjoyed once a year since 1998 by the villagers on all three sides, of walking across the fields and socialising with the neighbours around the Triplex Confinium, came to an abrupt halt.

Until 2019, Kübekháza was a complete dead end, without even the little accommodations that allow contact with the places just the other side of the line. The tracks and pathways across the fields to Serbia were fenced off. It was still physically possible to walk, presumably under surveillance, across to Romania but driving meant a long detour. Orbán's fence ends at the border post I visited, part of what made my trip there so surreal; it was the end of the rainbow but there was no pot of gold.

The Kübekháza border post was opened only in October 2019. I am not sure of the regulations, but it seemed that my trip to the border post might have hit a very narrow window of time when I was able to pass through. Smaller border posts are often only open for nationals of the countries on either side (Serbia and EU in this case) and my British passport was shortly to stop counting for this purpose. The new crossing I saw was opened as part of a paradoxical process, whereby having put up the fences at the edge of Hungary and the EU, the Hungarian government and the EU have been working together to increase the number of border crossings. There are European misgivings about some of the way that Hungary runs its border, though; the lack of access to the law and appeals, and the criminalisation of voluntary assistance trouble European consciences. The 'pushback gates' appearing every couple of kilometres along the fence enable the Hungarian border patrols to summarily deport individuals back into random Serbian fields, without judicial hearing and sometimes without documents. There is an 8km zone inside the Hungarian fence where border patrols, just as I had been warned, roam around asking anyone they feel like for ID and chucking out those whose faces and documents don't fit.

At the gates of Vienna

When a terrorist murdered 51 people at two mosques in Christchurch, New Zealand on 15 March 2019, one of his semi-automatic rifles bore the name of the 15th-century Hungarian regent János Hunyadi. The gunman had painted Hunyadi's name alongside other historical figures he revered because he believed he was continuing the resistance to Islamic conquest that Hunyadi had fought in his battles against the Ottoman Empire. The Norwegian terrorist Anders Breivik's anti-Islamic manifesto in 2011 referred to the Battle of Vienna in 1683, when Ottoman armies unsuccessfully besieged the Austrian capital.

Extreme Hungarian, Serb and Greek nationalism all represent a borderland complex of ideas about invasion by an alien other, and about being the shield of an undeserving and uncomprehending West. The warrior takes up arms against the Muslims, not shrinking from ethnic cleansing and genocide, for he is the sword of Christ and he is serving a heavenly cause.[37] The theory and practice of the Bosnian genocide of the 1990s are a link between these myths and contemporary extremism across the western far right.[38]

In contrast to the 1930s, when Croatian Ustaše fighters had bases in southern Hungary, official Hungarian nationalism does not support terrorism. It does endorse a great deal of the ideological framework that animates the contemporary militant far right. The journalist Zsolt Bayer, a founding member of Fidesz, has written that 'in the case of driving over a Gypsy kid, we should step on the gas', called Jews 'stinking' and equated Roma with 'animals'.[39] Bayer received the Order of Merit from Orbán's government in 2016. Orbán himself delivered an openly racist speech in 2022, warning that countries where Europeans mixed with people of non-European origin 'are no longer nations: they are nothing more than a conglomeration of peoples'. Official publications endorse 'Great Replacement' conspiratorial ideas, and indulge in anti-Semitic caricaturing of George Soros, the Hungarian-American financier and founder of the Open Society Foundations, as a manipulative enemy of the nation. The tone is often paranoid, with public agitation against the threat from 'Brussels' – the money received is less often mentioned. Culture wars against the liberal sexual mores of the west are nothing new: Hungarian propaganda circulated to Britain in 1922 claimed that the Czechoslovak government circulated pornographic literature and had voted for a resolution that there was no God.

The 'gates of Vienna' is a dangerous story to tell, but also bad history because it simplifies one engagement in centuries of European warfare into a clash of Christian and Islamic civilisations. There were Muslims and Christians on both sides of the battle; some Protestants fought for the Ottoman side, while Tatar Muslims were a valuable part of Jan Sobieski's Polish army that broke the siege. The Ottomans were not an alien interruption, but one of several large players in diplomatic and military affairs in Europe who allied and opposed mostly Christian powers at different times.

Hungary's engagement with Islam was not as hostile as one might imagine from Orbán's more rabble-rousing speeches. By the early 1900s, Austria-Hungary and the Ottoman Empire recognised that they had common enemies among Balkan nationalists. Following the occupation (1878) and annexation (1908) of Bosnia-Herzegovina to Austria-Hungary, there was an increase in curiosity about and sympathy towards the empire's new Muslim subjects. In Hungary there was even a sentimental celebration of Gül Baba, a Bektashi spiritual leader and rose-grower who died in newly Ottoman Buda in 1541; turn-of-the-century Hungarian children's books depicted him as a gentle holy man.

Post-communist governments in Hungary have, in their different ways, marked the country's links with Turkey. One of the main sights of the southern city of Pécs is the Mosque of Pasha Qasim, technically a Catholic church since it returned to Hungary but with its Islamic origins obvious from its architecture and interior. Nor, despite the rhetoric of Christian Hungary and the clash of civilisations, has the Islamic period been despised or downplayed under Orbán. The Turkish connection was celebrated in 2018 with the renovation of Gül Baba's tomb, an Islamic place of pilgrimage for over a century, and the inauguration of a small museum of Ottoman Buda by the tomb that is notably tactful and positive in its approach to its subject. The project was jointly organised by the Turkish and Hungarian governments, and Orbán and Erdogan presided at the opening, the mutual admiration of autocrats trumping any residual post-imperial discomfort.

Hungary under Orbán is an outlier on the rhetoric of migration and far right ideology, but in practical terms it is nearer to the European mainstream than it seems. When it comes to frontier enforcement, the self-perception as doing the west's dirty work again is not too far from the reality given the anti-immigration politics of countries such as Denmark and the UK far from the principal migration routes.

The bigger difference that has opened up since 2022 has been over Russia. Orbán's pro-Russian position does not result from a long-term alignment of Hungary with Russia: Russian troops, after all, suppressed Hungarian freedom in 1849 and 1956 and invaded the country in 1914 and 1944, and Hungary is a traditional enemy of pan-Slavism. Hungarian nationalism recognises Russia's imperial aspirations as akin to its own government's stance as a regime of 'nationality, not borders' and its disdain for successor states. A century ago, Hungarian leaders refused to recognise that Slovaks had their own identity. Putin's tyrannical belief that Ukraine is not real, and that the people should be forced to realise their Russian destiny, has its parallels in extreme Hungarian nationalism. In February 2023 Slovak foreign minister Rastislav Káčer warned that if the Russian invasion succeeded, then Slovakia would be facing territorial demands from Hungary. Experience in the 1930s tends to support Káčer; once the map started to be redrawn in 1938, further changes followed in a cascade.

The nationalist politics of hard borders was tested to destruction in interwar central Europe. It meant poverty, mutual suspicion about territorial claims and a bad deal for minorities in states that other groups believed were their property. The revival of this philosophy, under the guise of national populism, is destructive and dangerous. 'Borders make you poorer,' the former Czech prime minister Vladimír Špidla told me once; being obsessed with grandiose old borders makes you angry and backward-looking as well.

Ukraine

Ukraine from 1922

Areas of Western Ukraine
that were part of:
1 Poland (1945 and 1951)
2 Romania (pre-1940)
3 Czechoslovakia (pre-1945)
4 Russia (pre-1954)

Ceded by Ukraine to:

A Poland (1945 and 1951)
B Soviet Russia (1924)
C Moldova (1940)

PART FOUR

East

15

Where is my home?

(Ukraine/Russia)

The border between Russia and Ukraine is not a redundancy or a formality, but an essential need for our survival. It seems that we all are doomed to constantly make mistakes about where our home, the safe space of trust, ends and which of its borders should be especially well-guarded.[1]

Victoria Amelina, 2022

On 27 June 2023, the author and war crimes investigator Victoria Amelina was having a convivial dinner with some Colombian writers in a pizza restaurant in the European city of Kramatorsk in Ukraine. Someone had told the Russian military that the area was busy, and during her meal a missile crashed through the building. She was fatally injured and died on 1 July at the age of only 37. Eleven other people were killed in the same attack.

I only read Amelina's essay 'Expanding the Boundaries of Home' after she had been murdered, and it is full of wisdom about borders, hard-earned from disillusioning experience. She wanted to believe in a world without borders, but 'the idea of a world where every neighbour is a friend is a nice thing to sing about, but where Russia is concerned, it is unfortunately not so realistic'. The same attitude can be found in Finland and Estonia; that the border with Russia is a line to be fortified and defended, that the front door to one's home should not be left open for predators to enter. But where was that home, where were its other boundaries? Amelina found an answer in February 2022 when her country was invaded while she was in Egypt; there were no flights to Ukraine but she and her son managed to board a flight to Prague. Amelina remembered that when they were admitted to Czechia:

I started crying and I couldn't stop, and when my son asked why I was crying, I replied to him: 'Because we are home' 'But this is not Ukraine' he argued. 'This is Europe' I answered, as if this word 'Europe' should explain everything to my child. We were falling, and our fellow Europeans were ready to catch us. The limits of home may have just expanded, I thought.

Russia's unwillingness to accept the boundaries between its territory and neighbouring independent countries is at the root of the war. But there is an even deeper sense, to which Amelina referred, in which the war is about boundaries. Where is 'home'? To Amelina, Ukraine had the right to choose its home, and to regard the multiple boundaries separating Kyiv from Prague as being internal within a European home. She rejected the assertion that a state could, by imposing or changing a border, impose limits on one's human sympathy and sense of belonging. Soviet and Russian imperialism insisted that historic boundaries and cultural connections meant that Ukraine was locked inside the 'Russian world' dominated by Moscow.

'Historic boundaries' are often cited in arguments about territory, as if they establish a natural state from which departure is undesirable. Just one of the many problems with this is that each set of historic boundaries only reflects a moment of history, one balance of forces, and one can try to justify nearly any territorial claim with a careful choice of starting point. Old boundaries layer over each other like scar tissue. Given that the sufferings of previous generations cannot be undone, historical arguments must take at best a distant third place behind the legitimacy granted by international law and the wishes of the people who live there now. The history is formative, but it does not determine by itself where borders belong.

Go back far enough, before the Mongol conquest in 1240, and you will find a polity known to historians as Kyivan Rus, regarded by both Russians and Ukrainians as the origin of their nations. The history of 'Rus' as a political and cultural sphere and its continuing importance is the starting point for Vladimir Putin's 2021 essay 'On the Historical Unity of Russians and Ukrainians'.[2] But the name 'Rus' should not be taken as relevant to modern history. Compare it to 'Rome'. The name of Rome formed part of the title of two entirely separate polities for centuries (the eastern Roman Empire ruled from Constantinople, and the Holy Roman Empire in the west), neither of which controlled the city of Rome for very long. 'Rum' was the name of the Balkan region under Ottoman control once the eastern Empire was defeated in 1453, and had also been used for an earlier Muslim regime in Anatolia; the appellation 'Rumelia' was used to describe parts of both Bulgaria and Albania while 'Romania' became the state created in the former Ottoman provinces of Wallachia and Moldavia. It is impossible to use the presence of 'Rome' on a map or in language as the basis for anything at all in modern Europe. The same is true of 'Rus' and 'Slav', which shared similar vague meanings; Russia, Ruthenia, Belarus and Slovenia, Slovakia, Slavonia are all cognates without implying that they are identical. There is no historical law assigning them to the same state, let alone validating the Russian imperialist claim that Moscow should lead that state.

Ukraine's traditions as a state are bound up with the idea of Cossacks, and therefore paradoxically with the concept that allegiance to states is temporary and conditional. For all of history, mercenary armies and bands of freebooters have been troublesome for large states, whatever their efforts to harness or pacify them. The Cossacks are part of a tradition that encompasses Visigoths and Crusaders. In the mid-16th century the Commonwealth of Poland-Lithuania started to organise them into a military force, with the idea of protecting its territory in Ukraine from Tatar incursions. Ukraine is therefore an early example of the military frontier, contemporaneous with the Habsburgs' line in south-east Europe: establishing a border force of citizen-soldiers with privileges such as freedom from servitude or taxation being the reward for their duty to the state. But the frontier breeds a different mentality from that in safer territory, and that can be the seed for the idea of independence. In 1648 the Cossacks under Bohdan Khmelnytskyi rebelled against the Commonwealth and after a turbulent few years of shifting alliances, Khmelnytskyi signed the Pereiaslav agreement with the Tsar of Muscovy in 1654.

The Cossacks were not an ethnicity as we would understand it today, and the extent to which a hetman would control a territory would vary greatly from year to year, as would the extent to which the hetman was influenced by higher authorities in Kraków or Moscow. On the sparsely populated but fertile steppe frontier, if you did not like the local situation you could just leave and set up your own society a safe distance from your previous overlords. You might have to pay some protection money to a distant capital, or to the warlord you previously served. It did not make much difference to anyone's life, it was just another tax, but on a historical map centuries later, that transaction means that a falsely precise area around your main settlement gets shaded in the appropriate imperial colour.

The south of modern Ukraine looked to the Ottoman Empire until the late 18th-century empire-building period of European history, when Poland was partitioned. The history of the Black Sea shore and Crimea were part of the wider eastern Mediterranean world of Islamic and Hellenic culture. Ukraine has the northernmost Ottoman minaret in Europe, at the fortress town of Kamyanets-Podilskyi. It stands by a Polish Catholic church in the old city, a reminder not only of the Islamic past but also a symbol of honouring one's word. The minaret was protected when the Ottomans handed over the city to Poland–Lithuania in one of many territorial changes over the centuries in the region, and it is still there.

Minaret attached to a church, Kamyanets-Podilskyi, Ukraine, September 2019.

Catherine The Great's Russian state had no concept of legal or natural borders. Russia reached the far north-east corner of the Afro-Eurasian landmass, annexing Chukotka in 1778 and then founding a Russian colony in Alaska in 1784, before turning its annexationist appetite to the south-west. Russia seized Crimea and the land to its north and east in 1783 (dubbing it 'New Russia') and then took the regions to its west. Arguments were sometimes made with reference to history, or the spread of the Orthodox Christian faith, or protection of Christians in the Ottoman Empire, or imaginative interpretations of agreements like those with the Cossacks, but the common denominator was rapacious demand for land and subject people, and the strategic desire for a warm-water port on the Black Sea.

Ukraine was a more attractive colony than the endless taiga and tundra of Siberia, particularly before the railway made that vast land at all accessible. The climate was moderate, the soil fertile, and it was progress towards control of the Black Sea and eventually the Bosporus strait, Constantinople and the eastern Mediterranean. New Russia became a model colony, overseen by Grigori Potemkin, and forts and cities appeared across the territory populated by local Ukrainians, settled Cossacks, Russian migrants and settlers attracted from across Europe by generous deals.

Ukraine in 1815, therefore, was divided between two empires, with the Russian tsars controlling the east, including a fair chunk of what had previously been Polish territory, and the Austrians in charge of a smaller section in the west, in which Ukrainians, Poles and Jews were a mixed population. On the Russian side, Ukrainian literary culture – in both Ukrainian and Russian languages – developed but political and religious distinctness was suppressed. In eastern Ukraine the Donbas region industrialised, sucking in and mixing population from Ukraine and Russia. On the Austrian side, Ukrainian or 'Ruthenian' nationalism was tolerated by the authorities, who saw it as a counterbalance to Polish nationalism.

Ukraine emerged, just as other central European nations did, with the defeat of the Russian, Austro-Hungarian, Ottoman and German empires in 1917–18. Despite being divided by the border between Austria and Russia, the idea that there was something in common, distinct from the surrounding countries, had taken hold during the 19th century. Ukrainian unity was a stronger feeling than Yugoslavism or Czechoslovakism.

Provisional governments with claims to be Ukraine broke out across the area and sought unification with each other. The outline of modern Ukraine is very similar to the land claimed by Ukrainians in 1919.

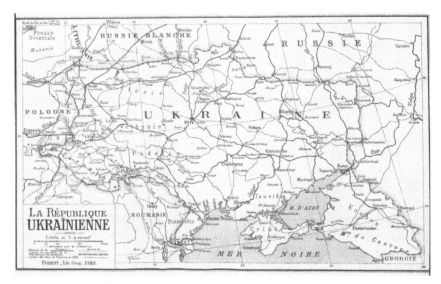

Ukrainian claim at the Paris Peace Conference, 1919.

This speculative map includes nearly all of modern Ukraine, plus territory that is now in Russia and Poland and smaller sections in Moldova, Romania, Slovakia, Belarus and Georgia. As with most other nations, the limits of what could be considered Ukrainian territory and who could be considered Ukrainian were vague when state borders were drawn after the First World War.

While one could take maps to Paris, there was a limited amount that the peace conference could do to make it happen, particularly if the map concerned the former Russian Empire. The Allies had military expeditions in Russia that aimed to overthrow the Bolsheviks, and if a White government could be restored, they did not want to see it losing too much territory. Nor were the Allies very sympathetic to Ukraine, which they were inclined to see as a German-Austrian ally. In the western regions, there was more than a passing regard among Ukrainians for the Habsburg heritage of multinational tolerance that ran against the programme of drawing nation states.

238

A section of claimed Ukrainian territory in the west was parcelled out to Romania, Czechoslovakia and – after the war of 1920–21 – to Poland. The remainder returned to Moscow's embrace as a part of the new Union of Soviet Socialist Republics (1922), despite the consolidation of a sense of national identity in Ukraine. It resembled Poland's treatment at the Congress of Vienna in 1815; instead of a country, they got a semi-sovereign unit under Russian leadership. The Ukrainians were the most populous nation of Europe without a state of their own.

Unification under the Red Star

The borders between Soviet Russia and Ukraine were changed in 1924; the cities of Taganrog and Shakhty in the south-east left Ukraine, and a smaller pocket of territory around Putvyl further north came in. Russian populations extended into the Ukrainian SSR but then there were also Ukrainians native to what were now parts of Soviet Russia such as Belgorod and Kuban. Other than Crimea, the legal boundary between Russia and Ukraine has been the same since 1924.

Stalin's determination to extend Moscow's control in Europe meant that Ukraine was the beneficiary of several annexations from the USSR's neighbours. With Crimea joining in 1954, the boundaries of Soviet Ukraine were broadly those that Ukrainian nationalism had wanted at the turn of the century.

There was a terrible price for this unification under the Russian-dominated USSR. Encouragement of local autonomy in the 1920s was followed by repression and centralisation in the 1930s, and the horrifying Holodomor famine in 1932–33 that killed around 4 million Ukrainians as a genocidal act of Soviet policy. Ukrainian cultural life was devastated in what Polish writer Jerzy Giedroyc (1906–2000) called 'the executed renaissance'. Many of the most vicious battles of the Second World War were fought on Ukrainian territory in 1941–44 and the German occupation regime was exceptionally savage. Under the administration of Erich Koch, 4 million died in executions, famines and the 'Holocaust by bullets'. Koch's racial hatred and deter-mination to destroy what was left of the Ukrainian elite after Stalin were clear: 'If I find a Ukrainian who is worthy to sit with me at table, I must have him shot.'[3]

In 1954 – the 300th anniversary of the agreement between the Russian government and Khmelnytskyi – Ukraine gained Crimea from Russia. The transfer of Crimea was the last legal alteration to Ukraine's borders. There is some mythology and propaganda about this change being drunken, guilt-fuelled generosity on the part of Khrushchev after his repressive actions under Stalin, but in reality it had more to do with agriculture and hydrology, with the arid peninsula being the beneficiary of a vast irrigation canal from the Dnieper.[4] The majority of the population was Russian by ethnicity and language, particularly since Stalin's deportation of the Crimean Tatars in 1944.

By the time of the 2001 census, 8.3 million inhabitants of Ukraine, 17 per cent of the population, identified as Russian, making them the largest national minority in Europe. The Russian proportion reflected two Soviet legacies. One was the system of internal passports and nationality, in which no matter where one lived one's nationality was determined by parental nationality.[5] A third-generation resident of Ukraine could therefore be 'Russian' rather than assimilated. The other legacy was the dominance of Russian language and culture for anything high-level in the media, professions and science, and the low status of other languages such as Ukrainian. The pressure to assimilate worked at the all-Soviet level, not within Ukraine; to get on in Soviet society, as under the tsars, Ukrainians learned Russian and sometimes conformed to Russian identity. As in other mixed-ethnicity industrial regions like Upper Silesia, a hybrid dialect developed: surzhyk, spoken mostly in the regions of Kharkiv and Kyiv. The Russian-Ukrainian population was oddly well represented at the highest levels of Soviet politics; Nikita Khrushchev was born in Russia but had most of his political career in Ukraine, and Leonid Brezhnev was born in Ukraine.

Independence in well-defined borders: 1991

The founding event of modern Ukraine was the independence referendum of 1 December 1991, in which 90.3 per cent of voters approved the Verkhovna Rada's (Parliament) decision to declare independence, originally made in the context of the August 1991 coup against Gorbachev. Turnout was 84 per cent and the vote was in favour in every subdivision of Ukraine, including Crimea and Sevastopol. The referendum was the trigger for recognition of Ukraine as an independent country on its current legal borders. This recognition of borders and independence was cemented by the 1994 Budapest Memorandum, which supposedly settled outstanding Russian–Ukrainian issues such as nuclear weapons and naval bases; Ukraine disarmed in exchange for what proved to be flimsy security guarantees.

When a federal or union state breaks up, sovereignty in international law resides in the lower-tier units that made up the federation. The legal principles are particularly clear when, as was the case with socialist Yugoslavia and the USSR, the constituent republics themselves already had some recognised sovereign characteristics. Soviet Ukraine was a founder member of the United Nations in its own right. There are sound practical reasons for this principle, and it also minimises the incentives for armed aggression and ethnic cleansing. An uncertain border encourages claimant countries and communities to establish facts on the ground by force, hence grim sequences of events across Europe and the Middle East in 1917–22 and 1943–48, when future boundaries were up for grabs.

Russia's invasion of Ukraine in 2014, and the offensive in 2022, are incompatible with any notion of international law of borders as it has developed over the last century. In the modern age of nationalism and nation states, the invasion and annexation of a neighbouring state's territory is, almost of necessity, going to involve genocide – the physical and ideological extermination of one form of nationalism by another. Russia's invasion has certainly qualified, with the crude repression of Ukrainian language and culture, mass murder and the abduction of children. The idea that someone can have national false consciousness, that someone can 'really' be Russian while imagining themselves to be Ukrainian, is absurd, but as Voltaire said, 'whoever is able to make you absurd is able to make you unjust'. Putin's motives for invasion may seem a primitive reversion to the imperialism of Catherine the Great's era, but in the modern era of nationalism the demands on subject people are much heavier.*

Brecht's character Andrea in *Life of Galileo* said 'unhappy is the land that breeds no hero', to which the reply was 'No, unhappy is the land that has need of heroes'. Ukraine has needed heroes but has often

---

*The Moscow line now justifies the invasions of the Baltic states, Poland and Finland in 1939–40.

had to make them out of tarnished material, and regarded them with ambivalence. Khmelnytskyi fought for freedom against Polish domination in 1648, but massacred Jews and brought Ukraine into the orbit of the tsar of Moscow. Simon Petlyura failed to sustain a Ukrainian state and his name is stained by the verdict of a French jury, which acquitted Sholom Schwartzbard of Petlyura's murder in 1926 because it was a reprisal for his army's pogroms. Stepan Bandera (1909–59) fought for the national cause too (and like Petlyura died by assassination), but his UPA committed numerous atrocities against Poles and Jews. The degree of personal responsibility of Petlyura and Bandera can be debated by historians, but they are heroes only if one is desperate. Veneration of Bandera is a stumbling block in Polish-Ukrainian relations, but Ukrainians will also point out that there are streets named after the anti-Semitic, anti-Ukrainian Roman Dmowski in Poland.

In a tragic and paradoxical way, the war of resistance to the Russian invasion has at last given Ukraine heroes to be proud about. For most of its history, Ukraine has been, as Kundera observed about central Europe as a whole, an object to which history happens rather than an actor in its own political destiny. Zelenskyy has genuinely written a new chapter: 'I need ammunition, not a ride' was the moment when a new dispensation began. The defenders of Snake Island and Azovstal will have streets and statues, as will the generals. Ukraine has always had its literary and artistic heroes like Taras Shevchenko (1814–61) and Ivan Franko (1856–1916), who were celebrated even under communism, but a new generation has joined them, in life like Andrey Kurkov or in the wastefulness of death like Lyubov Panchenko (1938–2022) and Victoria Amelina. As a Briton, I see similarities with our own experience of the Second World War, which even though we were already an old country has become our founding myth; the war has brought an idea of Ukraine that was already there – European, democratic, liberal – into sharp focus and made it nearly universal.

16

The chosen path

(Ukraine/Poland)

Ukraine and Poland have chosen one path. This path. On it we learned to distinguish enemies and appreciate friends. Appreciate each other and most importantly – respect.[6]

Volodymyr Zelenskyy, 22 May 2022

The boundary between Poland and Ukraine is a straight line on the map, a piece of crime scene tape stretched between L'viv and Rzeszów. The region, sometimes called eastern Galicia, was one of the bloodiest borderlands anywhere in Europe. Violence escalated through the 19th and early 20th centuries before it culminated in a murderous frenzy in the years after 1939. Both Polish and Ukrainian nationalisms claimed eastern Galicia as theirs, and both were victims and perpetrators of oppression and atrocity. But the friendship between modern Poland and Ukraine is not just unity in the face of the common Russian enemy, but reflects the efforts of people on both sides to modernise, normalise and live with the border despite its legacy. There are, as there always will be, disputes between governments about history and contemporary differences of interest, but the response of Poland's civil society to the invasion told an important story of reconciliation. If it can happen at the Polish–Ukrainian border, it can happen anywhere.

The road east from the Polish town of Sanok runs through a hilly landscape of lush, damp forests. There are a few small villages, one or two wooden churches and a spiky Gothic mansion house enclosed by a moat, but curiously few people live in the valley of the upper reaches of the San river. I was going to Ustrzyki Dolne, a small town tucked away in the far south-east of Poland near the Ukrainian and Slovak borders. I was curious about the town's tortuous history, seeing it as a microcosm of what a lot of small towns had endured during the 20th century. Ustrzyki is a centre for hiking and relaxation, although the attentive eye will spot that nearly all the buildings in the centre of town are modern constructions despite the town's long history. If you follow the hiking trails into those green hills, you will find the detritus of war such as anti-tank concrete 'dragon's teeth'.

Before Ustrzyki was a resort, it was a small country town like many others, saved from complete obscurity because it sat on the Galician Transversal Railway, a pet project of the Austro-Hungarian state that never paid its way. The Transversal was a highland line that ran from a junction near what is now the Czech–Slovak border, through a series of small upland Polish and Ukrainian towns to the oilfields around Krosno and Drohobych and out to the eastern edge of the empire at Stanisławów (now the Ukrainian city of Ivano-Frankivsk). In what is now the far south-east of Poland, the Transversal tracked the undulations of a little brook called the Strwiąż, in whose valley sits Ustrzyki Dolne, lower Ustrzyki, whose name means 'the place where the streams meet' in an ancient language once spoken in Wallachia (Romania).

The countryside around Ustrzyki was the typical east Galician mix of Poles, Jews and Rusyns, some of whom were starting to think of themselves as Ukrainians at the turn of the century, but the town was a cosmopolitan little place. The majority of the population were Jews, and as well as Poles and Rusyns there were Germans who had lived there for generations. The first shock came in 1914 when Russian troops invaded Galicia, accompanied by looting and violent anti-Semitism. When the Russians were expelled again, the Austrians did not control the valley for long; when their empire collapsed, there was fighting between Polish and Ukrainian forces. Interwar Poland restored Ustrzyki to its accustomed sleepy state of provincial diversity, but the fabric of the town was systematically destroyed in the 12 years from 1939 to 1951. Ustrzyki did not rip itself apart; the damage was done by empires and ideologies that could not tolerate the sort of tolerance that made the old town function.

German troops reached the little valley of the Strwiąż in September 1939 but pulled back because the Molotov–Ribbentrop line ran along the San river, flowing through Sanok 40km to the west. After some bogus legalities, the area was incorporated into Soviet Ukraine and the grisly NKVD police state. The first community to leave Ustrzyki were the Germans, who were sent 'home' to the Reich as raw material for Germanising the conquered territories in western Poland. In June 1941 the Germans reconquered Ustrzyki's valley. Those Jews of the town and the surrounding villages who had not fled into the Soviet interior were systematically murdered by December 1942, either in local mass killings or at the Bełżec extermination camp. The Nazis eliminated most traces of the Jewish life of the town, although the old synagogue is used as a library and there is a hill overlooking the town where, among the apple trees, I found the resting place of past Jewish generations.

Ustrzyki Dolne Jewish cemetery, September 2022.

The next people to be deported were the Poles, because Ustrzyki Dolne again became part of Soviet Ukraine in 1944–45 and the Soviet and Polish authorities imposed ethnic homogeneity on the formerly mixed areas of the borderlands. The Poles had been permitted in the Soviet lands, albeit as an oppressed minority in 1939–41, but now Stalin wanted rid of them all; across the new border they went. Any Germans who had remained were also expelled or killed. But for poor Ustrzyki, there was a postscript. Stalin's regime had a free hand to draw boundaries where it wanted in 1945, but there were one or two places where on reflection over the next few years the USSR decided it wanted a little bit more territory from its neighbours. One of these was the area around the small town of Sokal, which had been returned to the reconstituted Poland. There was coal under Sokal, and the USSR wanted it. But while the USSR could do what it liked, this was an occasion for a genuflection in the direction of respectful mutual relations with its allies. In 1951, in return for the coalfield, the USSR disgorged some of its own territory (since 1945), which included Ustrzyki Dolne.

This led to the final round of ethnic cleansing, in which the Ukrainian inhabitants of the area – the last people standing from the formerly mixed population – were moved to other areas of Soviet Ukraine. Poland took back an empty, nearly ruined town, set in depopulated countryside. Four thousand Poles displaced from Sokal were moved to what was left of Ustrzyki Dolne, so – unlike many of the villages in the far south-east of Poland – the town did not entirely die. The centre of the resort town is strewn with monuments – to the Polish Home Army, to the victims of the Nazis, to the Poles killed by Ukrainian insurgents in 1943–47, to the lost Polish settlements of the Sokal area, and a wooden totem recalling the pagan people who lived in the valley centuries before these brutal modern conflicts.

The post-1951 border created an odd situation where the railway from Ustrzyki Dolne to Przemyśl ran across a little bit of Soviet territory. Polish trains made the journey, but under strange conditions. The border between the fraternal nations was marked with barbed wire, and a gate stood across the railway line. When the train came by, the Soviet border guards opened the gate and boarded the train, standing armed with submachine guns at the end of each carriage throughout the journey; two more guards rode outside at each end of the train, an unpopular duty in cold Carpathian winters. The authorities did not fear Poles trying to escape into the USSR, of course – they were alert for people dropping letters or propaganda from the train, and for Soviet citizens trying to cross illegally into Poland. While technically passengers were supposed to keep the windows closed, a blind eye was turned on hot summer days. The journey attracted nostalgists, for this had all been Polish territory before 1939, and the adventurous and curious. The last trains ran in 1994.[7]

Although they were more relaxed than the Soviets, the communist rulers of Poland initially saw the depopulated border region around Sanok and Ustrzyki Dolne as a security threat, but over time their thinking turned to how the area might be useful. Some of it was developed for logging and reservoirs, but industrialisation was resisted, particularly by a younger generation who discovered the joys of hiking in a pristine wilderness away from Poland's polluted industrial cities. As the historian Patrice Dabrowski describes,[8] it was a lively debate in the context of Poland's authoritarian system. The conservationists won and the Bieszczady National Park was designated in 1973 and expanded several times. Walking in these hills, either as part of official youth activities or freelancing, was a formative experience for many young Poles in the late People's Republic.

The Bieszczady wilderness – part natural, part the consequence of the brutality of humans – shares the sinister beauty of old border woodlands across Europe, from the Vosges to the birch forests of Bukovina. Bison, bears, wolves and stags roam the hills; there are occasional casualties from bear attacks on forestry workers. The undercurrent of fear and brutality in the dark woods was brought out in the 2014 Polish television series *Wataha* (*The Pack*, broadcast in the UK as *The Border*), which juxtaposed the hunting element of tourism and culture in the Bieszczady with the border guards' patrols aiming to stop illegal migration from Ukraine. It was a dark, ambivalent series – the border country was sinister and threatening, with the migrants being both dangerous and vulnerable, and the guards themselves being pawns in political and criminal games. This border line has a dark place in the Polish imagination, which has only recently started to acquire more benevolent connotations.

Brothers and enemies?

The First World War had grim consequences for the Polish-Ukrainian borderlands right from the beginning. The violence of the contending imperial armies brought brutality into the delicate balance of relationships between the communities. On the Austro-Hungarian side of the front lines, Ukrainians were suspected of having sympathies with Russia and civilians evacuated from forward areas were sometimes treated with appalling brutality. Thousands of people died in the region of Lemberg (L'viv) and Przemyśl in ill-directed communal violence in 1914.

The temporary Russian occupation was also a plunge back into primitive anti-Semitism that shocked the local population. Pogroms followed wherever the tsar's army went; Jewish houses in Joseph Roth's home town of Brody went up in flames on 14 August 1914. Up to 400,000 Jews fled, or were expelled, from Russian-occupied Galicia.[9] The wave of refugees encountered an anti-Semitic backlash in the heart of the Austrian empire; the chain reaction of prejudice and discrimination led Europe into the depths.

After the defeat of the empires, Poland and Ukraine struggled for control of the mixed territories that lay between Sanok and the eastern borderlands past Ternopil. As elsewhere across Europe, the literal battle was fought on the ground while the parties also contended for the ear of the western powers at the Paris Peace Conference. On the ground, the ex-Austrian Ukrainians were first to declare their control of the main city of Lemberg (Lwów, L'viv) in November 1918, but they were chased out by Polish forces before the month was out, and the more organised nascent Polish state pressed the Western Ukrainian People's Republic ever eastward. Poland also had more friends in Paris than Ukraine, her claim for a sovereign state recognised as Wilson's Thirteenth Point, while the ex-Russian authorities of the Ukrainian People's Republic in Kyiv faced an uncertain future after the collapse of their German and Austrian allies.

The Polish authorities were divided in their own estimation of where their eastern border should be. Their first claim in February 1919 was ambitious, the 'Dmowski Line' running well to the east of the Polish ethnic majority and including large territories in what is now central Ukraine and Belarus, where Poles made up less than 20 per cent of the population even by their own estimate.

There are, as we have seen, few geopolitical situations that cannot be worsened by an Englishman brandishing a map and a pen. The Curzon Line of 8 December 1919 was one of many proposed courses of Poland's eastern border that were circulating among the Allies immediately after the First World War. In fairness, the Curzon Line was far from the worst piece of British export cartography. It attempted to separate areas of Polish ethnic majority from the borderlands to the east where Poles were a minority, albeit one with an outsized cultural presence. In the north, it traced a frontier that corresponds more or less to the current state boundary with Belarus. The line between Poland and Ukraine came in two variants, one running each side of the city known to the Austrians as Lemberg, the Poles as Lwów and the Ukrainians as L'viv. The dilemma was that the city's population had a clear Polish majority, but the countryside around it was mostly Ukrainian, so there was no line that could be drawn without leaving hundreds of thousands of people on the wrong side.

Further, the borderlands between Poland and Ukraine were rich in Jewish life, as were the fertile plains of central Ukraine. Uman was the centre of the Hasidic movement. The intellectual life of Lemberg, and Żółkiew/Zhovkva to its north, produced – as the British-French lawyer Philippe Sands writes in *East West Street* – Raphael Lemkin (1900–59), who originated the term 'genocide', and Hersch Lauterpacht (1897–1960), who developed the concept of crimes against humanity. The Jews, city and rural, could have little faith in either nationalist alternative.

The Curzon Line and its meanderings were rendered moot by the outcome of the Polish-Soviet war that was fought in 1920–21 and ended with the Treaty of Riga. Poland's military success meant that the agreed boundary in Ukraine was much closer to the original Dmowski Line than either variant of the Curzon Line. Poland annexed all of Austrian Galicia, plus the former Russian province of Volhynia, where the Ukrainian ethnic majority was even larger than in eastern Galicia.

Poland's new borders did not reconstruct anything like the pre-1772 Commonwealth, but neither were they tightly drawn around the ethnic Polish heartland. It was too big to be comfortable as a nation state, too small to be a multinational federation, and the politics of all its borders and minorities were troubled throughout the 1920s and 1930s. The future of the Ukrainian–Polish mixed regions was overshadowed by the prospect of future violence to settle the conflict that had been left unresolved in 1921.

Poland's policies in its Ukrainian east were not liberal. Having suffered from German settlement policies of a colonial nature after 1908, Poles inflicted similar indignities on Ukrainians after 1921. Land reform was accompanied by attempts to encourage Polish settlers, and education policy favoured the Polish language.[10]

After the defeat of the Ukrainian movement in 1918–22, some nationalists – as elsewhere in the troubled Europe between the wars – became radicalised, violent and hostile to other nationalities, including Jews. A militant nationalist group, the Ukrainian Military Organisation (OUN), formed in 1929 and began sabotage and terrorism; the Polish state responded with a 'pacification' campaign in 1930. But the underground

remained active and its leader in eastern Galicia, Stepan Bandera, organised the assassination of the Polish minister of the interior in June 1934
and other lethal attacks on the Polish state and more moderate Ukrainian
political rivals.

The simmering conflict within Poland was overtaken in summer 1939
by the Molotov–Ribbentrop pact between Poland's enemies to the east
and west, followed rapidly by invasion and partition of the country
between the two. The Soviet Union moved the Ukrainian border far to
the west, to the banks of the San river at Sanok (Sianik) and Przemyśl
(Peremyshl) beyond Ustrzyki. Przemyśl became a divided city, the city
centre falling under Soviet control and the northern suburbs part of
Nazi-occupied territory.

The Soviet military built concrete defences along the partition line
they agreed with the Nazis, conscious that this 'Devils' Alliance', as the
historian Roger Moorhouse put it, might dissolve at any time.
Construction went fastest at the southern end of the line around
Przemyśl, but the forts were little use when German troops came pour-
ing across the line on 22 June 1941. They obstructed the advance for a
couple of days – the concrete carcasses of what is left of the Molotov
Line are still there, broken, in the woods – but the Germans reached
L'viv on the eighth day of the assault.

The scale of the violence that took place in the 'bloodlands'[11] of
Poland, Belarus and western Ukraine in 1939–45 has few parallels in
history. The German invasion was accompanied by atrocities against the
local population, particularly the Jews who were the victims of mass
extermination, at first by firing squads and then from extermination
camps. After the tide of battle turned at Stalingrad, the grinding Soviet
progress westwards was war at its cruellest, and there was a spiral of parti-
san warfare and atrocities against civilians.

Most Ukrainian nationalists had no love for the Soviet Union, which
had inflicted the Holodomor famine on the part of Ukraine it controlled
in 1932–33, and many welcomed the arrival of the Germans in June
1941. They had the same enemies – the Soviets, the Poles and, for the
many anti-Semites among the radical nationalists, the Jews. There were
some fond memories of Austrian rule. But these Germans were different, regarding Ukrainians with scarcely less racial contempt than they
regarded the Poles. They squashed the intended declaration of
a Ukrainian republic in L'viv on 30 June. Instead of having even a

Slovak-style puppet state, eastern Galicia was attached to the Generalgouvernement, which was a Nazi colonial regime in central and southern Poland. In the longer term, the Nazis intended that the native people – Jews first, then Poles and Ukrainians – would be exterminated, enslaved or deported and the region would become German, but in the short term it was a labour reserve.

Not having the powers of a state, the extreme Ukrainian nationalists of the UPA used terror to kill and expel much of the Polish population of Volhynia in particular, although the campaign extended into Galicia. Estimates of the death toll are contested and imprecise, but around 60–100,000 Poles were killed in spring 1943 and 15–30,000 Ukrainians died in Polish reprisals.[12] The Nazi authorities let them fight each other. When the Soviets arrived in 1944, they brutally suppressed both combatant forces and decided that the two peoples would have to be permanently separated. Many of the region's Poles were already running westwards, away from the Scylla of the UPA and the Charybdis of the NKVD, which had committed mass murders targeting Poles in the 1930s.[13]

The Second World War in Europe ended, for the most part, more definitively than the First World War. The Axis defeat was total, and the US and the USSR still had sufficient power and ruthlessness to put out the brushfires. But there were a few areas in which war continued for years afterwards in some form, including the parts of former Poland incorporated into the USSR. The UPA engaged Soviet forces in brutal fighting that took the lives of perhaps 30,000 people in the years after 1945. It was not until the 1950s that western Ukraine was fully pacified, even after the deportation of 76,000 to the Gulag in October 1947. This phase of the conflict enabled the UPA to present itself as a patriotic, anti-Communist, anti-Russian militia, a reputation burnished by Soviet propaganda that described any non-approved manifestation of Ukrainian nationalism as 'Banderite'.

Drawing the new border

In a legal sense, the USSR repudiated the Molotov–Ribbentrop border in an agreement with the Polish government-in-exile in 1941, but it was clear that Stalin still believed he had a legitimate claim to the territory east of it. In talks with the western allies, the Soviets dredged up the line drawn by Lord Curzon in 1919 and claimed – rather preposterously, given that the British Foreign Office still had their files – that the 1939 boundary was basically the same thing. Churchill and Roosevelt were prepared to accept the real Curzon Line, which approximated the pre-war line between Polish majority and minority areas, but Stalin traded it off for the Soviet acquisition of Königsberg. The Polish communists also negotiated some concessions, including the Polish share of the primeval Białowieża forest on the Belarus border where the legendary żubr, European bison, live.

Developments on the ground had, again, overtaken the negotiations of the Great Powers. The USSR had captured L'viv in July 1944 and had agreed with its Polish communist subordinates at Lublin in September that not only would it keep L'viv, but that there would be mutual ethnic cleansing to end the border issue once and for all. After the violence of 1943–44, the Soviet authorities started organised transfers of the remaining Poles from Volhynia and Galicia. Polish officials protected some of the interests of the deportees.[14] At first, deportations had to go slowly because the Red Army had not conquered enough of central and what was to become western Poland – they reached the pre-war border in Silesia in the south only at the end of January 1945. There was the ever-present risk with deportation that the train would go east, to Siberia and the Gulag, rather than west to the new frontier of the 'recovered' German lands.

Whichever side won control of L'viv, the city could never be its old self because nearly all its Jews – an essential part of its personality, and that of many smaller Galician towns – had been murdered during the Nazi occupation. There were savage pogroms when the Germans arrived in June 1941, with local nationalists encouraged to participate. The vicious concentration camp of Janowska was established in the north of occupied L'viv; 35–40,000 people died there, some after unspeakable cruelty. Many L'viv Jews died in the Bełżec extermination camp, which is now just across the border in Poland.

L'viv is another of those palimpsest cities of the borderlands, where the people have gone but many physical traces and even an intangible spiritual presence remain. Neither Polish Lwów nor Austrian Lemberg have entirely vanished, despite the replacement of much of the population in the 1940s by Ukrainians from further east and the efforts of

the Soviet Union to create a proletarian industrial city.[15] It is a paradoxical place, strongly nationalistic despite its border location and
history; its nationalist culture at once the most pro-western and the
most tone-deaf to how discussion of the past might sound to the west
of the border.

The intact physical condition of the inner city, with manifestations of
centuries-old diversity such as an Armenian cathedral, makes the past
instantly accessible. It is a city where one looks up, for unexpected details
like a stone owl that marked a bookshop when it was placed there in
1895, or a drunk centaur where there was a pub. L'viv is a Viennese-style
city of cafes and neurosis. When I first went, in 2007, I looked for the
birthplace of Leopold von Sacher-Masoch,* one of many unusual citizens. I found the location, an apartment block just west of the centre, but
the expedition was too easy and painless to be really satisfying.

Neighbours and friends?

It would be understandable if the 1940s, on top of the long history
between the nations, had permanently ruptured Polish and Ukrainian
national identities from each other. But the horror of those years inspired
determined work from the post-war dissident generation to make sure
that it never happened again; having suffered the cruelty of Stalin's border
work, there would be no more grasping for territory.

Healing the breach and recognising the harm done has been a
long-term effort for both Poles and Ukrainians. Polish intellectuals,
particularly the circle around the exiled Jerzy Giedroyc, who published
the literary-political *Kultura* magazine in Paris from 1947 until his death
in 2000, challenged the traditional attitude of Polish nationalism towards
its eastern neighbours. Instead of nostalgia for the Polish Kresy – the old
borderlands of big skies and multi-ethnic villages with Polish landlords
– or the politics of cultural condescension or resentment, there would be
reconciliation and neighbourliness. The Ukrainian émigré historian
Bohdan Osadchuk (1920–2011) first met the *Kultura* circle at the inaugural meeting of the (CIA-sponsored) Congress for Cultural Freedom in

---

*Sacher-Masoch (1836–95), author of *Venus in Furs*, was the unwilling inspiration
for Richard von Krafft-Ebing's term 'masochism'.

West Berlin in 1950. He became an integral part of the *Kultura* circle, although even within post-war intellectual circles people would still provoke each other with contentious claims about borders and history. In wider culture there was a deep freeze of ignorance, chilled by Soviet censorship.[16]

The conversations and essays of Giedroyc and Osadchuk had their influence on the dissident generation in Poland in particular, and seeped into the idea of Ukraine as a modern European nation. Osadchuk's project was as much a cultural initiative as a geopolitical one, and culture is always a work in progress – a cultivation of spiritual, as opposed to economic or military, bonds. In his address to the Verkhovna Rada alongside Polish President Duda, Zelenskyy proclaimed 'the time that Jerzy Giedroyc and Bohdan Osadchuk dreamed of has come'. Even before the war, Zelenskyy and Duda had discussed building a joint memorial on the border.

It has proved convenient for both Poland and Ukraine since 1990 to process the trauma as part of a shared history of oppression at the hands of Stalin and Hitler, who stirred the conflict, and the long history of Russian hostility to both countries. Repudiating communism meant that it was possible to accept the historical reality of the many crimes of the borderland, but attribute them to inauthentic non-national actors rather than regard them as stains upon national honour. Poland could disown the ethnic cleansing of Operation Vistula, Ukraine could recognise the Polish heritage of L'viv. Poland was the first country to recognise Ukrainian independence within its legal borders in 1991, a gesture of respect that was appreciated in Kyiv. The bloody futility of re-litigating the border was quickly acknowledged by the post-1989 Polish government. It, and the final abandonment of the vestiges of German claims elsewhere in the 1990 treaties, represented the new Europe's determination to draw a line under drawing lines.

Significantly, steps towards symbolic and practical Polish–Ukrainian reconciliation took place under governments of all political colours on both sides. In 2003, presidents Kuchma of Ukraine and Kwaśniewski of Poland unveiled a memorial in the Volhynian village of Pavlivka commemorating hundreds of Poles massacred by the UPA in 1943. In 2006 their successors, Yushchenko and Kaczyński, met in the Polish village of Pawłokoma, west of Przemyśl, where Polish fighters had killed hundreds of Ukrainians in 1945.[17] Duda and Zelenskyy attended a commemoration of the murdered Poles of Volhynia in July 2023.

While there is a will to move beyond the bitterness, the historical issues still rankle.

The Pawłokoma commemoration was vexed; the memorial to the murdered Ukrainians is non-specific about who actually did the killing, while a parallel monument to murdered Poles specifically names 'Ukrainian nationalists' as perpetrators.[18] As with Poles and Germans, the bishops have advanced the process of reconciliation. Alongside a July 2023 service conducted by Polish Catholic archbishop Stanisław Gądecki and Ukrainian Greek Catholic primate Sviatoslav Shevchuk, they issued a joint statement:

> Reconciliation is not an easy process; today, after the discovery of mass graves in Bucha, Irpin and Hostomel, we all understand how important it is to clearly name the perpetrators, exhume the victims, respect their right to a dignified burial and memory.[19]

Poles are understandably offended by Ukrainians who use symbols linked to the UPA, or glorify the memory of Bandera, and politicians and churchmen urge that Ukraine should acknowledge the Volhynia massacres as 'genocide', to use the word of the Jewish Galician Raphael Lemkin. Progress on exhuming and reburying the victims has slowed, but will be one of the historical issues to be addressed after the peace. Polish–Ukrainian friendship is to the forefront when issues of present and future are addressed, even if historical issues are recognised as difficult and there are the normal inter-governmental disagreements on matters like agricultural produce.

When the countries to the west of Ukraine joined the European Union in 2004–07, it vindicated Kundera's 'Central Europe' but also exposed the problems with the concept. 'Old Europe' and 'New Europe' had their happy reunion, while places such as Ukraine that were not included became the 'other' – regarded as a wilder eastern frontier. As Ben Tallis observed:

> This stigmatised them as not only more dangerous but also part of one of Europe's constitutive others – the 'Orthodox/Russian East' – the very perpetrators of [Kundera's] 'kidnapping' of Central Europe.[20]

Polish–Ukrainian reconciliation and integration at a practical level acquired an extra dimension, because the border became the edge of the Union (in 2004) and of Schengen (in 2007) and had to follow the rules for all external frontiers of the EU. The previously permissive approach to visas for Ukrainians had to be tightened. As with Ireland, the border is both an important political and economic distinction – Union or not-Union – and a place with its own distinctive features and historical baggage, where people's local connections overlap the line.

The European rules on the external Schengen border are not quite the cliché of 'Fortress Europe', much as that description fits places like the Spanish enclaves in North Africa and, increasingly, the frontier with Russia and Belarus. The Ukraine-Polish border has become an efficient filter rather than an inefficiently closed barrier around which smuggling and other criminality took place in the 1990s and early 2000s. The principal border crossing at Medyka, between Przemyśl and L'viv, saw waiting times reduced to hours; borders where drivers need to wait with their vehicles for days tend to become litter-strewn zones of petty crime and sex work.

A more orderly border enabled Poland (and therefore the EU) to sign a Local Border Traffic (LBT) agreement with Ukraine in 2008. This is one measure in the armoury to reduce the negative impact of a hard border on people who live near it and the arrangement with Ukraine is not unique (there was one with Russia around Kaliningrad for a time). Locals living within 50km of the border (i.e. not as far as L'viv), who had been resident for over three years, were allowed to obtain permits that exempted them from visa requirements. They were allowed to travel up to 30km into Poland, i.e. to Przemyśl but not much further. It freed up a lot of border control resources and for the local smuggling community the downside of the LBT agreement was greater surveillance and record-keeping. The proportion of people abusing the system was vanishingly small.[21]

Even before the war, Ukrainian migration into Poland had been increasing; 250,000 Ukrainians had full residence permits in Poland in 2021, and there were well over a million with year-long visas or visa-free. Just as Poland had supplied large quantities of labour to western Europe including the UK after 2004, the rapid growth of the Polish economy has sucked in workers from neighbouring countries, of which Ukraine is the friendliest and most familiar. Under a supposedly anti-immigration government, Poland had become more of a mixed country than it had been at any time since the deportations of the late 1940s. With the influx after the Russian invasion of February 2022, the proportion of Ukrainians among residents of Poland rose to 9 per cent, the largest foreign community within the EU.

The border at war

One of the original functions of the Transversal Railway cut through the Carpathian foothills was as a way of getting soldiers and supplies from the heart of the empire to places in what is now Ukraine, such as Stanisławów (now Ivano-Frankivsk), via a route that was better protected against the Russian military. These considerations suddenly became relevant again in 2022. When I visited in September, work was underway to restore the Transversal as an alternative route into Ukraine.

The south-east of Poland has traditionally been one of the most conservative, nationalist and anti-Ukrainian areas of the country. It is still both conservative and nationalist, but the anti-Ukrainian feeling melted away nearly completely on 24 February. An extreme Polish nationalist organisation organised a demonstration against Ukrainian workers and refugees in the main city, Rzeszów – a cause that would have enjoyed significant sympathy in 2021, when a majority in Polish public opinion opposed accommodating refugees, but proved a laughable failure in 2022. As war grinds on and other concerns come to the forefront, the fervour of unity may not last, but permanent foundations have been laid.

Rzeszów airport became part of the principal route for military and other supplies across the land border of Ukraine. In October 2022, it was a place of strange juxtapositions, the taxiways along which my Ryanair plane trundled being lined with Patriot missile batteries and the terminal a mixture of Polish families and uniformed and plainclothes military from all over NATO.

Ukraine's lifeline in the war runs across the Polish land border. In the early stages, refugees crossed in their millions and many people still come and go for family reasons. The road crossing at Krakovets[22] rumbles day and night with lorries heading into Ukraine. The train crossing from Przemyśl has become the place where foreign leaders steel themselves and enter a country under siege. In February 2023, US president Joe Biden boarded 'Rail Force One' for the ten-hour overnight journey from the border to Kyiv to talk to Zelenskyy in the embattled capital. President Duda of Poland is a frequent traveller. As Zelenskyy told him on one of his visits:

> We are defending a common universe for us called freedom and inde-
> pendence, at a time when someone is committing barbarism of a
> cosmic scale. Today the understanding, interaction, friendship and
> brotherhood of Ukraine and Poland reach the same scale. On February
> 24, we began writing a new volume of our history. Our common
> history – it is important. The unity of our nations must last forever . . .[23]

History is made by events, not memories.

17

'I came from nowhere'

(Ukraine/Slovakia/Hungary)

Khust is not a sophisticated metropolis. As I walked by a block of flats just outside the town centre I was startled by a hollow, knocking sound. I turned around and there by the bins was a dog with a calf's head in its jaws, shaking it vigorously to break the bones or rub off some meat. You will see horses pulling carts in the muddy and unpaved old side streets in the town centre, and the horizon is made up of forbidding green mountains. The market in Khust is full of old women in head-scarves selling handicrafts and herbs and mushrooms and fruit, just as their ancestors have done for centuries. Khust's population is a little under 30,000, comparable to, say, Kendal. What drew me to the town, apart from a desire to see life in western Ukraine away from the coffee bars of L'viv, was its unlikely history as a national capital, which is just about within living memory. Khust was the seat of the independent republic of Carpatho-Ukraine in March 1939, the romantic lost 'republic for a day'.

The ruins of Khust castle sit on top of a steep, lonely hill just south of town. Walking up the winding path to the top, one comes past several old cemeteries, one each for the Catholic, Uniate and Orthodox denominations, and a commemorative area for the short-lived independent republic. The USSR tried to suppress the memory and Ukraine was ambivalent about the experience of 1939 for a while, but in 2002 President Kuchma rehabilitated Avgustyn Voloshyn, its president, and the history of the little republic was incorporated into the official narrative. It did, after all, fly the blue and yellow flag and hoist the trident that are now both symbols of independent Ukraine.

The view from the top of the hill is worth the climb. Khust sits on a small, pastoral plain where cornfields and vineyards have long grown, as the Tisza river flows westward and the green hills separate the area from Ukraine-across-the-mountains to the right, Romania to the left and the next folded valley of Transcarpathia straight ahead. I went there as sunset fell and looked out on the landscape, but even here there were reminders that I was in a contested place. The Ukrainian flag flew tall, but a Hungarian tour party who puffed up the hill alongside me had a different perspective. Led by their guide, they sang a mournful-sounding song at the foot of the flagpole, looking out on what had once been part of their country.

Khust castle, March 2019.

The hills, the lack of industry or natural resources and the history of being in the shifting borderlands but away from the main trade routes have made this a poor, remote and mysterious region, whatever one chooses to call it – Transcarpathia, or Subcarpathia, depending on which side of the hills you are coming from. Communications with neighbouring parts of western Ukraine are slow, as the railway lines are chopped up by the current and former national boundaries and rugged geography. Getting from Khust to Kamyanets-Podilskyi, a journey of about 215km as the crow flies, takes 27 hours on the train, with a long stop in L'viv. The British historian A.J.P. Taylor (1906–90) quotably referred to

Bukovina, the province south-east of Carpathia, as being 'cut off from everywhere, a meaningless fragment of territory for which there could be no rational explanation'. The description fits Subcarpathia better than it does Bukovina. Perversely, it is at the junction of Slavic, Romanian and Magyar language groups, and the Catholic/Orthodox frontier, and a hill near the village of Dilove has a vigorously contested claim to be the geographical centre of Europe. But Ruthenia is still in the middle of nowhere.

Carpathian Ruthenia: the people of the hills

Intellectuals like Herder and the poets and linguists and politicians of the 19th century were creating a reality rather than describing one. Well into the 20th century, there were a lot of people in the borderlands who were basically indifferent to national labels. When asked to vote in plebiscites, such as the Upper Silesia vote in 1921, they made surprising choices, such as Polish-speakers choosing to stay with Germany. Sometimes states bid for their allegiance, sometimes they oppressed and expelled them. Sometimes nations even looked for purer versions of themselves in the borderlands. The process whereby nationality emerges is contingent on lots of factors. As we have seen, some areas are not naturally part of any particular state and lots of people have identities that do not neatly correspond to a 'national' area within a line on the map. Do they come from 'nowhere'?

Hill country and borders often go together because high ground is an obstacle to social exchange between lowland areas on each side, and therefore tends to result in differences of language and culture. The hills are also barriers to invasion. The highlands are often sparsely populated and rural, lagging the lowlands in economic development and connectedness and therefore, historically, nationalism. The hill people themselves were insulated from the corpus of literature and the formal language that were the building blocks of national identity. They often speak dialect rather than the literary form of the language, and have music and folk costumes that have been abandoned – or, more likely, never seen in that form – in the lowlands.

Nationalism is a paradoxical intellectual movement that tends to revere a supposed state of nature. The most developed nationalism in the

19th century was to be found among urban poets and university lecturers, but the ideology of nationalism itself was an aspect of the forces of modernity that conservative nationalism deplored as eroding what made their nation distinctive; hence the search for purity and rustic authenticity that took, for instance, Polish intellectuals into the hills in the 19th century. Sometimes the people of the highlands are slow to throw their lot in with a nation. The same hill culture can serve as inspiration for more than one national myth, as the Hutsuls of the eastern Carpathians do for both Poles and Ukrainians, or remain uncertain for a long time as different states and cultures contend for their allegiance.

One such ambiguous people is to be found where the modern borders of Poland, Slovakia, Hungary, Romania and Ukraine come close together. Once upon a time, most of the region was known to cartographers and travellers as Carpathian Ruthenia, but that name has faded from the map just as 'eastern Galicia' – covering some of the same land – did a century ago. The land is divided between modern states, the largest part being in Ukraine and smaller parts being in Slovakia, Poland and a tiny corner of Romania. To get to the country of the Rusyns still requires planning; to leave has often been a once and for all journey into the unknown. It is famous for those who have left, and the children of these emigrants, rather than those who have stayed.

Ruthenia is an elusive concept, related as it is to the old and vague idea of Rus. The hill country of the Rusyns, in the north-west of 'Ruthenia', never quite gelled into a country; it is one of the 'might have been' countries on the European map.[24] But it has its own national myth, largely – like most other national stories – the work of 19th-century poets. The Rusyn legend is of Prince Laborec, a ninth-century Slavic duke who resisted the advance of the invading Hungarians in the hills north of where Uzhhorod is now. The historical Laborec may well not have existed[25] but this Rusyn King Arthur is now commemorated in a majestic statue on a hill near the village of Habura, just on the Slovak side of the border with Poland. Laborec's plinth is packed with soil from Slovak-Rusyn villages.

From the 11th century onwards, most of Carpathia was part of the Hungarian crown lands of St Stephen, and its frontier location gave it impressive castles including the squat, functional one in Uzhhorod (Ungvár in Hungarian) and the romantic ruined edifice overlooking Khust (Huszt), though there was a shadowy portion that was on the

Polish (later Austrian) side of the hills. Carpathian Ruthenia was too small and poor to break through into existence in the heyday of the formation of nation states in the 19th and 20th centuries. It was surrounded by covetous and powerful rivals when the empire collapsed. The Rusyns were also divided among themselves, and shared their country with many other ethnic groups. Under Habsburg Hungary it was a particularly variegated multinational, multicultural corner of the central European world. Baedeker's *Austria* of 1896 notes of Maramaros Sziget,* the main market town of the eastern end of the region: 'The fairs annually held here present a curious mix of nationalities (chiefly Ruthenians, also Roumanians, Germans, Magyars, Gipsies, Slovaks, Armenians etc.)'[26]

One approximate indicator of Ruthenia was that many of the villages in the green hills of their region have wooden churches, usually Greek Catholic but occasionally Roman Catholic or Orthodox. Some are recent restorations, but a surprising number are original. Their survival in a region where armies have frequently marched through, burning and looting, is miraculous. Each church is different but similar; built on higher ground, with bulbous Eastern towers, devotional altars and icons and a creaky floor. Some of them are enclosed by a round protective wall. They are modest, artisan constructions, built without nails and held together by an ingenious system of interlocking beams and notches. Their glory is often in the wall paintings, vivid, centuries-old depictions of Bible stories and the hierarchies of angels and archangels below God, and the occasional grinning demon. My travelling companion, František, was keen on visiting them, both for aesthetic and family history reasons – an ancestor was priest in the village of Krempna, which is now in Poland. He was on a tour of wooden churches and lost villages; I was interested in learning more about the hilly Slovak–Polish borders and finding my way to the place where Andy Warhol's family came from. Realising that we were in the same region, doing the same sort of journey, we linked up through the unusual medium of Twitter. His company, and his car, were extremely welcome. We went to the UNESCO-listed Roman Catholic church at Hervartov, which meant obtaining the key

---

*Now Sighetu Marmatiei in Romania, separated from adjacent Solotvyno by the Tisza river and therefore the other side of the national boundary 1919–40 and since 1944.

from the volunteer caretaker, who was a bit surly and reluctant. František told him that I had come all the way from England to see the church, but he wasn't impressed: 'your new Prime Minister is terrible. She's even worse than ours.' The spectacular unravelling of the Truss administration accompanied me through the Polish–Slovak Carpathians; sterling collapsed overnight between making the taxi booking and taking the ride across the border from Svidník to Krosno, raising the cost by a couple of unexpected pounds.

The caretaker relented and let us in, and František and I marvelled at the place. The wooden Gothic church dates from 1499 and the art is mostly 17th-century. As another example of the fractal complexity of the borderlands, the Catholic faith and the village name indicate that at some stage the village was a settlement of Croats. There was a 'White Croat' population of great antiquity in the Carpathians, who were there in early medieval times before Croats settled the region that is now Croatia. Had Prince Laborec existed, he might have been classifiable as a White Croat. But people also moved around during the Habsburg empire, and there were many Croats and Serbs who fled across the contested borders between it and the Ottoman realm.

Hilly lands tend to be poor, particularly if they are distant from the main cities and lacking in coal or iron. Galicia was regarded as a backwater of the empire, and hardly anyone knew enough to form any stereotypes about the Rusyn region on the Hungarian side of the hills. Although Carpathia did not industrialise, its people did. 'Give me your tired, your poor/Your huddled masses yearning to breathe free' wrote the Jewish-American poet Emma Lazarus in 1883, raising funds for the Statue of Liberty, and Carpathia had many of those to give. From the 1880s until 1914, around 225,000 people left the hills for the United States. Young men crossed the ocean in search of prosperity but mostly went into mining and heavy industry in Pennsylvania. They said they wanted to work in America, but ended up working under America, breathing coal dust rather than free air. Some returned home, but the majority stayed and their families joined them. The east side of Pittsburgh, and the grimy industrial towns of the Monongahela valley such as Homestead in the shadow of Andrew Carnegie's steel works, became Rusyn country.

Andy Warhol used to say that he 'came from nowhere' – and he did invent and reinvent himself in the New York art scene. But he could not shake off his origins quite so easily. He was born into a working-class Rusyn family in Pittsburgh in 1928, the son of Ondrej and Julia Warhola, who both came from villages near Medzilaborce (now in eastern Slovakia). His friends John Cale and Lou Reed sang that he came from a 'small town' but Pittsburgh is pretty big; what was small and constricting was the ethnic working-class world of America that replicated Medzilaborce in smoky industrial Pennsylvania. Modern Pittsburgh has its glittering side, including Andy's museum in North Shore, but where the Warholas actually lived is now a neglected and ramshackle corner. Most of Medzilaborce looks better, and Medzilaborce is far from the most dynamic town in Slovakia. Homestead's population peaked at over 20,000 in 1920 but is now less than 3,000 and the steel works has been bulldozed and replaced by a mall.

There is a Warhol museum in Medzilaborce. As communism crumbled in the 1980s, a local teacher, Michal Bycko, became interested in Andy, and contacted Warhol's brothers and the US-based Warhol Foundation. Bycko was able to travel around the region to talk to Warhola relatives and collect artefacts. Communism's fall came just in time to remake many living connections severed by war and the Iron Curtain. There are still members of the Varchola family in the region, particularly at their home village of Miková. The local authorities were interested because the connection raised Medzilaborce's world profile above the run of obscure Rusyn Slovak towns, and a museum opened in 1991 in a brutalist concrete building given a splash of Pop Art colour. A statue of Andy stands outside, his skeletal umbrella a poor shelter against a rainy day in the Carpathians.

Like many people of my age, I've been through several stages in how I think about Warhol. When I was 16, he was the coolest man who ever lived; when I was 36, he was a derivative, superficial hack. But I see him through a different lens now, as an artist of the Rusyn borderlands, dislocated but unable to escape his origins however much he claimed to come from nowhere. As a child, little Andy went with his beloved mother and fellow artist[27] Julia to the local Rusyn church in Pittsburgh, losing himself among images imbued with spiritual significance. It was not until I went to Medzilaborce that I understood how Warhol's art reflected that Rusyn, Orthodox side of his identity. He was constantly creating and reinventing icons, reflecting on the adulation that western society was awarding

Andy statue at the Warhol Museum, Medzilaborce, September 2022.

commercial and celebrity images. I caught a glimpse of myself in the museum, my arms raised in reverence, holding a phone to take a photograph, in front of one of Warhol's images. I felt like an Orthodox pilgrim contemplating an icon at a holy place.

The politics of central Europe and western Pennsylvania were entangled, just as the personal lives of families like the Warholas were lived in a connected world of migration, return and blurred identity. The Pittsburgh Agreement of May 1918 put Czechoslovakia on the – future – map, and the July 1918 Homestead resolution of the Rusyn-Americans set out three options: autonomy within Hungary, autonomy with another state, or an independent country with their compatriots from the Austrian side of the hills. Their community organisations recruited a lawyer for General Motors, Jerry (Gregor) Zhatkovych of Homestead, to represent their interests.[28] He was good value in that respect; on 21 October 1918 he, other than Masaryk, became the only exile leader to arrange a personal meeting with President Wilson, where the president advised him that he would be best off seeking autonomy within a larger state. Strangely, there was a plebiscite of Rusyns on 1 December in which the votes were cast in the United States rather than the Carpathians;* the vote went the way Wilson and the community leaders wanted, with 67 per cent for Czechoslovakia, 28 per cent for Ukraine and the rest for Hungary or independence. Back in the region itself there was more support for independence and a 'Hutsul Republic' was proclaimed at the large mountain village of Yasinia in February 1919 but rapidly dissolved by Romanian troops. But the exiles and realpolitik prevailed, and the ex-Hungarian Rusyn region nearly all went to Czechoslovakia.† The Czechoslovaks were largely indifferent; as Masaryk told Karel Čapek, the idea was an American one and it was for the Rusyns to decide between Czechoslovakia, Poland and Hungary (in the absence of a coherent Ukrainian bid).[29]

It is hard to detect much enthusiasm from anyone involved. Decisions about nationality in this period were more about trying to back the right horse rather than the expression of a deeply held identity. Czechoslovakia probably was the best bet at the time for the Rusyns. One of the attractions of belonging to Czechoslovakia was integration with a wealthy state that had the best chance of any in the region of developing a democratic attitude to national minorities and therefore to the Rusyns. The principal alternatives were Hungary, which had a poor record with minorities and was regarded as a defeated power, and Ukraine, whose future was itself being fought over in a complex set of wars between the nascent Ukrainian state, Poland, the Bolsheviks and the Russian Whites.

Jerry Zhatkovych returned to Carpathia via Paris in March 1919 for the first time since he left with his parents in 1891 at the age of four. His mission, complicated by the continued conflict in the region involving local nationalists, Hungarian factions and Romania, was to co-ordinate the various nationalist councils in line with the American solution. He was successful and Masaryk's government appointed him the region's first governor under the Czechoslovak flag in 1920. Zhatkovych had a replica of the Liberty Bell sent from Philadelphia to Carpathia. The bell

---

* We do not know whether Ondrej Warhola had a vote or a voice in the plebiscite as it was somewhat informal, and his own national affiliation was fluid between Rusyn and Slovak, which was far from unusual.
† Part of the Rusyn claim, Maramureş went to Romania.

had been commissioned for the meeting of the Mid-European Democratic Union, Masaryk's association of stateless nations, at Independence Hall in October 1918.[30]

Zhatkovych did not stay long in what he considered the sovereign state of Rusinia. The Rusyn-Americans had demanded autonomy for the region, but like the Slovaks they were disappointed by the centralised paternalist Czechoslovak state that emerged. The borders of the region were also upsetting to the Rusyns, whose American advocates had claimed nine northern Hungarian counties, some of which had only tiny Rusyn populations. They ended up with less than half what they had considered theirs. The western border with Slovakia that was designated in 1919 was supposed to be provisional but rapidly became a permanent line, hence the inclusion of towns such as Medzilaborce and Svidník in Slovakia to this day.

Zhatkovych resigned in April 1921 to return to his law practice and political life in western Pennsylvania; he never visited his ancestral homeland again, although he engaged intermittently with its affairs until his death in 1967. Immigration restrictions imposed in the United States in the 1920s choked off the two-way flow of people and the Rusyn-Americans and their compatriots in Czechoslovakia and Ukraine had drifted apart even before they were cut off by the Iron Curtain.

The lost replica Liberty Bell from the Independence Hall meeting of 1918 is a rather direct metaphor for the failure of the Wilsonian attempt to export American idealism to a new Europe of free nation states governed by democratic republics. Even Masaryk's Czechoslovakia proved a disappointment. To Americans like Woodrow Wilson, self-determination was the solution to Europe's problems. But Wilson himself represented the dark side of America as well as the compromised ideals. The United States expanded with little regard for the self-determination of indigenous people, and ideas of American liberty co-existed with a rigid and ruthless system of racial segregation and oppression throughout the South, which Wilson extended into the federal civil service in Washington, DC. The dictatorships looked to America just as the national democrats did: Nazi Germany emulated American racial laws, the Soviet Union copied Fordist industrial production.

The idea of the continental empire and the frontier of settlement were reimported from America to Europe. In *Mein Kampf*, Hitler saw only a few possible dominant powers in the world – the United States, Soviet Russia, the British Empire and Greater Germany; before he rejected America, he admired its continental scope of ambition and its frontier mentality. Frontier and border have similar meanings, but they have different connotations. A border is a limitation, a place that acts upon the traveller and the states on each side. A frontier, in the American sense, can be a place of freedom rather than restriction. A border has two sides; the frontier purports to have only one. It is a place that is remade by the frontier settler, and a place where the settler can reinvent his own self.

Before the Wild Wests of post-1945 western Poland and the former Sudetenland, before the American West and British Australia, there were frontier territories in Europe. Ukraine after Russia's conquests under Catherine the Great and the lands of south-east Europe opened to the west by the long, slow Ottoman retreat after 1683 were settled at the command of the empires. But the freedom of the frontier comes at a high price, because there have been so few truly virgin territories in the tens of thousands of years that humans have been migrating around the world. One people's utopia is always built on another people's grave-yard.* The Nazi project for the settlement of Lebensraum involved neo-medieval fantasies of German soldier-settlers and their kitsch family homesteads stretched out along a long line north from Crimea, guarding the frontier from the barbarians of the east. It was no mere personal quirk that Hitler enjoyed Westerns, particularly those by the German author Karl May (1842–1912). They painted a picture of the inevitable advance of white civilisation against lesser races – sometimes noble and romantic, but destined for history's rubbish heap. Lebensraum was the German version of America's Manifest Destiny.

An appendage to Czechoslovakia

People were still leaving the Rusyn lands between the wars, even though the passage to America had closed. One such person was Robert Maxwell, born Ján Ludvík Hoch in what was then the Czechoslovak–Romanian border town of Solotvyno in 1923. Although he was dubbed

---

* The only exceptions are 'reclaimed' land – the Oderbruch of Frederick the Great, the polders of the Netherlands. But even there, the ecological costs may be high.

the 'bouncing Czech', Maxwell was never a Czech at all. He was a Jewish Ruthenian who joined the British Army after a wartime journey via Budapest, and made an even more circuitous journey via the House of Commons and newspaper barony to a grave at the Mount of Olives in 1991. Another Jewish refugee from the region, from the village of Ruscova just over the Romanian border (and, just like Solotvyno, in Hungary in 1940–44), was Bernat Hecht. Hecht fled to Wales in 1939 and his son Michael – the family name was anglicised to Howard in 1948 – became leader of the Conservative Party in 2003–05. Another Jewish family in the region produced the philosopher and humanist Elie Wiesel (1928–2016). Many of the Hoch and Hecht and Wiesel families who remained in their homeland died in Auschwitz in 1944.

International borders becoming fluid again at Munich was dangerous for regions like the Rusyn lands, caught between the longer-term interests of Germany in expanding to the east, the more limited territorial ambitions of Hungary and the persistence of rival ideas about the nature of the Rusyns.

The rapidly drawn border was a mess. The strokes of the pen on the map at Vienna sliced randomly across rural communities, disrupting the patterns of commerce and everyday life. The areas ceded to Hungary were the lower lands, with the towns and the communications routes, while Czecho-Slovakia kept the higher ground. Travelling to the eastern hill country left inside Czecho-Slovakia involved a lengthy bus ride on bad roads over the hills from the Slovak-Rusyn town of Prešov to Khust, which took over from Uzhhorod as the local capital. To the detriment of both sides, a hard border separated market towns from their rural hinterlands and legal commerce shrivelled overnight.[31]

This situation could not last, particularly as the authority of the Czecho-Slovak central government was crumbling and Rusinia was a pawn in the calculations of others. The little Carpatho-Ukrainian state assumed a strange degree of importance in the politics of Europe as a whole – in March 1939, it became the first place in Europe where shots were fired in anger in pursuit of territorial annexation since the early 1920s. In 2022 this history, which seemed a quirky byway, returned to relevance in a bizarre and unexpected fashion.

Republic for a day: Carpatho-Ukraine, 1939

The Carpatho-Ukrainian regime within Czecho-Slovakia held an election for the national parliament, the Soim, in February 1939. It was neither free nor fair – no opposition candidates were presented and there was a 92 per cent vote for the unity list proposed by the regime. Ruthenia was diverging rapidly from its recent Czech period; by early March, all Latin script and Czech language signs had been removed from Khust. There was an uneasy relationship between anti-Czech rhetoric and the concrete reality that the province's budget depended on Prague's generosity and the Czech armed forces and border guards were standing between Ruthenia and the obvious wolfish interest shown in the territory by Hungary and Poland, with an occasional glance in their direction from Romania, which claimed a section near Sighet.[32] The Ukrainians hoped that Germany would step in to fill the gap.

Czecho-Slovakia finally fell apart in March 1939. There had been increasingly bad relations between the nationalist government and the remaining bits of the Czecho-Slovak state in Ruthenia, which culminated in gun battles breaking out in Khust between Czechoslovak gendarmes and Sich militia. The streets of the town were immediately festooned with the bright blue and yellow of the Ukrainian flag. But it could not last. Hitler was ignoring the requests of what was now the Ukrainian government for recognition and assistance.[33] He had instead given Hungary the green light to invade and even as the independence-day parties were continuing in Khust, the Hungarians were crossing the border.

The Hungarian invasion was not bloodless, despite the disarray of the defending Ukrainian forces and the departing Czechs. The Ukrainians took refuge in the hills, fertile territory for irregular warfare, but the Hungarians closed in and they were squashed against the Polish frontier overnight on 17 March. Several hundred Sich fighters died in these battles, and when the conflict was over the defeated forces were either deported into Poland or, according to reports, massacred on the banks of the Tisza after being rounded up by 'mopping up patrols'.[34] The Carpatho-Ukraine leadership escaped into Romania. Although in western memory it was a quirky 'republic for a day', it is memorialised in Carpathia as having lasted from 14 to

18 March. In practice, it had been quasi-independent for four months before the formal declaration.

The Hungarian invasion was a real war with all the brutality that implies.[35] A legitimate successor state to the Czechoslovak Republic had been invaded by a foreign power; a red line in European affairs had been crossed. It was also an early lesson in how little Nazi Germany respected the nationalism of others; it was not Germany for the Germans, Poland for the Poles and Ukraine for the Ukrainians – it was German domination over their presumed racial inferiors.

The synagogue of Khust

The most remarkable building in Khust is the synagogue. Transcarpathia had a large and well-established Jewish population before 1939 – about 13 per cent overall, and much more in the urban areas where Jews were strongly represented in the skilled trades and commerce. Most of the tailors making the colourfully embroidered, quintessentially Rusyn clothes worn by the Hutsuls were Jewish. There had always been anti-Semitism in the region as well, and as in much of eastern Europe it was growing in the interwar period, but the events of November 1938 turned up the heat. The nationalist Sich militia harassed Jews, seized their property and relied on money extorted from them to sustain its activities. Although the government tried to reassure the Jewish population, the atmosphere of foreboding and lawlessness under the autonomous government in 1938–39 had many Jews trying desperately to obtain the right of residence in Britain or anywhere.[36]

From haphazard anti-Semitism under the post-Munich republic, things got rapidly worse when Hungary occupied Khust in March 1939 and applied its anti-Semitic laws to the region. When Hungary and Nazi Germany invaded the USSR in summer 1941, the mass murder began. In July 1941, the Hungarian authorities deported Jews who could not prove Hungarian citizenship across the border into Nazi-occupied Galicia. Most of them were murdered by the SS in mass shootings around Kamyanets-Podilskyi in August 1941, and some were drowned in the Dniester river. The local survivors' organisation estimates that 4,000 of the deportees were refugees who had sought sanctuary in Czechoslovakia (or Hungary 1939–41) and 14,000 were

Hungarian citizens who did not have their papers in hand. It was hardly surprising that a lot of people did not have the documents given that this rural, distant territory had only been absorbed into Hungary two years before, but no mercy was shown. 'May the Lord revenge their blood! May Their memory be blessed forever and ever!' as the memorial tablet at the Khust synagogue says.

When the Jews of Hungary proper fell victim to the Holocaust in spring 1944, the surviving population of Khust and the surrounding shtetls was rounded up and deported. Most, around 10,000 people, were sent to Auschwitz at the end of May but some were death-marched towards camps such as Mauthausen, deeper in Nazi-controlled Europe, and others were thrown in the Tisza river. Scattered survivors started to return as they were liberated from Nazi captivity by the advancing Red Army, and by summer 1946 there were 400 Jews again in Khust. There is still a Jewish community of around 165 people in the town.

Khust synagogue exterior, March 2019.

The synagogue's survival as a building is an extraordinary story. It was built on the main square of Khust during the flowering of emancipated European Jewish culture in the late 19th century. Huszt's position in the far east of Hungary meant that actual Nazi occupation lasted only a short time – from March 1944 until the town was taken by the Red Army on 24 October. The surviving synagogue was the depository for religious items and property looted from other synagogues and Jewish people and institutions in Khust, and escaped the vandalism and destruction that was the fate of so many Jewish buildings. When the Soviets arrived, they tried to take possession of the building for secular purposes, but in an astonishingly brave act of defiance the returned Jewish population, led by local women, kept vigil in the synagogue to stop it being Sovietised. Eventually, the communist authorities gave up and it remained with the Jewish community.[37]

Visiting Khust synagogue, as I did thanks to the kindness of Ze'ev, who was looking after the old scriptures there, packs an emotional punch. It didn't want to be special, it wanted to be a place that was patched up and evolved with the life of the community who gathered there, like the synagogues of countless towns across central and eastern Europe, like the places the Hochs and the Hechts attended in Solotvyno and Ruscova. Now, the building is a battered, beautiful survivor that still needs a lot of love. The floorboards are uneven and the wall paintings need a bit of restoration. The synagogue has a library of pre-1940s scriptures and books; these, sometimes dog-eared, books and the old stalls and seats spoke to me of the everyday religious life of the people who lived here. The Jewish community of Khust still worships here each Shabbat, in a modernised section of the same synagogue building that served the community before catastrophe struck. Standing in Khust synagogue one can marvel, and weep, at that poignant, fragile golden thread of continuity that endures in the borderlands, in defiance of the very worst the world can do.

Transcarpathian Ukraine

Despite its timeless air, modernity did come to Transcarpathia in the Soviet era. Khust lacked running water and mains drainage in 1939, and the pumps even in prime locations like Government House and the

Koruna Hotel sometimes produced nothing more than mud.[38] New housing blocks appeared around all the towns. The Carpathian region became increasingly popular for holidays, with its clean air, green hills and seasonal skiing providing a refreshing contrast to the flat plains and heavy industry of central and eastern Ukraine.

Little Transcarpathia had autonomous status under the Ukrainian SSR and preserved a sense of being a bit separate. In the independence referendum in 1991, the west was nearly unanimously enthusiastic, except for Transcarpathia — it voted for independence but turnout was comparatively low. There was nowhere else for it to go. It was culturally and politically distinct from the rest of western Ukraine; Transcarpathia was the only part of the west to vote for Viktor Yanukovych's 'Party of Regions' in the 2010 presidential election. Like nearly everywhere else, it voted for Zelenskyy in 2019. As well as its Hungarian minority, before the war some people still felt ambivalent about Ukrainian identity and feel that they are Rusyns first.

The Hungarian border attracts most of the traffic and most of the ill-feeling, but Transcarpathia has two other borders. Near Khust, the Romanian border is a forbidding range of hills, but further east it is along the Tisza river and there are several crossing points that unite the Ukrainian and Romanian sectors of the former Hungarian province of Maramureş. The towns of Solotvyno (Ukraine) and Sighetu Marmatiei (Romania) face each other across the river via a fragile-looking narrow metal bridge, although Ukraine is busy upgrading its crossings into Romania. A new railway bridge near Dilove — perhaps no longer the middle of nowhere — opened in January 2023.

The other border is with the eastern tip of Slovakia. This is an amended version of the line drawn on a provisional basis in 1919 between two constituent parts of Czechoslovakia but which now divides the Rusyn communities of eastern Slovakia and western Ukraine. This border grew steadily in significance and it is now part of the formidable external frontier of the EU and the Schengen zone. Queues on the main cross-border road at Uzhhorod could be epic before 2022.

I experienced some stern border control myself when I crossed from the Ukrainian rail checkpoint at Chop in 2019 — a vast, gloomy hall of a station in a very small town, once upon a time the entry point for trains from Czechoslovakia to the Soviet Union. The Ukrainian exit controls were in a customs zone of the station, after which I and the two other passengers were escorted by border police to a small, shabby and slightly smelly train that was travelling westwards to the Slovak town of Čierna nad Tisou, a distance of about 5km that took an hour to cover. This was not because of the decrepitude of the train, but because it ground to a halt at a border post where Slovak customs and immigration officers boarded the train and conducted a painstaking investigation. My three cans of Ukrainian beer – intended to anaesthetise me for the long night-train ride from Košice to Prague that was ahead of me – were duly declared and approved. The officers unscrewed all the ceiling panels in the train in search of contraband.

The glamour of international train travel, Čierna nad Tisou, March 2019.

Nevertheless, Uzhhorod prospers, as attractive border towns sometimes do. Arriving from Kyiv, one has to remind oneself that this is in the same country, so different is the atmosphere and landscape. No doubt a certain quantity of cigarettes and alcohol is sold for clandestine export, but from what I could tell on a wander around the town it was full of clothes shops, of which there were many more than a town of its size usually sustains. It is an easy-going sort of town, and tolerant of national ambiguity. In the castle there is a large iron Turul, a mythological creature from Hungarian legend resembling an eagle and said to have impregnated Emese, the mother figure of the Magyar tribes.[39] It was cast to commemorate the Hungarian millennium of 1896.

Carpathia has a Hungarian minority population. A relatively small proportion actively identify as Hungarians, but a larger number have Hungarian antecedents. Under Hungary's 2011 citizenship law, people able to prove their descent from pre-1920 or 1941–45 Hungarian citizens and who pass a loosely defined language test were entitled to apply for citizenship.[40] The criteria have been very generously applied. As of 2015, around 100,000 Carpathian Ukrainians had received Hungarian nationality through this route and about another 50,000 qualify in principle. This is a significant proportion of Transcarpathia's population of 1.2 million. The attractions are obvious for those that are eligible; it is a quick route to a prized Schengen area passport and the right to live and work across the EU. The emigrant tradition that sent the Warholas to the USA is still strong, and Transcarpathia's borderland history of changes in sovereignty is still relevant to people down to the present day.

The Hungarian law produced conflict with Ukraine long before the war, as it has with Slovakia. Ukraine is the territorial government of the region with a legitimate interest in building a united society within its borders. After a video of a citizenship ceremony appeared online, the Ukranian government took diplomatic action, expelling the Hungarian consul in the Carpathian town of Berehove, in the most Magyar section of the region in October 2018. Ukrainian law is less than clear about dual nationality, but there are accounts of hostility from border guards towards people with two national ID cards and the controversial video contained advice to hide Hungarian nationality from the authorities. Hungarian nationality is certainly useful, but getting the documents does not mean that the Magyar minority is anxious to secede from Ukraine, or is in any way disloyal to Ukraine in the current war.

Relations between Hungary and Ukraine got even worse after the Russian invasion of February 2022. Hungary's overt dependence on Russian energy, unwillingness to help Ukraine and persistent trash-talking of Ukraine's military efforts put it out of step even with other nationalist regimes within the EU and NATO, such as Italy under Giorgia Meloni. The Hungarian government has allowed Russian espionage and influence operations to flourish in Budapest and has repeated

Kremlin propaganda for domestic and international consumption. On at least two occasions in 2023, Russia released captured Ukrainian soldiers of Hungarian ethnicity to Hungary rather than Ukraine, highly suspect treatment of prisoners of war.

Many Ukrainians are suspicious that Hungarian complicity goes even further than that – that Putin told Orbán about his intentions and that he had dangled the idea of parcelling out Zakarpattiya to Hungary. In the early stages of the war, when Russia hoped for a quick victory, speculative maps appeared in Russian media suggesting that the western sections of Ukraine might be disbursed to Poland, Hungary and Romania – while Poland and Romania had no interest in this, Hungary might. As we have seen, there is a mutual understanding of autocrats who do not accept that borders are fixed, and regard the status quo as reflecting a disadvantageous balance of power. But it is contrary to the principles of the EU and NATO. Hungary has not been forced to choose, yet, between the geopolitics of Putin and membership of western organisations. But in Victoria Amelina's terms, it is not part of her European home.

18

The secret capital of Europe

(Ukraine/Romania)

The city of Chernivtsi (Czernowitz in German, Cernăuți in Romanian) is a little jewel. As soon as I arrived in the old centre, on a blustery rainy September day in 2019, I knew I was going to like it. It was the ultimate borderland, a place whose historic national identity was misty, and which stood on the frontiers of eastern, central and southern Europe while looking a long way to its west for its cultural roots. I stepped from the steamy trolleybus into a fantasia of elegant late 19th-century architecture, a townscape that resembles parts of Prague or L'viv. There is beauty in the ordinary here: an unexpected decorative flourish on a modest house, a sudden view down a hill and over the countryside, a street opening out into an exquisitely proportioned square. The public buildings, all dating from the same period, are ebulliently confident statements – particularly the crenelated red-brick university complex that occupies the highest point in the undulating city landscape. I sat writing in the Grand Café, a proudly nostalgic *Kaffee und Kuchen* establishment on the finest street in Chernivtsi, and imagined myself for a moment as a central European intellectual. But I also feel pain – not nostalgia, exactly, but a sense of loss that although I am in a beautiful and cultured place, it is also less than it should be. It represents a vanished civilisation that was systematically destroyed in the 20th century. Old Czernowitz was the property of no tribe or nation, but the achievement of many. Walking the streets of modern Chernivtsi, I feel almost within touching distance of this other Europe.

Bukovina, the region around Chernivtsi, was and is a borderland par excellence, at the fluctuating frontiers of empires, denominations and religions. Chernivtsi changed hands multiple times in the 20th century – in Ukraine since 1991 but before that in the USSR (1944), Romania (1941), the USSR (1940), Romania (1918) and the Austro-Hungarian Empire. Its personality remains mostly Habsburg, at least in the centre

279

(some outer suburbs are unmistakably Soviet), because its formative years in 1860–1910 were under the double eagle. The empire had acquired Bukovina in 1774–75 as part of a joint Russian–Austrian war against the Ottoman Empire, at a time when there were many territorial changes across Europe.

During the next century, Bukovina came to occupy a special place in the heart of the rulers of the increasingly complex multinational Habsburg empire. Precisely because it was such a blank slate, it could be made into a model province. The Bukovina project was based on the idea of extending 'civilisation' in the east through education and enlightenment, and thereby reflecting greater glory on the empire. The empire brought running water, paved streets, law and bureaucracy, schools and concert halls. Functional bits of open space in Czernowitz were transformed into elegant urban squares – Fischplatz became Theaterplatz, a grain-trading yard became Rudolfplatz* in honour of the heir to the throne now known mostly for the murder–suicide at Mayerling in 1889. The architecture was stylish and modern; Czernowitz was proud that leading architects from across the empire planned its new centre. In 1866 the railway came to Czernowitz, four years before there was a station in Kyiv, as people here will proudly tell you. The population swelled from 20,500 in 1851 to over 67,000 in 1900, making it one of the fastest-growing cities in the empire. As it grew, the city became increasingly Jewish and the community fglowered after the empire granted equal civil rights in 1867.

In 1875, Bukovina looked back with self-congratulation on a century of progress. The emperor decided to grant Czernowitz a university, an honour indeed for a distant province and a symbol of benevolence and enlightenment. Josef Hlávka(1831–1908), the Czech architect of the Vienna opera house, designed the university, which also served as a seminary and headquarters of the metropolitan (bishop) of the Orthodox Church. In deference to its borderland situation, chairs were established in Romanian and Ruthenian studies.[41] South of the university, a dusty piece of land on the edge of the rapidly growing city was laid out as Austria-Platz and a marble statue of Mother Austria was put up. Mother

---

*Prince Rudolf visited Czernowitz, and his square, in 1885 to acclaim from the local inhabitants. The square is now Filarmonia square, after its concert hall.

Theatre Square, Chernivtsi, September 2019.

Austria was clothed in imperial robes but the sculptor had made her voluptuous, a maternal archetype alongside the stern but kindly father Emperor.

The Bukovina project was about more than civilising public works. It was based on the co-existence and equal political rights of all the groups who made it their home. No national or ethnic group came close to an overall majority in Bukovina or Chernivtsi. Romanians and Rusyns predominated in the countryside, in roughly equal numbers, but the cities were extremely diverse. The largest single nationality in Czernowitz was Jewish (33 per cent) with 15–18 per cent each for Romanians, Rusyns, German-Austrians and Poles.[42] The city's middle class and skilled artisans were predominantly Jewish. The vague identity and sense of Chernivtsi as a crossing point applied even within the Jewish community, which was a blend of eastern and western cultural traditions – from people who could slot easily into a Viennese salon to mystical Hasidic devotees of the Baal Shem Tov, who walked these hills in the 18th century.[43] There were no pogroms in old Bukovina.

Bukovina's pluralism helped it function during the rise of nationalism as a political force within the empire. Alliances formed between different groups on different issues, with a general tendency for the Germans and Romanians on the one hand, and Jews and Ruthenians (Ukrainians) on the other, to co-operate.[44] Each nationality had its infrastructure of clubs and churches and its own community *Haus*, usually a rather grand building in the centre of Czernowitz. The Jewish community centre made no apologies for its presence in the Theatre Square, one of the most prominent places in this cultured town. It was and is impressive, decorated at the front by four Atlas sculptures representing the Jewish response to oppression: one assimilates, two shoulder the burden, and one looks to a far horizon – of equality, of Zionism?

The idea of Bukovina as a harmonious place, where people from different ethnic and religious communities lived tolerantly together under the benign aegis of the paternal emperor, was a seductive vision. Its regional identity was as a place of diversity, while there was also a strong sense of allegiance to imperial institutions; while there was consciousness of 'national' differences, what was missing for the most part was nation-state nationalism. As the historian Jeroen van Drunen recently observed, the notion of a 'Bukovinan people' conflicted directly with the core idea of nationalism, but the concept clearly had validity.[45] There is enough truth in the legend of Bukovina for it still to inspire as an example of unity in diversity, although the reality inevitably came with its messy and problematic aspects and popular sovereignty was tightly restricted.

Czernowitz was and is a city of stories and storytellers. I was shown some of the city's sights by Halia Marchenko, an illustrator who is a graduate of the university. She told me about Eugen Hackmann (1793–1873), Bukovina's first civilian governor who went on to become the metropolitan of the Orthodox Church in the region and had been a tutor to the imperial family in Vienna.[46] There was the illustrious Anton Kochanowski (1817–1906), a Polish aristocrat who was elected seven times to the city's mayoralty for a German political party and did much to establish the civilised way of life that characterised the city and is still an important influence. The great civic works of its squares and theatres were erected during his rule, but so were less prominent but more important amenities – piped water, sewage, electricity and a tram line. He lived in an apartment in City Hall for much of his term, and when he retired he paid for a new, modern clock for the tower of City Hall – the building still has two clock faces. Jewish politics was led by the redoubtable Benno Straucher (1854–1940) – the power broker of city politics who led the largest block on the city council and represented the area in the Austrian Parliament.

Perhaps because of the youth and heterodoxy of most Czernowitz intellectuals and the city's juxtaposition of many cultures, its intellectual climate could be eccentric. Old Czernowitz produced more than its share of inventors and authors and dreamers. Joseph Schumpeter (1883–1950) taught economics at the university; his ideas about long cycles of development and decline and his non-Marxist prophecy of the eventual self-destruction of capitalism have long seemed intriguing and quirky, difficult to fit into mainstream frameworks. Perhaps it is time now for a rediscovery of Schumpeter, who is mostly known for his concept of 'creative destruction' as the engine of progress under capitalism. Not to be outdone by Lemberg (L'viv) and its native son Leopold von Sacher-Masoch, Czernowitz educated Wilhelm Reich (1897–1957), the wayward apostle of psychosexual liberation and orgone energy, and Freud's disciple Wilhelm Stekel (1868–1940), the principal early analyst of paraphilias and sadomasochism.*

While Czernowitz was known as an outpost of civilisation, Bukovina had a distant, exotic mystique about it – Half-Asia (*Halb-Asien*), as the Jewish Czernowitzer Karl Emil Franzos 1848–1904 called the province in an 1876 book. To Franzos and many others, the city was a little island of western enlightenment in a sea of superstitious eastern backwardness. Gregor von Rezzori (1914–1998), another son of Bukovina, evokes the sense of his small town as a distant outpost on the perimeter of civilisation:

> Especially at night, when you approached it from a distance, its forlornness under the starry sky touched you to the quick: a handful of lights scattered over a flat-topped hill at the bend of a river, tied to the world solely by the railroad tracks, which glistened in the goat's milk of the moonlight. The firmament was as enormous as the huge mass of the earth, against whose heavy darkness these signals of human presence asserted themselves with a bravery that could scarcely be called reasonable.[47]

*Reich and Stekel were in local high schools rather than the university.

Czernowitz, as a beacon lighting the frontier, depended on the Austrian Empire, an always improbable political entity that did not cope well with the colossal strains of the Great War. Bukovina was on the military frontier between Austria-Hungary and Russia and was conquered and lost several times by the Russian army. Russian occupation was a shock to tolerant Czernowitz, particularly its Jewish population, who faced discrimination and violence. But the other local communities did not abandon them; their Torah scrolls were kept safe by the Orthodox metropolitan and returned to the Jews after the war.[48]

Although the threat from Russia's empire was repelled, Austria-Hungary staggered on to defeat against a host of lesser powers. The relevant one in Bukovina was Romania, which had coveted the territory because of the large Romanian-speaking element of its population. Somewhat improbably, Romania did well out of the end of the Great War. The country had only joined the fighting in August 1916, hoping to gain long-coveted Transylvania from Austria-Hungary, but fared poorly in the war and was left isolated when Russia was knocked out and came to an armistice with the Central Powers in December 1917. The draft Treaty of Bucharest in May 1918 was reasonable in its territorial terms but would have made Romania constitutionally more or less a German vassal state, and it had not been ratified by the time Germany and Austria-Hungary were collapsing in autumn 1918. Just in time – on 10 November 1918 – Romania re-entered the war. As well as gaining credit for being on the winning side, Romania also benefited from having a functioning state and military in a chaotic region. Romania was therefore able to create facts on the ground in Transylvania and Bukovina that helped shape the Paris settlement in her favour. One of many short-lived Ukrainian states was formed in Czernowitz in November 1918 but it was taken over by Romania within a week. The British-born Queen Marie led a successful delegation to Paris in 1919 that pressed home the Romanians' advantages, while in central Europe Romanian forces launched a successful invasion of communist Hungary and occupied Budapest. Romania's borders after 1920 were about as wide as they ever possibly could be; the interwar state fulfilled the century-old nationalist idea of 'Greater Romania'.

Like many states in the reorganised eastern Europe, the new government insisted on a rapid conversion to the language of the new dominant population, in this case the Romanians. Czernowitz quickly became

Cernăuți, the street names changed and the monuments that dotted the city were taken down or restyled to fit the new regime. The Mother Austria statue was first to go; she vanished in 1918 soon after the Romanians arrived. The language of instruction at the university was abruptly changed to Romanian, and many of the faculty left never to return. Ukrainian-speaking teachers and civil servants lost their jobs. Jews, free of anti-Semitic laws since 1867, felt the net tighten from the moment in 1920 when they were restricted to a maximum proportion of students at the university. Anti-Semitic incidents, previously rare, became more commonplace, particularly in areas where the Romanian nationalist Iron Guard operated.[49]

Despite these conditions, Cernăuți's lively literary and intellectual scene continued to make it a little Vienna beyond the mountains. The 'Bukovinan Caruso' Josef Schmidt (1904–42) was one of the most sought-after singers in Europe. The Ukrainian community politician Volodymyr Zalozetskyj-Sas was another legendary interwar Czernowitzer. A doctor of law (Czernowitz) and philosophy (Vienna) and art historian, he lived in a fine house on Herrngasse* in Czernowitz, earning fame – and a lifetime supply of milk – by chasing a thief out of the nearby dairy. He had a swashbuckling career: taken prisoner by the Russians but returning in time to be involved in the short-lived Ukrainian government in the city in 1918, and returning – after a brief period of exile – to take a seat in the Romanian Parliament. He was one of the best-received ambassadors for the Ukrainian cause, speaking to British MPs in July 1937 about the Holodomor. He was also an architect and the promoter of a puppet theatre that toured across western Europe and appeared on German and Austrian television in the post-war years. Following the Soviet seizure of power he left home again, living in Vienna and leading the Ukrainian and Bukovinan exile community in Austria until his death in 1966.[50] Multiculturalism survived, and there are a few architectural flourishes from the Romanian period, but the light was fading.

The Russians came back to Cernăuți in June 1940 as the pact of Hitler and Stalin cast its dark shadow over Bukovina. The fall of France was quickly followed by a series of ultimatums from the Soviet Union to its neighbours and in the harsh new Molotov–Ribbentrop Europe there

---

*Known as Yanka Flandor Street during the Romanian period, Olga Kobylyanska Street today.

was little hope in fighting as Finland had done the previous winter. The tribute demanded from Romania consisted of the territory of Bessarabia, whose annexation Russia had never accepted,* and the northern part of Bukovina, including Chernivtsi. Romania was allowed to keep the southern part of the province around Rădăuți and Suceava. Hitler suggested to the Romanian leader Ion Antonescu (1882–1946) that Romania would have a chance to win back the lost territory before long, but the Romanians also had to swallow the humiliation of being forced to give up some more of its 1918 gains to its other neighbours Hungary and Bulgaria in the Second Vienna Award in August 1940.

The NKVD set up shop in a grand house in Chernivtsi's Herrngasse, and their arrival in the province had its usual gruesome consequences – executions, deportations and terror, which fell on all the communities that were part of Bukovina's multicultural life. The Bukovina Germans were encouraged to go 'home' to Germany – a country many of them had never visited, ruled from a city, Berlin, that had never been their capital. They, like Baltic and Volga Germans, were fodder for Nazi racial settlement schemes in Poland, whether they liked it or not.

When Bukovina reverted to Romania in June 1941, the terror continued at the hands of Hitler's allies. Deportations, pogroms and the burning down of a synagogue preceded the establishment of a ghetto in Chernivtsi in October 1941. The Antonescu government in Romania was one of the nastiest home-grown fascist regimes in eastern Europe. It had its own peculiar blend of anti-Semitism and xenophobia. It would engage in mass murder of foreign Jews without compunction, massacring tens of thousands in the camps of occupied Transnistria; the Romanians had a worse reputation than the Germans in occupied Odessa.

At home, and this included Bukovina, Romanian terror was more chaotic and haphazard; the regime refused to deport Romanian Jews to Auschwitz not out of any human feeling but because it regarded them as a Romanian problem for Romanians to deal with. It was possible, with enough persistence and if one caught the authorities in a good mood, to

---

* The legal status of Bessarabia as Romanian territory under the 1920 Treaty of Paris had also been incompletely ratified, although international law was not a primary concern of the USSR. Bessarabia overlaps substantially with the modern state of Moldova.

navigate through the many cracks in the structure of oppression. The government imposed a new mayor, Traian Popovici (1892–1946), when Chernivtsi was reoccupied in 1941, but he proved to be anything but a pliant tool of the oppressors. He argued that Chernivtsi could not survive economically without its Jews and pragmatically argued that among other things all the plumbers were Jewish and the city would start to rot and stink if they were deported. He stopped the deportations in November 1941, although thousands had already gone. He then got permission to issue a few hundred exemption certificates but used this as the thin end of the wedge and by the time he was dismissed in summer 1942 he had issued 19,500. In terms of numbers, Popovici was one of the most notable Righteous Among the Nations. Although things in Chernivtsi got worse after his dismissal, the Romanian government's purges were wound down as the Nazi empire reached its limits at Stalingrad. Popovici had saved Jewish Czernowitz from complete destruction.

The turning of the tide of war meant that sooner or later the Russians would be back at the frontiers of Romania. The Red Army took Chernivtsi on 29 March 1944. When they launched the big offensive on the rest of Romania in August 1944, the result was devastating. King Michael of Romania dismissed Antonescu and sued for peace with the allies.

Stalin, however, was not going to disgorge his Molotov–Ribbentrop gains at Romania's expense and Bessarabia and northern Bukovina were returned to the USSR in 1944. Most of Stalin's borders across eastern Europe were deliberate violations, impositions of lines on the map that would work only with mass deportations and cruelty. The border that divided Bukovina was an exception, in that it did a reasonably fair job of separating mostly Romanian southern Bucovina around the city of Suceava, and mostly Ukrainian northern Bukovina around Chernivtsi. There were minorities left on both sides, but in communist Europe and afterwards they were allowed a certain amount of cultural autonomy and rights to cross the local border.

There is little demand now, even among the more extreme Romanian nationalists, for the restoration of northern Bukovina to Romania. The one slight exception that rankles is the Hertsa Land, a tiny region of a few villages that had previously been associated with the Romanian province of Moldavia but was annexed to Soviet Ukraine. Perhaps Stalin could not draw a boundary line without some element of wilful devilry. The people encouraged to leave Chernivtsi were replaced by what was intended to be a population of standard-issue 'Soviet citizens'[51] but the mysterious charm of the city proved impossible to expunge.

Chernivtsi slept in the Soviet era. It was of little strategic interest anymore and the Bukovina border generated little trade. It was given a collar of concrete suburbs and a course of renaming of streets. The university did little of note, in contrast to its lively Austrian origins, until in a piece of very late Soviet opening-up in 1989 an academic led a successful campaign to name the institution after Yuriy Fedkovych, a 19th-century Ukrainian man of letters. As the Soviet system eroded, one of the biggest, earliest international trading markets was established in a yard in the north of the city. Traders from the USSR and Romania, and not long after that all over eastern Europe and the near east, converged on Kalynivskyi market to wheel and deal and the market grew to huge proportions. Chernivtsi was returning to its roots. Kalynivtskyi is still there, a maze of sea containers and hawkers where one can buy nearly anything – or at least, one could before February 2022.

Soviet Chernivtsi's population became steadily less diverse, as the remaining Germans left for the west, Romanians drifted south, and many Jews migrated to Romania prior to emigration to Israel, France or the US. For Jews from the rest of the USSR, Chernivtsi's surviving community infrastructure and its southern location felt like a warm breath of freedom and the city became a centre for the 'refuseniks'.[52] Chernivtsi's exiles included the important German-Jewish poets Paul Celan and Rose Ausländer, who wrote from the vantage point of their lost city about Heimat, language, the Holocaust (both had experienced the ghetto and the camps) and the pain of belonging to and estrangement from German civilisation; Celan rejected the German philosopher Theodor Adorno's concept 'no poetry after Auschwitz': he tried to express the horror in his work such as 'Todesfuge' (Death Fugue). Celan died in Paris in 1970; Ausländer felt the call of Germany and lived her last few years in Düsseldorf, dying there in 1988. To people who had grown up in the benevolent world of Czernowitz, the bond between Germany, Europe and civilisation was too strong even for the Nazis to break. Selma Meerbaum-Eisinger was another poet from the twilight of old Czernowitz; she died in a work camp in Ukraine in 1942 at the age of eighteen but had already emerged as a talented poet and translator.

Literary Czernowitzers were often prodigiously multilingual – Celan could translate from nine languages and at eighteen Meerbaum could work in German, French, Ukrainian and Hebrew. The breadth of understanding and knowledge that was available to these people without leaving their home town! It is to the journalist Georg Heinzen that I owe my chapter title, in his affectionate, half-parodic description of old Czernowitz:

> Czernowitz, auf halben Weg gelegen zwischen Kiew und Bukarest, Krakau und Odessa, war die heimliches Hauptstadt Europas.[53]

> (Czernowitz, halfway between Kiev and Bucharest, Krakow and Odessa, was the secret capital of Europe.)

The city was:

> where the sidewalks were swept with roses and there were more book-stores than bakeries. Czernowitz was a perennial intellectual discourse that invented a new aesthetic theory every morning and had rejected it by the evening. Where the dogs bore the names of Olympic gods and chickens scratched verses from Hölderlin into the ground.[54]

How dare, *how dare*, anyone ever say that the multilingual, the cosmopolitan, the intellectual, are 'citizens of nowhere' or do not have the connection with territory that 'authentic' people feel? I had vaguely heard of Celan and Ausländer before I wrote this chapter, but Meerbaum was new to me. I wish she had been given the time to say more and I wish the unique culture that nourished her had flourished for longer.

Chernivtsi is still difficult to get to, except from Kyiv where there are two night trains in each direction and a very occasional flight. It takes considerably longer from Vienna than it did in 1900. Crossing the border to Suceava and southern Bukovina involves a tedious wait at the featureless border station of Vadul-Siret if you go by rail, or a long queue at the road border. The university now has a medical school, progress since its day as Franz-Joseph University, and in that section of it the language of education is English (no more tedious debates between different forms of nationalist here). The sense of Chernivtsi as a crossing point, where cultures meet, is slowly seeping back. Walk along the elegant showpiece avenue of the city, Olha Kobylyanska* (formerly Herrngasse, making its current name a pleasing and unusual bit of street-name feminism in central Europe), and it is looking as splendid as it ever did, with its grand mansions, coffee houses and institutions of the Romanian and Polish communities all restored.

The proximity to the Romanian border is evident in modern Chernivtsi. The statue of the Romantic poet Mihai Eminescu (1850–89) is garlanded by yellow and red wreaths, laid by admirers of his epic poem *Luceăfarul*. As with other parts of western Ukraine, the complex history creates loopholes and back doors for its people. Many qualify for Romanian passports based on the 1918–44 period, and therefore the right to live and work in the EU. Bucovina was less contentious within the EU than Moldova, many of whose working-age citizens acquired Romanian nationality and instantly seized the opportunity to go west. Romania, and the Romanian minority, were apprehensive about the impact of the Ukrainian government's nation-building policies and the education law of 2017, which required primary education to take place in the Ukrainian language. But there was no breach, in contrast with Hungary.

As the region passed from the USSR to independent Ukraine, and the Habsburg-era city centre started slowly to be restored to vitality, people occasionally wondered where the Mother Austria statue had gone but nobody who knew was telling, and it is quite possible that nobody alive knew at all after the horrifying upheavals of 1940–46. In 2003, she was rediscovered in a storage chamber below a bank, a few metres away from the square where she had stood. She was missing a head and her right hand, but otherwise in good condition. There was an exhibition in 2006 in which replicas of the truncated Mother Austria were given to contemporary artists to modify; one was given a Lara Croft body modification, one was plastered with advertising, one was covered with a burqa. They now reside in the entrance hall to the university. The missing pieces of the statue have not yet turned up, but even a century later there must still be some chance of recovering them. The search for Mother Austria is a heavy-handed metaphor for people of Chernivtsi trying to re-establish

---

* Kobylyanska (1863–1942) was a feminist, novelist and, like everyone in the city it seems, multilingual and multicultural. She was Ruthenian by identification but had German and Polish family background as well and wrote mainly in German.

the cosmopolitan origin of the city, which was covered over by commun-ism and nationalism but is now tantalisingly accessible, if in a neglected and mutilated form.

Mother Austria, in the entrance hall of Yuriy Fedkovych
Chernivtsi National University, September 2019.

Chernivtsi, with its legacy of Mother Austria, brought together many of the threads that I picked up in my exploration of the borderlands of Europe. As I travelled, I learned to love borderlands for more than the quirky anomalies of Baarle, Clones or Campione. Borderlands upend the false opposition of the local, rooted and connected to the liberal and cosmopolitan. The life of Robert Schuman, a provincial bourgeois in his life and politics, straddled France, Germany and Luxembourg and there are millions of people like him, who know where their home is but do not regard their national affiliation as all-important. Chernivtsi is the true home of the local cosmopolitan, just as much as Luxembourg, Berlin or London.

Chernivtsi's history renders foolish the idea that multiculturalism was new to European history; the ethnically cleansed straight-line borders such as the Oder–Neisse Line or the Curzon Line were the real innovations. They were there because of the escalation in hatred and violence in mid 20th-century Europe that had resulted in catastrophe. Different peoples have lived together – not always comfortably, of course – for longer than they have lived apart. A living continent is constantly changing, as Friedrich Naumann imagined his *Mitteleuropa* pullulating with life; the rigid, sterile classifications that Hitler and Stalin imposed on Europe and with which we lived for decades are deadly as well as boring.

Liberating nationalism, of the sort championed by Herder and the poets and politicians of the early 19th century against the rule of empires, has its positive side. But I came to dislike, even more, the hectoring nature of official nationalism, which tries to eliminate the pluralism that emerges around the edges and in the large cosmopolitan cities alike. In Poland and Czechia, I learned that nationalism and communism were not opposites; that communists were capable of cynical and successful appeals to popular nationalism, particularly in the ethnically cleansed borderlands, that mobilised people behind the red flag.

Russia's way of war has been genocidal for a lot longer than Putin's bloody adventures in what he thinks of as rebel imperial territories. But the attitude to treaties and borders is also a radical repudiation of international law and the understandings that make civilised life possible. Wars of conquest, if permitted, make every border on Earth potentially just a provisional line of control before the next war starts. Annexation is much more serious in the world of nation states than it was in the pre-1815 dynastic empires, where it did not imply forced submission of one nationalism to another. Part of the purpose of this book, as it evolved in the years between 2017 and 2023, has become to explain the profound evil of annexing a territory, and that in modern times it means oppressing, expelling or killing the local population.

For the borderlander, exchanging one set of majoritarian oppressors for another is usually not much progress. Better that national identity is conceived as something civic and capacious, rather than ethnic or monocultural. As St Stephen, the founding and greatest monarch of Hungary, put it a millennium ago:

> The utility of foreigners and guests is so great that they can be given a place of sixth importance among the royal ornaments . . . For a country unified in language and customs is fragile and weak[55]

Revising borders, even without evil intent, is a fool's errand. There can be no ideal state of national borders, so there is merit to sticking with what one has even if it is unsatisfactory, as is the case to a much greater extent in Africa than Europe. History and ethnicity are too slippery to be valid ways of defining borders. Being obsessed with old borders or ethnic grievance, the direction in which Hungary and Russia's governments have tried to influence their societies, is a quick way to become sadder, angrier and poorer. Just across the Hungarian–Romanian border, in the city of Oradea, there is an example of prosperity and progress that embraces its multicultural identity; the gap will surely widen as years go by.

Looked at through the perspective of Oradea, or Luxembourg or Switzerland, the mixed borderland is a strength rather than a weakness. The people of the borders can offer a way towards understanding one's neighbours, making peace and trading with them, rather than fighting for territory. A borderland is a place where connections are made as well as where lines are drawn; the question is the balance between the two. A hard border defines the limit of trust; while we cannot trust indiscriminately, a world without trust is a bleak place indeed. Donald Trump promised in 2016 to 'build a great, great wall. On day one, we will begin working on an impenetrable, physical, tall, powerful, beautiful, southern border wall.'[56] Trump's celebration of the virility and power of border walls struck me as profoundly sinister, a sign of a fascist mentality. Border walls are not beautiful; they are some of the ugliest places on Earth. A hard, sterilised border creates a miasma of human misery on both sides; desperate people, a degraded environment, fear and barely suppressed violence all around. Most defenders of hard borders regard them as a necessary evil, not as something 'beautiful'.

'Borders make you poorer,' as the former Czech prime minister told me. But conscious of the Russian invasion and Victoria Amelina's idea of 'home', perhaps we can say instead that borders are expensive and need to be paid for; we need to be sure that putting up barriers to states and peoples is worth it when we do it. The ease with which the British can forget that their state has a land border, and that the sea has always been a place of exchange and commerce, is an obstacle to a clear-sighted accounting of the costs and benefits of restricting life at the borders. The countries of mainland Europe have been forced to face this, and have chosen to have open borders with each other – albeit with a pragmatic web of special cases and temporary exceptions. Political trends in many countries in Europe have recently been hostile to migration, and therefore suspicious of open borders. However, it is unlikely that decades of progress and integration in the borderlands will go into reverse. Even on as troubled and fortified a border as Hungary's with Serbia, anti-migrant politics is combined with measures to soften the impact of the border on its immediate neighbours.

As I conclude the book, I ache to return to Chernivtsi, be that in wartime or peacetime. My visit in September 2019 generated many powerful memories. I find myself drifting back to a particular moment there when all my inchoate feelings about local and European history and culture came together for me. I was sitting, overcome by nostalgia

Former Austriaplatz, Chernivtsi (September 2019).

by proxy, in Soborna Square, Austria-Platz as was, between the heavy red marble memorial to the Soviet Unknown Soldier and the terrace that looks out over the little park in the middle of the square. Gradually, music filtered into my consciousness, a gentle but occasionally halting Chopin melody on a solo piano, as if time had become jumbled and I was hearing an auditory fragment of old Czernowitz. A few minutes later, another less practised piano player took over the piano at the music school across the street and bashed out the start of Bach's Toccata and Fugue. The ominous thudding brought me out of my reverie and back to 2019. I looked out at the square, at the flower bed where Mother Austria once stood and where now two flags fly side by side – the blue and yellow banner of Ukraine and the blue with gold stars of Europe. Even a secret capital should fly its flag. Under those flags, Chernivtsi aspires to reconnect with its past as a sophisticated city, and live once more in ambiguity alongside the other treasured jewels of Europe's scintillating borderlands.

Acknowledgements

Family is the first debt. This book owes its origins to my father, Vic Baston, and my mother, Jill Baston, who encouraged my interest in travel from an early age. As I write in the Introduction, they took me over my first land border in 1984. They, and my sister Ros Baston, put up with a long coach journey across Europe because they thought, correctly, it would fire my imagination. They have supported and encouraged me ever since. Hannah Nicholson, my wife, has lived with this book – and the heaped towers of other books I have been consulting at home – for five years, although it must feel like longer sometimes.

Two friends deserve special thanks. Samantha Sharp has constantly encouraged me to get on with it, had faith in the project, asked intelligent questions and given much valuable research assistance. Her lively mind and endless curiosity about our world have given me an idea of what the book's reader will be like. Donna Sharpe has been with 'Das Buch' ever since the beginning and has read many sections in drafts that have gradually come into focus, her scriptwriter's eye alert for dullness and infelicity and their opposites. The book would not be what it is without Donna and Samantha.

Several of my journeys along the way have been brightened by the company of others. I have been on road and rail trips with Jon Worth to at least five border zones, some as part of his own #CrossBorderRail project to encourage better public transport in the borderlands. Hannah Nicholson, as well as putting up with me for years, came to the German-Polish-Czech Dreiländereck and conducted interviews in German. I joined forces with František Konstantinovic in Slovakia and Poland – taking a chance that a stranger on Twitter would be a friend – and was hugely rewarded by sharing his insights and his company. Tanweer Ali and Eva Kellnerová have been reliable friends in Prague, introducing me to Eminent Czechs and people with stories to tell. Ben Rawlings put me up in Nicosia. Étienne and Barbara Augris, and Étienne's colleagues – particularly Marie-Pierre Takir – showed me Meurthe-et-Moselle and the Vosges, and Étienne took me on a never-to-be-forgotten pilgrimage to Verdun. Małgosia Szpara showed me around the mysterious environs of Wałbrzych and we bonded over our shared love of Bebok, the fierce guardian of the Silesian hills. Joanna Lamparska took me to the dark side of Silesia.

I am grateful to the Finnish Border Guard, especially Colonel Kimmo Elomaa, and to the Estonian Police and Border Guard, particularly Ilmar Kahro in Tallinn and those officers around the country who shared their time and expertise with me. I'm also appreciative of the border officers of Hungary and Serbia based at Kübekhaza. Thanks also to the organisers and speakers of the January 2023 conference on Vibrant Cross-Border Labour Markets at the European Commission in Brussels.

Many people have been generous with their time and their stories. In Helsinki, Essi Lindstedt White, Maria Mekri and Mikko Veinonen; in Baarle, Willem van Gool and Ad van Boxel; in Croatia, Marko Rakar and Nada Jovanovic; in Northern Ireland Fergal Barr and Paul Smyth; in Basel Tina Lawton and Julien de Salaberry; in Prague, Vladimír Špidla, An Eminent Czech, Petr Strabawa, Tereza Vavrova, Antikomplex and the Institute for the Study of Totalitarian Regimes; in Warsaw, Pawel Markiewicz; in Berlin, Matthew Tempest, Bridget Heal and Rose Sharpe; in Frankfurt an der Oder, Jeannette Wheatley; in Guben, Rurik von Hagens; in Ostritz, fighting the good fight against the Nazis, Michael Schlitt; in Budapest, Tamas Ibolya and Viktoria Serdült; in Khust, Ze'ev, custodian of the synagogue; in Chernivtsi, Halia Marchenko; about Romania, Chris Terry-Enescu and Craig Turp-Balasz. Victoria Amelina, whom I never met, illuminated this book with her wisdom.

For support from people who have trod borders and written about it before me, ranging from generously provided advice to a quick word that gladdened the heart: Jonn Elledge, Alexandra von Tunzelmann, Timothy Garton Ash, Tim Marshall, Philippe Sands and Garrett Carr. My mentor Sir Anthony Seldon, author of *The Path of Peace*, which traces a journey along the scar left by the Western Front, will see his influence in these pages. My other mentor, Sir David Butler (1924–2022), to my sadness, will not.

For reading sections of the draft to save me from error and awkwardness, I am grateful to several people named above, particularly Jill Baston,

Donna Sharpe and Guy Rowlands, and also to the indefatigable Steven Seegel, Tony Thorne, Jonathan Bousfield, Tanweer Ali, Nicholas Blincoe, Claire Bisdorff, Matthew Happold, Gary Gibbon, Viktoria Serdült, Aliona Halivco and Ben Tallis. Any error and awkwardness remaining is, of course, my own.

This book has been written in the age of social media. I put many of my travels and thoughts online through Twitter at @BastonBorders and felt part of a warm, appreciative community (most of the time). It forged connections and introduced me to people and perspectives I would not have had the chance to engage with otherwise. I am grateful to everyone who encouraged, warned and advised, whether we met in person during the work or not. There were over 2,500 people who were listening to what I had to say by the time the book was finished, and probably around 1,000 (across two Twitter accounts) I was following for European border knowledge. I am bound to forget some friends if I try to list those who gave something special, so no offence to anyone else, but thanks to: Patrice Dabrowski, Grant Harward, Christopher Lash, Uilliam Blacker, Nick Short, John Paul Newman, Anna Tuckett, Christopher Guyver, Philip Blood, Dustin Du Cane, Nancy Wingfield, Arnold Platon, Stefan Czarniecki, Will Mawhood, Bogdan Mateescu, Gabriele Paleari, Lucy Coatman, Katja Hoyer, Giovanni Vale and the *Hidden Europe* team.

Libraries, museums and workspaces all play their part in the life of a writer. This book has been written in many places, including the British Library, the Royal Society of Arts, the Grand Café in Chernivtsi, the Café Wien in Sibiu and HomeWork in Southfields in London, which has been a friendly base across the river.

My agent, Tom Killingbeck of the A.M. Heath Literary Agency, has been an indispensable ally in getting this book into shape. The role agents play in negotiating contracts is well enough known, but Tom has done so much more for me and this book. He has helped me sharpen and structure my thoughts, and offered priceless encouragement and practical and moral support.

Kirty Topiwala at Hodder & Stoughton took a chance on me as an author who has changed lane from electoral politics to history and boundaries and has been supportive and constructive and an immensely skilled and sensitive editor. Her colleagues Naomi Morris Omori and Juliet Brightmore also contributed to the shape of the final book, as did the wonderful copy editor Jenni Davis. In publicity, Louise Court, Olivia French and colleagues made sure that people heard about *Borderlines*.

The final months of writing up were anything but straightforward because of the loss of my esteemed father-in-law, Hugh Nicholson, in April and my deteriorating health. In June, I was diagnosed with a neurological condition called a Dural Arterio-Venous Fistula (DAVF), which took its toll on my energy and attention span as I concluded and edited the book; I can only pay tribute to the efforts of the skilled, caring and underpaid people at the National Hospital for Neurology and Neurosurgery and the Royal National Throat, Nose and Ear Hospital.

References

PART ONE

1 As cited in Diarmid Ferriter, *The Border* (Profile Books, 2019), p141.
2 Marc Geagan, *Bordertown Blues* (Stracomer Press, 2015), p70–73.
3 Richard Blanke, *Orphans of Versailles* (University of Kentucky Press, 1993), p32–60.
4 As cited in Terence Dooley, *Burning the Big House* (Yale University Press, 2023), p169.
5 As quoted in Gina Sigillito, *The Daughters of Maeve* (New York: Kensington Publishing , 2007), p87.
6 www.dib.ie/biography/fox-william-billy-a3348 'William (Billy) Fox' by Patrick Maume and Diarmaid Ferriter in *Dictionary of Irish Biography*.
7 John Bruton interview with Aaron McElroy for Northern Sound radio, 16 March 2018 www.northernsound.ie/podcasts/the-wider-view/hear-former-taoiseach-john-bruton-remembers-senator-billy-fox-134321, accessed 4 July 2023.
8 www.irishtimes.com/news/politics/oireachtas/call-for-leinster-house-memorial-to-courageous-senator-killed-by-ira-1.4509057
9 Alsace-Moselle Memorial Museum installation, Schirmeck, Alsace seen May 2019.
10 Mark Mazower, *Hitler's Empire* (Allen Lane, 2008), p108–109.
11 Margaret Lambert, *The Saar* (Faber & Faber, 1934), p213, 259.
12 ibid., p268.
13 Interview with Catherine Hanly for *Hot Dinners* website www.hot-dinners.com/Gastroblog/Interviews/my-hot-dinners-howard-marks-picks-his-favourite-restaurants, accessed 19 July 2023.
14 Howard Marks, *Mr Nice* (Secker & Warburg, 1996).
15 Film script, *The Third Man* (1949).
16 Anthony Seldon, *The Path of Peace* (Atlantic, 2022), p15–17.
17 Carl Zuckmayer, *A Part of Myself* (Secker & Warburg, 1970), English translation Richard and Clara Winston, p63; original German edition 1966.

18 ibid., p71. A plaque at Feldkirch station commemorates the events of March 1938 and all the other inhumane uses to which the railway had been put.

19 Ernst Kamm interview (1997), exhibit at the Jewish Museum in Hohenems.

20 Yad Vashem citation of Paul Grüninger www.yadvashem.org/righteous/stories/grueninger.html, accessed 5 August 2019.

21 https://www.swissinfo.ch/eng/jewish-refugee-policy_-the-boat-is-full---75-years-later/43531288, accessed 5 August 2019.

PART TWO

1 Robert Gerwarth, *The Vanquished: Why the First World War Failed to End 1917–23* (Penguin, 2017).

2 Rachel King, 'Whose Amber?' edoc.hu-berlin.de/bitstream/handle/18452/8206/king.pdf?sequence=1&isAllowed=y

3 Ibid., p3–4.

4 Immanuel Kant, *Anthropology from a Pragmatic Point of View* (1798), as translated by Robert B. Louden for Cambridge University Press edition (2006), Preface p4.

5 See Patten, Alan, '"The Most Natural State": Herder and Nationalism', *History of Political Thought* 51.4 (2010): 657–689.

6 J.G. Herder, *Outlines of a philosophy of the history of man*, tr. T. Churchill (1800), p53.

7 Ibid., p413.

8 See Patten, p37, for an exploration of Herder's argument.

9 Ernest Gellner, *Nations and Nationalism* (Cornell University Press, 1983), p2.

10 *Kaliningradskaya Pravda*, 30 April 1949.

11 Catherine Scott-Clark and Adrian Levy, *The Amber Room* (Atlantic, 2005).

12 Anne Applebaum, *Between East and West* (Pan Macmillan, 1994) p23.

13 sobor-kaliningrad.ru/en/content/40

14 www.csmonitor.com/World/Europe/2015/0726/Living-on-Prussia-s-ruins-Kaliningraders-embrace-Germanic-past

15 www.dw.com/en/row-over-traitor-german-philosopher-kant-riles-russian-hometown/a-46587360

16 Robert Service, *Russia: Experiment with a People* (Macmillan, 2002) p273.

17 Winston Churchill 'Sinews of Peace' speech at Fulton, Missouri, 5 March 1946. For full text, see for instance the National Archives transcript available at www.nationalarchives.gov.uk/education/resources/cold-war-on-file/iron-curtain-speech

18 Churchill, 'Sinews of Peace', op. cit.

19 John Quincy Adams, *Letters on Silesia*, Silesian Museum, 2019, originally published 1800, p10–11/30.

20 Tim Blanning, *Frederick The Great* (Allen Lane, 2015).

21 From a soldier's memoir published in 1793, as cited in Blanning, p230.

22 www.vfdgKüstrins.de/texts/kk-back.html

23 J.Q. Adams, p10–11/30.

24 'Man darf nicht warten, bis der Freiheitskampf Landesverrat gennant wird. Man muss den rollende Schneebal zertreten. Die Lawine hält keiner mehr auf.' The saying is from Erich Kästner (1899–1974), the anti-Nazi author of *Emil and the Detectives*.

25 See for instance https://www.aljazeera.com/news/2018/04/german-town-alert-neo-nazi-festival-counter-events-held-180421200541064.html

26 See for instance https://www.welt.de/politik/deutschland/article173176932/Neonazi-Festival-in-Ostritz-Sind-Bands-fuer-die-nicht-nur-der-Dorfnazi-kommt.html

27 Michael Schlitt interview, 10 October 2019.

28 Michael Schlitt interview, 10 October 2019.

29 Sebastian Siebel-Achenbach, *Lower Silesia from Nazi Germany to Communist Poland* (Springer, 1994), p87.

30 John Quincy Adams *Letters on Silesia*, Silesian Museum, 2019 originally published 1800, p14 original, p34 museum edition.

31 Anon. Editor, *Nie Vergessene Heimat* (Hamburg: Verlag Johannes Thordsen, 1950), p144. Original: 'Neumark und Niederlausitz – brandenburgisches Land, von dem gesungen worden ist: Wiesen, Wasser, Sand, das ist des Märkers Land, und die Grüne Heide, das ist seine Freude. Das Verlorens mag immer glänzender in der Erinnerung stehen, als es in Wirklichkeit war.' Translation LSB.

32 When Adams visited the area, there were glass-blowing workshops set up either side of the border post, rather like the way that handicraft and souvenir stores line the approaches to many modern-day borders. p78–80 old numbering, 106–109 museum edition.

33 Adams p47,111 original 68, 142 museum edition.

34 www.rozhlas.cz/toulky/vysila_praha/_zprava/141284 via en.wikipedia.org/wiki/Northern_Moravia_witch_trials

35 Norman Davies and Roger Moorhouse, *Microcosm: A Portrait of a Central European City* (Jonathan Cape, 2002), p190.

36 Julius Ruff, *Violence in Early Modern Europe 1500–1800* (Cambridge University Press 2001), p21–22.

37 vomanomalous.blogspot.com/2014/10/1673-original-frankensteins-monster.html

38 https://dolnyslask.travel/kompleks-riese/?lang=en (accessed 14 December 2023) and the tunnel sections under Książ Castle that were opened for visitors in 2018.

PART THREE

1 Friedrich Naumann, *Central Europe* (1916 edition), p65.
2 Also titled *The Kidnapped West*. It was published in English translation (Edmund White) in the *New York Review of Books* Vol 31, No 7, 26 April 1984.
3 Keiron Pim, *Endless Flight: The Life of Joseph Roth* (Granta, 2022), p100.
4 Sir Walter Runciman, Lord Runciman of Doxford from 1937.
5 Jonathan Wallace, 'The Political Career of Sir Walter Runciman'. PhD Thesis, University of Newcastle, 1995, p393.
6 Ibid., p402.
7 *Encyclopaedia Judaica* 'Cheb' p585–586. The anti-Semitic Pan-German politician Georg Schönerer represented Eger in the Austrian Reichstag before 1907.
8 Mazower, *Hitler's Empire* (2009), p59, p586–587.
9 Ibid., p56.
10 R.M. Douglas, *Orderly and Humane* (Yale University Press, 2012) describes the process in detail.
11 As cited in Glassheim, p167.
12 *Guardian* 26 November 2016, 'The Czechs and Germans trying to deal with the ghosts of the past' by Robert Tait.
13 Tereza Vavrova interview, 26 February 2019.
14 *Daily Telegraph* 8 August 2012, 'Soviet era ruse that tricked "escapees" into thinking they had fled Czechoslovakia' by Matthew Day.
15 Eagle Glassheim, *Cleansing the Czechoslovak Borders* (Pittsburgh University Press, 2016). Chapter 5 concentrates on the story of Most.
16 Glassheim, p121.
17 József Borbély, *Breakthrough/ Áttörés: Páneurópai Piknik 1989* (Ad-art, Győr, 1999), p22.
18 Ibid., p24.
19 Ibid., p4.
20 Ibid., p35.
21 Ibid., p38.
22 Kundera, *The Kidnapped West* op. cit.
23 *Annual Report* (2022) VW Slovakia, p22 via https://sk.volkswagen.sk/en/company/facts-and-figures.html
24 Chrena tells the anecdote at the Iron Curtain Stories website www.ironcurtainstories.eu/?lc=en&id=854&rt=37
25 Tony Thorne, *Countess Dracula* (Bloomsbury, 1997); Aleksandra Bartosiewicz 'Elisabeth Bathory: A True Story', *Przegląd Nauk Historycznych* 17(3), December 2018; Ronan O'Connell, 'The bloody tale of Hungary's serial killer countess', *National Geographic*, 21 October 2022.

26 www.pewresearch.org/global/2020/02/09/nato-seen-favorably-across-member-states/#are-there-parts-of-neighboring-countries-that-really-belong-to-us. Greece, Bulgaria and Turkey also had majorities for irredentism, and Poland and Slovakia had pluralities. The UK was reasonably happy, 72 per cent denying that there were parts of it governed by someone else and 23 per cent saying that there were.

27 R.W. Seton-Watson, *Treaty Revision and The Hungarian Frontiers Eyre & Spottiswoode*, 1934, p52.

28 Lord Rothermere, *My Campaign for Hungary* (Eyre & Spottiswoode, 1939), Chapter 11.

29 Ibid., p140.

30 Translation taken from Balazs Ablonczy's *Pál Teleki (1879–1941): The Life of a Controversial Hungarian Politician.*

31 www.rferl.org/a/hungary-serbia-Orbán-fidesz-no-bid-contract-investigation/31994585.html, accessed 17 March 2023; ODIHR Election Observation Mission Final Report 3 April 2022, p15–17, 37: https://www.osce.org/files/f/documents/2/6/523568.pdf accessed 5 January 2024.

32 OSCE ODIHR report, op. cit., p20.

33 hungarytoday.hu/hungarian-borders-commissioner-diaspora-interview-peter-szilagyi/, accessed 18 March 2023.

34 Luiza Ilie and Gergely Szakacs, 'Romania quietly catches up with richer neighbours, helped by EU cash', Reuters Europe online, 9 January 2023.

35 www.euronews.com/2017/11/23/hungarian-mayor-the-Orbán-government-needs-an-enemy

36 www.ironcurtainproject.eu/en/stories/the-return-of-barbed-wire/

37 Branimir Anzulovic, *Heavenly Serbia: From Myth to Genocide* (New York University Press, 1999).

38 Jasmin Mujanovic, 'The Balkan Roots of the Far Right's "Great Replacement" Theory', *New Lines Magazine*, 12 March 2021.

39 United States Holocaust Museum, 23 August 2016 www.ushmm.org/information/press/press-releases/museum-condemns-conferring-of-hungarian-order-of-merit-to-zsolt-bayer

PART FOUR

1 Victoria Amelina, 'Expanding the Boundaries of Home: a Story for Us All' www.iwpcollections.org/victoria-amelina, accessed 13 July 2023.

2 http://en.kremlin.ru/events/president/news/66181, accessed 9 July 2023.

3 Timothy Snyder, *Bloodlands: Europe between Hitler and Stalin* (Vintage, 2011), p319.

4 Rory Finnin, 'Why Crimea is the Key to Peace in Ukraine', Politico, 13 January 2023 https://www.politico.com/news/magazine/2023/01/13/peace-ukraine-crimea-putin-00077746

5 There were a few cases where nationality changed but these were anomalous. For most people, it was a fixed designation. See Rogers Brubaker, *Nationalism Reframed: Nationhood and the National Question in the New Europe* (Cambridge University Press, 1996).

6 Speech by President Zelenskyy to the Ukrainian Verkhovna Rada, 22 May 2022, alongside President Duda of Poland. www.president.gov.ua/en/news/vistup-prezidenta-ukrayini-volodimira-zelenskogo-pid-chas-sp-75261, accessed 2 April 2023.

7 https://podroze.onet.pl/polska/podkarpackie/pociag-z-przemysla-do-ustrzyk-dolnych-i-zagorza-przez-teren-zsrr-historia-trasa/he4rvwt, Dawid Smolorz, 22 November 2019.

8 Patrice Dabrowski, *The Carpathians: Discovering the Highlands of Poland and Ukraine* (Cornell University Press, 2019), p168–181.

9 Alexander Watson, *The Fortress* (Allen Lane, 2019), p117–119.

10 Serhii Plokhy, *The Gates of Europe: A History of Ukraine* (Penguin, 2016), p236–237.

11 Timothy Snyder, *Bloodlands: Europe between Hitler and Stalin* (Vintage, 2011).

12 Plokhy, p281.

13 Christopher Lash, *Moving West: The Transfer of Eastern Poles to Post-Yalta Poland, Urban Reconstruction and Post-war Relief, 1944–8*, University of Manchester PhD thesis, 2010 p51.

14 Ibid., p57.

15 Tarek Cyril Amar, *The Paradox of Ukrainian L'viv* (Cornell University Press, 2019), p163–173.

16 https://notesfrompoland.com/2022/11/17/fulfilling-osadczuks-dream-polish-ukrainian-reconciliation/, Samuel Tchorek-Bentall

17 www.rferl.org/a/1068362.html 'Analysis: Ukraine, Poland Seek Reconciliation Over Grisly History' *RFE/RL* 12 May 2006 by Jan Maksymiuk, accessed 2 April 2023.

18 Tatiana Zhurzenko, 'Memory Wars and Reconciliation in the Ukrainian–Polish borderlands' in *History, Memory and Politics in Central and Eastern Europe: Memory Games* (Palgrave, 2013) p187–188.

19 'WW2 massacre of Poles by Ukrainians must be called genocide, says head of Polish church', *Notes from Poland*, 7 July 2023.

20 Ben Tallis, *Identities, Borderscapes, Orders* (Springer, 2023), chapter 2.

21 Ibid., chapter 4.

22 Bernard Wasserstein, *A Small Town in Ukraine* (Allen Lane, 2023) is about this little border town.

23 Speech by President Zelenskyy to the Ukrainian Verkhovna Rada,

22 May 2022, alongside President Duda of Poland. https://www.president. gov.ua/en/news/vistup-prezidenta-ukrayini-volodimira-zelenskogo-pid-chas-sp-75261, accessed 2 April 2023.

24 Norman Davies, *Vanished Kingdoms* (Allen Lane, 2011).

25 Paul Robert Magocsi, *With Their Backs to the Mountains* (Budapest: Central European University Press, 2015), p45.

26 Baedeker's *Austria* 1896, p364.

27 On Julia Warhola www.warhola.com/andysmother.html

28 Paul Robert Magocsi, 'The Fellow Who Made Himself President of a European Republic' *Nationalities Papers* (2021) 49:5, 838–854 www. cambridge.org/core/journals/nationalities-papers/article/fellow-who -made-himself-president-of-a-european-republic-gregory-ignatius-zhatkovych/84CDFF05C5EC12F881F300352F99CC0B/share/ 40275cb6899386a6a9560c8f7405d763fec8c543

29 Karel Čapek, *Talks with T.G. Masaryk* (North Haven, CT: Catbird Press, 1995), p233. First published in Czech and English in the 1930s. English translation: Dora Round and Michael Helm.

30 Magocsi (2021), p841–842. The present whereabouts of the replica bell are not clear.

31 Robert Winch, *Republic for a Day* (Robert Hale, 1939), p138.

32 George Kennan, *From Prague After Munich: Diplomatic Papers 1938–40* (Princeton University Press, 1968), p63.

33 Kennan, p89.

34 Davies, p631; Kennan, p90.

35 Norman Davies, *Vanished Kingdoms: The History of Half-Forgotten Europe* (Penguin, 2011), p621–634.

36 Winch, pp25, 171–172.

37 The website http://shtetlroutes.eu/en/khust-putvnik has been a valuable source on the history of the Jewish community of Khust.

38 Winch, p12.

39 Magocsi (2015), p43.

40 Judit Toth, 'The Curious Case of Hungary', GLOBALCIT, January 2018 http://globalcit.eu/the-curious-case-of-hungary-why-the-naturalisation-rate-does-not-always-show-how-inclusive-a-country-is

41 Jeroen van Drunen, *"A Sanguine Bunch": Regional Identification in Habsburg Bukovina, 1774–1919* (Amsterdam: Pegasus 2015), p592.

42 Figures from the 1910 census.

43 David Rechter, *Becoming Habsburg* (Liverpool University Press, 2013), p4–5.

44 Van Drunen, p606.

45 Van Drunen, p595.

46 For Hackmann, see www.bukowina-portal.de/de/ct/102-Eugen-Hackmann

47 Gregor von Rezzori, *Memoirs of an Anti-Semite* (Picador, 2002), p6–7. The

German original was first published in 1979. The English translation here is the work of Joachim Neugroschel for the 1981 Penguin edition.

48 Museum of History and Culture of Bukovyna Jews, installation.

49 Museum of History and Culture of Bukovyna Jews, 2010.

50 With thanks to Halia Marchenko for sharing the story of the remarkable Zalozetskyj.

51 See for instance Svetlana Frunchak, *The Making of Soviet Chernivtsi: National "Re-unification" World War II and the Fate of Jewish Czernowitz in Post-war Ukraine*, Thesis submitted to University of Toronto, 2014.

52 Vladislav Davidzon 'Everything is regurgitated', *Tablet*, 28 November 2012.

53 *Rheinischer Merkur*, 1 February 1991, cited Chernivtsi Bukovina – Where People and Books Lived (czernowitz.de)

54 'Wo die Bürgersteige mit Rosenstraussen gefegt wurden und es mehr Buchhandlungen gab als Backereien. Czernowitz, das war ein immerwährender intellektueller Diskurs, der jeden Morgen eine neue ästhetische Theorie erfand, die am Abend schon wieder verworfen war. Wo die Hunde die Namen olympischer Götter trugen und die Hühner Hölderlin-Verse in den Boden kratzten.' From Marion Tauschwitz, *Selma Merbaum – Ich habe keine Zeit gehabt zuende zu schreiben: Biografie und Gedichte* (Klampen-Verlag, 2014), introduction. Translation LSB.

55 As cited, Benedict Anderson, *Imagined Communities*, 1983, p104.

56 *Washington Post*, 31 August 2016. www.washingtonpost.com/video/politics /trump-says-he-will-build-impenetrable-physical-tall-powerful-beautiful-border/2016/08/31/34eceacc-6fb6-11e6-993f-73c693a89820_video.html

Picture acknowledgements

Most of the photographs are from the author's collection.

Additional sources:
Alamy Stock Photo: 25/The Print Collector, 202/Keith Corrigan.
Courtesy of Archive Antikomplex: 176.
CCI/Shutterstock: 212. dmg media licensing: 110. Courtesy of
Willem van Gool, Chairman Tourist Office/Baarle-Hertog-Nassau/The
Netherlands & Belgium: 44. © Lorenz Kienzle: 140. Public domain: 73,
121 above, 136, 210, and 238/Wikimedia Commons. Jon Worth:
119/Polenmarkt Hohenwutzen, 23 September 2020, CC-BY 2.0.

Index